# The European Council and the Council

# The European Council and the Council

New Intergovernmentalism
and Institutional Change

Uwe Puetter

# OXFORD

UNIVERSITY PRESS

Great Clarendon Street, Oxford, OX2 6DP,
United Kingdom

Oxford University Press is a department of the University of Oxford.
It furthers the University's objective of excellence in research, scholarship,
and education by publishing worldwide. Oxford is a registered trade mark of
Oxford University Press in the UK and in certain other countries

First Edition published in 2014
Impression: 2

Published in the United States of America by Oxford University Press
198 Madison Avenue, New York, NY 10016, United States of America

British Library Cataloguing in Publication Data
Data available

Library of Congress Control Number: 2014937672

ISBN 978–0–19–871624–2

Printed and bound by
CPI Group (UK) Ltd, Croydon, CR0 4YY

# Acknowledgements

Research for this book started exactly five years ago in 2009. The intention was to start a first round of interviews with policy-makers who had close familiarity with European Council and Council decision-making before the Lisbon Treaty came into force, and then to engage in a second round of intensive fieldwork thereafter. Though this plan was realized, the European Union's responses to the economic and financial crisis have almost made it impossible to conclude the research on the institutional setting as modifications started to occur almost every semester. This motivated further research and follow-up interviews. Many thanks go to all my interviewees in Brussels and the different capitals for being available for this project, and especially to those who were available more than once.

The book benefited very much from feedback at various workshops and conferences and from colleagues who were happy to share their own work with me and who commented on drafts. In particular I would like to thank Chris Bickerton, Simon Bulmer, Paul James Cardwell, Thomas Christiansen, Mai'a Davis Cross, Deirdre Curtin, Mark Dawson, Youri Devuyst, Gabriel Glöckler, Marie-Pierre Granger, Dermot Hodson, Markus Jachtenfuchs, Christian Joerges, Jakob Lempp, Katarina Areskoug Mascarenhas, Stephanie Nowak, John Peterson, Karolina Pomorska, Sabine Saurugger, Jonas Tallberg, Zbigniew Truchlewski, Antje Wiener, Jonathan Zeitlin, and Eva Zemandl. Special thanks go to three anonymous referees, my editor Dominic Byatt, and Adina Maricut for excellent research assistance in relation to the compilation of the European Council agenda dataset.

Agnes Batory and Antje Wiener very kindly allowed me to evaluate interview data that were generated in the context of two respective research collaborations with them. The project on the Council trio presidency with Agnes Batory benefited from a research grant provided by the Central European University. The research on bifocal foreign policy analysis with Antje Wiener took place within the context of the RECON consortium, which was financed as an Integrated Projected by the European Commission's Sixth Framework Programme for Research. The Stiftung Wissenschaft und Politik in Berlin hosted me at the beginning of this project during a sabbatical in 2008–9. Finally, I would like to thank the students of my MA and PhD courses at the Central European University in Budapest for all the interesting debates around the issues that are covered in this book.

Uwe Puetter

Budapest
28 February 2014

# Contents

## Contents

# List of Figures and Tables

## Figures

## Tables

# List of Abbreviations

| | |
|---|---|
| CFSP | Common Foreign and Security Policy |
| CIVCOM | Committee for Civilian Aspects of Crisis Management |
| COREPER | Committee of Permanent Representatives |
| CSDP | Common Security and Defence Policy |
| DG | Directorate-General |
| DG ECFIN | Directorate-General for Economic and Financial Affairs, European Commission |
| EC | European Commission |
| ECB | European Central Bank |
| ECOFIN | Economic and Financial Affairs Council |
| EDA | European Defence Agency |
| EEAS | European External Action Service |
| EES | European Employment Strategy |
| EFC | Economic and Financial Committee |
| EFSF | European Financial Stability Facility |
| EFSM | European Financial Stabilisation Mechanism |
| EMCO | Employment Committee |
| EMS | European Monetary System |
| EMU | Economic and Monetary Union |
| EP | European Parliament |
| EPC | European Political Cooperation |
| EPSCO | Employment, Social Policy, Health, and Consumer Affairs |
| ESM | European Stability Mechanism |
| EU | European Union |
| EU2020 | European Union's growth strategy for the decade, 2011–2020 |
| FAC | Foreign Affairs Council |
| GAC | General Affairs Council |
| GAERC | General Affairs and External Relations Council |
| HR | High Representative |

## List of Abbreviations

| | |
|---|---|
| JHA | justice and home affairs |
| NATO | North Atlantic Treaty Organization |
| OMC | open method of coordination |
| PSC | Political and Security Committee |
| QMV | qualified majority voting |
| SEA | Single European Act |
| SGP | Stability and Growth Pact |
| SPC | Social Protection Committee |
| TEC | Treaty Establishing the European Community |
| TEU | Treaty on European Union |
| TFEU | Treaty on the Functioning of the European Union |
| TSCG | Treaty on Stability, Coordination and Governance |

# 1

# The Integration Paradox and the Rise of New Intergovernmentalism

Contemporary European Union (EU) decision-making confronts scholars of European integration with a puzzling scenario. Though the EU has adopted three new treaties since the 1992 Maastricht Treaty, including the most recent Treaty of Lisbon, and expanded its membership to 28 in 2014, member states have repeatedly rejected new major transfers of ultimate decision-making powers to the supranational level. Yet there seem to be no signs of integration fatigue. Quite to the contrary, the EU has expanded its policy-making activities to almost all sectors of public policy-making, including controversial domains such as economic governance, foreign, security, and defence policy, social and employment policy, and justice and home affairs (JHA). During the last two decades especially the broad areas of socio-economic governance and external affairs have moved to the centre of EU policy-making, and increasingly determine how the EU in general is perceived domestically and in global politics. The expansion of the EU agenda to these new areas of activity has not so far been reflected in a more powerful role for the most important supranational institution—the European Commission ('the Commission'). In all new areas of EU activity the Commission's traditional right of initiative is either formally or de facto limited, or does not exist at all. Moreover, the Court of Justice of the European Union ('the Court of Justice'), once known for its landmark decisions that shaped the character and scope of European-level policy-making, is largely banned from interfering with substantive policy decisions in economic governance, foreign affairs, and social and employment policy coordination. Also, the JHA field did not originally fall under the jurisdiction of the Court of Justice. Instead the European Council and the Council of the European Union ('the Council') are at the centre of attention. Moreover, the European Council has obtained a leading role in policy-making in all new areas of EU activity. It sets the main policy objectives and reserves the right to finalize decisions that are considered to have fundamental

1

repercussions on domestic policy-making. It also regularly instructs the Council and the Commission to work towards certain objectives. The meetings of the heads of state and government have become the focal point of EU politics. Starting in 2008 the EU's fight against the consequences of the global economic and financial crisis has provided a powerful illustration of this. The future of the single currency, if not of the Union itself, was considered to depend on European Council action.

Yet the centrality of the European Council was apparent even earlier. The top-level forum played a key role in setting up, implementing, and later reforming the EU's Stability and Growth Pact (SGP). Foreign policy crisis situations regularly triggered European Council intervention, and there was hardly any major EU policy initiative—for example, the so-called European Employment Strategy (EES), the Lisbon agenda or the Tampere Programme—that did not involve the 'heads', as European Council members are referred to in EU jargon, taking a leading role. The most senior formations of the Council—the Economic and Financial Affairs Council (ECOFIN) and the Foreign Affairs Council (FAC), as well as the Eurogroup of euro-area finance ministers—are at the centre of the complex day-to-day intergovernmental coordination processes, dealing with the review of national policies and organizing the pooling of member state resources for collective policy action. All major treaty reforms starting with the Maastricht Treaty have endowed the Council with new political responsibilities in this regard. These new responsibilities trigger Council decision-making beyond legislative politics—the traditional domain of the Council.

In short, a new intergovernmentalism has been on the rise ever since then. It dominates decision-making in the new areas of EU activity in the post-Maastricht era. The classic 'community method', with its focus on legislative decision-making that continues to apply to traditional so-called community policies, such as regulatory and competition policies in the context of the single market and agriculture, was no longer considered the preferred option when it came to developing the new areas of EU activity.

The new intergovernmentalism in EU politics is still not fully understood despite the fact that all indications are that it is there to stay for the foreseeable future. Despite attention being paid to alternative forms of EU decision-making, created by the literature on new modes of governance, many scholarly contributions about decision-making in the post-Maastricht EU are still focused on legislative decision-making in the context of the community method rather than on the question of why and how the role of the European Council and the Council in EU policy-making is changing. Moreover, the internal transformation of the two institutions, especially with regard to their role in non-legislative decision-making, has received surprisingly little attention. Some of the changes highlighted above were noted, but were discussed mainly in connection with instances of treaty change and, thus, not studied empirically as a novel practice of decision-making. Helen Wallace (2002) was one of the very few voices that explicitly highlighted the growing importance of non-community method decision-making within the Council, and called for new research.

The present study responds to this call. Indeed, the transformation that has taken place in the way the European Council and the Council operate is hard to ignore. There are more frequent and longer European Council meetings than ever before. Once a forum for discussion, which was convened three times a year, the European Council has developed into an institution for regular policy debate that meets several times a year and is also frequently convened on an ad-hoc basis. The meetings of the heads are presided over by a full-time elected president who operates independently of the rotating presidency of the Council.

Similarly, the agenda of Council decision-making reveals important changes. Once known predominantly as Europe's primary legislative institution, the Council now spends more and more time on non-legislative decision-making and policy debate than ever before. Those Council formations with responsibility for the new areas of EU activity have repeatedly adjusted their internal proceedings to the fact that legislative decision-making is no longer always the dominant activity when ministers meet in Brussels. Political and scholarly debates about the expansion of qualified majority voting (QMV) and the risk of legislative deadlock in the Council of the enlarged Union have drawn attention away from these developments. Many scholars of European Council and Council decision-making in the post-Maastricht era have ignored the increasing importance of non-legislative activity, which relies on unanimous agreement among ministers. In the post-Maastricht EU the most senior formations of the Council—ECOFIN and the FAC—as well as the informal Eurogroup focus predominantly on intergovernmental policy coordination rather than legislative decision-making. Moreover, the coordination agenda is constantly expanding, leading to even more and longer gatherings of ministers in Brussels. Meetings are no longer convened only according to a long-agreed schedule, but additionally take place at short notice so as to resolve open issues and respond to crisis situations. The working schedules and political activities of national finance and foreign affairs ministers are tied increasingly to the meeting schedules of the FAC, ECOFIN, and the Eurogroup, and the coordination agenda set by these forums. Traditional patterns of internal Council leadership and organization are changing too. Elected presidents, rather than the rotating presidency, have come to lead the Eurogroup and the FAC. A whole family of designated high-level expert committees has been put in charge of preparing the work of these bodies, leaving formerly important actors such as the Committee of Permanent Representatives (COREPER) side lined. Meeting activity among ministers and senior civil servants has increased dramatically compared to the early 1990s. Bureaucratic networks span Brussels and the capitals, and increasingly influence the domestic processes of policy formation. Moreover, despite the enhanced constitutional status of QMV as the standard decision-making mechanism in the field of EU legislative politics following the adoption of the Lisbon Treaty, European Council, and Council, decision-making relating to the new areas of EU activity follows predominantly the unanimity rule.

This book proposes a novel conceptual framework for understanding this particular phase of integration and the related process of institutional change in the European Council and Council environment: *deliberative intergovernmentalism*. It seeks to explain the foundations of the rise of new intergovernmentalism in EU politics and aims to identify the underlying mechanism of institutional change in the post-Maastricht era. It locates institutional change at the level of European Council and Council decision-making. It is argued that, post-Maastricht, integration is characterized by the paradoxical insistence of member states that the EU's independent supranational powers should not be expanded, while at the same time they pursue the rapid expansion of the EU's policy-making agenda. This *integration paradox* motivates the surge in demand for more and closer intergovernmental policy coordination as an alternative method of integrating European public policies. The emphasis on intergovernmental policy coordination, it is argued, inevitably triggers a constant quest for consensus generation among all involved actors as policy implementation in the new areas of EU activity depends crucially on the decentralized resources of the member states. These resources largely escape the direct control of supranational actors and are mostly not subjected to binding EU legislation, which would regulate and steer their use or activation. Building new areas of EU activity—economic governance, the common foreign, security, and defence policy, social and employment policy coordination,[1] and JHA cooperation—requires individual member state governments' permanent commitment to implementing commonly defined EU policy objectives within their own jurisdictions. Due to the decentralized character of policy-making in the new areas of EU activity, a lack of strong political support at the highest level of government immediately leads to implementation failure and stops policy initiatives from being effective. Defection from EU-level policy objectives is easy and, indeed, regularly occurs.

Yet this is an intended feature of the post-Maastricht EU. As they agree in principle that the development of the new areas of EU activity is vital for the Union and its member states, key actors are aware that specific policy

---

[1] These are the domains beyond the existing EU social policy *acquis* that were previously exempted from EU policy-making altogether.

decisions require a convergence of otherwise diverse views. This explains their general commitment to the collective process of consensus seeking. EU policy coordination may be a tedious process; however, actors have consistently stood loyal to the process of EU-level policy debate. Instances of severe disagreement, such as during the disintegration of the former Yugoslavia or during the US-led military campaign that dismantled Saddam Hussein's regime in Iraq, it seems, have triggered an increase rather than a decrease in coordination activity. The European Council and the Council are at the centre of this process as they assemble the most senior political actors in each policy field. The two bodies representing the member state governments thus obtain a new role in EU policy-making. This change in focus is reflected in a series of attempts at *institutional engineering*, which are aimed at improving the potential of the European Council and the Council to facilitate consensus and deliberation over policy by modifying the framework conditions of EU decision-making, and thus are key characteristics of a new European intergovernmentalism.

Deliberative intergovernmentalism is the umbrella term for an analytical framework which holds that the dependency on permanent consensus generation among member state governments in day-to-day policy-making within the EU's new areas of activity determines intergovernmental decision-making practice and thus the way the European Council, the Council, and related comitology processes function. It allows the tracing of specific institutional dynamics against the background of the post-Maastricht integration paradox, which implies that the development of new areas of EU activity is achieved mainly through processes of intergovernmental policy coordination in which member states retain ultimate decision-making competences as regards legislative and executive action. Deliberative intergovernmentalism predicts that institutional engineering will occur in all spheres of European Council and Council decision-making that are relevant to the new areas of EU activity, with the aim of increasing the consensus generation capacity of these institutions so as to allow common, yet decentralized, policy action.

The argument is tested and applied with particular reference to three core domains of European Council and Council action: economic governance under Economic and Monetary Union (EMU), the field of foreign, security, and defence policy, and the area of social and employment policy coordination. All three domains are considered to embody the new intergovernmentalism in EU policy-making particularly well. They have very similar governance architectures and are thus well suited to investigating the link between new intergovernmentalism and institutional change. The book is structured as follows. This chapter further develops the idea of the integration paradox by reviewing the trajectory of major EU institutional reforms at Maastricht and beyond. The post-Maastricht era is identified as a particular phase of integration. The chapter illustrates the rise of new intergovernmentalism and highlights particular challenges to EU governance. Notably, it is shown that decentralized political authority requires a constant process of consensus generation among member state governments and the core institutions, so as to bring national-level legislative and executive decisions in tune with commonly agreed EU objectives. Chapter 2 advances the concept of deliberative intergovernmentalism as an analytical framework, and links the argument about the integration paradox to the various attempts at institutional engineering that are detectable during the post-Maastricht period and have changed the way the European Council and the Council operate substantially from the second half of the 1990s until today (2014). The chapter discusses how deliberative intergovernmentalism is linked to other scholarship on new modes of governance, the European Council, and the Council, and why it challenges in particular rational choice institutionalist assumptions about European Council and Council decision-making. Chapter 3 analyses the emergence of the European Council as the centre of political gravity in the post-Maastricht era. It shows that new areas of EU activity dominate the European Council agenda and explains why and how the high-level forum became subject to renewed attempts at institutional engineering. The chapter demonstrates that these changes were aimed primarily at enhancing the consensus generation potential of the European Council. The chapter offers novel insights into the work of the European Council, notably its working methods, the role of the elected president, and the introduction of the Euro Summit format. Similarly, chapter 4 applies the analytical framework of deliberative intergovernmentalism to the Council and especially the role of this institution in policy coordination. It focuses on those Council formations that are responsible for policy coordination in the new areas of EU activity, including the ECOFIN Council and the Eurogroup, the FAC, and the Employment, Social Policy, Health and Consumer Affairs Council (EPSCO). Moreover, the chapter demonstrates that a complex intergovernmental bureaucratic infrastructure consisting of senior expert committees such as the Economic and Financial Committee (EFC), the Political and Security Committee (PSC), and new organizational structures such as the European External Action Service (EEAS) have emerged in support of intergovernmental consensus generation at the political level. This technocratic infrastructure is constructed as a network infrastructure that is focused on the pooling and coordination of national-level and existing EU-level administrative resources. Finally, chapter 5 discusses the ramifications of Europe's new intergovernmentalism for the EU's key supranational actors including the Commission, the European Parliament (EP), the Court of Justice and the European Central Bank (ECB). The chapter considers the challenge of democratic control, and debates the outlook for EU policy-making under the Lisbon Treaty against the background of the main findings generated under the analytical framework of deliberative intergovernmentalism.

The main aim of this book is to advance the conceptual and empirical understanding of contemporary processes of institutional change in the European Council and Council environment. It aims to generate new theoretical insights as much as policy-relevant knowledge, as it presents theoretically informed propositions about the viability and appropriateness of alternative institutional options. The method of achieving this objective, applied here, is to construct a conceptual and theoretical framework that guides research about a quickly changing environment with *sui generis* features. Yet the rich tradition of European integration studies is the basis for generating insights into institutional developments, of which the full scope may only become visible later. The focus is on middle-range theory, process-tracing and lesson-drawing, as well as on making some informed guesses about future developmental pathways. In this sense the study emphasizes the relevance of social science theory in guiding policy-relevant research and emphasizes the usefulness of an open research design (Jentleson and Ratner 2011: 8).

## 1.1 The Legacy of the Maastricht Treaty

The journey in uncovering the paradoxical character of the EU's new intergovernmentalism starts with the Maastricht Treaty and the so-called pillar structure of the new Union. This is not to treat the Maastricht Treaty as an isolated historical event that constitutes a clear cut-off point between old and new intergovernmental decision-making practices. Obviously the Maastricht Treaty is heavily influenced by the phase of integration that immediately preceded it—notably the process of reinforced single market integration in the 1980s and the Single European Act (SEA), as much as the lessons member states drew from this experience. The same applies to the practices and routines of intergovernmental decision-making within the environment of the European Council and the Council, which are studied in detail in the subsequent chapters of this book. There are certainly traces of what is identified throughout this book as 'post-Maastricht' practice during earlier phases of integration. Similarly, institutional change does not occur from one day to the next and only in the immediate aftermath of the Maastricht Treaty. Changes occur over time and are informed by previous experience of collective decision-making and institutional learning.

Yet what this chapter seeks to demonstrate is that the Maastricht Treaty, as no other document, marks the constitution of a particular logic of integration to which all subsequent treaties have subscribed. The objective is to demonstrate that key decisions at Maastricht and beyond concerning the broader institutional architecture of the Union, and notably the new areas of EU activity, have played a pivotal role in informing the emergence of a new intergovernmentalism in EU policy-making and a related process of profound institutional change that is concentrated around the European Council and the Council. The main argument is that key institutional decisions that have shaped the role of the two decision-making bodies in EU politics as well as their internal operation were informed by an underlying integration paradox. At Maastricht and beyond, member states insisted on strictly limiting further transfers of ultimate decision-making powers to supranational actors, as they feared the irreversible dismantling of national sovereignty. Yet, and this constitutes the integration paradox, member states were equally eager to expand the scope of EU policy-making activities significantly so as to include all core areas of national sovereignty such as economic governance, foreign affairs and defence, welfare state policies, and JHA. The emergence of Europe's new intergovernmentalism cannot thus be understood as the result of integration fatigue or even the desire to roll back previous steps in the integration process. This study takes seriously the view that the desire to pursue the closer integration of European public policies did not fade away with the rejection of major new transfers of formal decision-making competences as understood in the context of the classic community method. Rather, it highlights the paradoxical character of integration in the post-Maastricht era. Member state governments largely converge in their analysis that the capacity of individual countries to act as sole providers of public policy is highly limited. Moreover, the constitution of new areas of EU activity beyond market integration, by virtue of the Maastricht Treaty, takes place not in a vacuum but on the basis of a complex single market integration *acquis*, which was developed over several decades following the principle of the selective delegation of legislative competences to the EU level. This single market *acquis* remains largely intact and is not questioned, though there are some adjustments to the way single market governance operates.

The single market *acquis* also represents an institutional legacy on the basis of which EU integration continues to evolve, even though the development of new areas of activity has taken a different path. Thus the new intergovernmentalism in the post-Maastricht EU cannot be explained in terms of an opposite model of integration, nor can it be reduced to a rudimentary form of decision-making in international organizations, as early accounts of intergovernmentalism in European integration scholarship might have suggested (see chapter 2.1). The new intergovernmentalism occurs within a highly developed institutional framework, which has been shaped by community method decision-making for a long time. The EU's core decision-making bodies, including the European Council, the Council, the Commission, and the EP, are at the heart of this institutional framework. The increasing emphasis on intergovernmental policy coordination, it is argued, occurred *because* of the renewed ambition to enhance the European dimension of national public policies, rather than in the absence of such ambition. It is in this sense that it is argued that the emergence of Europe's new intergovernmentalism is rooted in the Maastricht Treaty. In this context it is important not to conflate the debate about what dynamics informed the 'choice for Europe' (Moravcsik 1998) at Maastricht and how the Treaty was negotiated, with the intellectual task of tracing the consequences of the Maastricht decisions for the further evolution of the EU's institutional architecture. In any case there is no shortage of competing explanations for the Maastricht Treaty and the process leading to its adoption—be they inspired by liberal intergovernmentalism, neofunctionalism (Cameron 1992, 1998), historical institutionalism (Sandholtz 1993), a focus on supranational agency (Ross 1995), or process-oriented constructivist perspectives (Dyson and Featherstone 1999; Marcussen 2000). It is not the ambition of this book to revive the debate about how the Maastricht Treaty came about. The approach is rather to concentrate on one defining element of the outcome: the introduction of intergovernmental policy coordination as the main governance mechanism for new fields of EU policy activity.

The Maastricht Treaty marks a watershed in EU integration. It not only builds on and develops further the successful acceleration of the single market agenda, which evolved around the adoption of the SEA in the mid-1980s and the activist Commission under Jacques Delors. The Treaty constitutes the most radical expansion of the scope of EU integration so far, emphasizing the different political quality that the integration project assumes by moving from a community to a 'Union'. The new institutional framework established at Maastricht provides for a role for the EU in key areas of public policy that have hitherto been exempt from its influence, or have led a life outside the formal institutional framework of the Union. The Treaty marks the birth of EMU, including the introduction of a single currency and coordinated economic policies; it constitutes the EU as an international foreign policy actor by providing for a Common Foreign and Security Policy (CFSP), and foresees close cooperation in the field of JHA. At an institutional level the Maastricht Treaty emphasizes the principle of a single institutional framework for EU governance—all EU activities are decided upon by the same decision-making institutions, no matter what the decision-making procedure is. The European Council is singled out as the central institution for providing 'the necessary impetus' (Article D, TEU Maastricht) for the further development of the Union and for defining 'the general political guidelines'.

The complexity of the new institutional architecture is difficult to ignore. After Maastricht, the EU was referred to as to consisting of a three-pillar structure. Two of the new policy areas—foreign and security policy as well as JHA—constituted the two new 'intergovernmental pillars' (Denza 2002) of the

Union. Yet the so-called community pillar—the areas covered by the Treaty establishing the European Community (TEC)—also contained a distinct intergovernmental element. What reference to the concept of a pillar structure at the time tended to ignore was that the 'E' of EMU was organized as another intergovernmental pillar, which follows an institutional model that is radically different from EMU's supranational monetary policy. Economic governance under EMU is based on the principle of policy coordination. The ultimate responsibility for decisions over macroeconomic policies still rests with the member states.

## 1.2 The Peak and End of Legislative Activism

In order to better understand the emergence of the new intergovernmentalism in EU policy-making, it is helpful to recall briefly the integration steps taken immediately prior to and after the Maastricht Treaty came into force. The period between the adoption of the SEA in the mid-1980s and the signing of the Maastricht Treaty at the beginning of the 1990s is characterized by the most significant integration steps so far, following the logic of the community method. This also is true for the field of social policy. By the time the SEA was adopted, member states had transferred real decision-making competences regarding social policy issues to the European level—although in a very limited way. This included most prominently areas related to the free movement of workers and questions of equal pay (cf. Hervey 1998; Shaw et al. 2007). The wider field of social policy has always been under close scrutiny because of the potential impact of economic integration on domestic social standards. Like foreign policy and EMU, social policy constitutes an area that serves as a benchmark for the EU's ability to match market integration with political integration. Or, to use different terminology, to counter some of the detrimental effects of market or negative integration with positive integration or state-building at the European level (Leibfried and Pierson 1992).[2] However, the process of establishing EU social policy competences was cumbersome. Soon it became clear that the full harmonization of social standards, and in particular a potential pooling of resources related to the maintenance and development of (domestic) social safety nets, was out of the question.

Yet the period between the mid-1980s and the mid-1990s was characterized by a widening of the community's social policy competences (cf. Streeck 1995). The SEA introduced QMV in several areas related to the freedom of movement of workers. The SEA also established the concept of a 'high level of

---

[2] On the notions of negative and positive integration, see also chapter 2.1.1.

protection' (SEA, Article 100a.3) in the areas of health, workplace safety, the environment, and consumer protection. This empowered the Commission to propose new legislation in the relevant fields. The Delors Commission made use of these powers and advanced social policy legislation in the context of its single market offensive. Delors propagated the idea of a European social space to counter balance the adverse social consequences of market integration (Kuhn 1995; Waldschmitt 2001). The framework directive on health and workplace safety was an important advancement in this context (Smismans 2004: 105). The Social Protocol and the Social Agreement annexed to the Maastricht Treaty marked the next significant step in the extension of the EU's decision-making competences in the social policy field. The two documents provided the basis for finalizing a number of legislative initiatives— among them the much debated working time directive.

This extension of the EU's legislative competences in the field of social policy reached its peak in the mid-1990s. The Social Protocol and the Social Agreement were key components of the Maastricht package constituting the new Union. However, strong opposition from the United Kingdom and its desire not to be bound by these provisions resulted these competence changes being given only the status of annexes to the treaty. This showed how difficult progress in this area was. The Amsterdam Treaty eventually integrated most of the non-regular Maastricht social policy provisions in its new Title XI on social policy, and emphasized the role of QMV as the prevalent mode of decision-making in this area. Under the Blair government the United Kingdom became part of the EU's social policy *acquis*. However, the Amsterdam Treaty left the scope of the EU's legislative competences in this policy field largely unchanged, as did the Nice Treaty.

Though the trajectory of EMU is in many ways different from the more gradual evolution of the social policy field and its related legislative competences, the monetary policy arm of EMU also involved a formal transfer of substantial decision-making competences to the EU level. The monetary policy component of EMU marked a radical departure from the previous practice of monetary cooperation. Initially, the focus was on the control of inner-European exchange rates based on intergovernmental agreements and coordination between national central banks and finance ministries. The so-called 'Snake' and the more successful European Monetary System (EMS) were instituted following high-level political decisions by the heads (cf. Gros and Thygesen 1998; Ungerer 1997). The creation of the EMS in 1979 was closely linked to an initiative by French President Valéry Giscard d'Estaing and German Chancellor Helmut Schmidt. In addition to pushing for a reformed system of exchange rate coordination, the two politicians had developed further the practice of European-level summit meetings (cf. chapter 3.3).

Regular and confidential exchanges at the level of the heads were considered to be crucial for introducing initiatives such as the EMS.

Already the Treaty of Rome had identified monetary and economic policy as a field in which member states should coordinate their domestic policies. The interdependency between market integration on the one hand, and national monetary and economic policies on the other, was recognized in principle, and a development in this field following the community method was at least conceivable. The Maastricht Treaty constituted a landmark decision in this regard. EMU implies the full and irreversible transfer of decision-making authority over monetary policy. The ECB was created as a powerful and independent supranational institution to run monetary policy. National currencies and banknotes disappeared and were replaced by the euro as a supranational currency. Moreover, the Maastricht Treaty limited the scope of national budgetary policies by introducing a binding deficit rule that foresaw financial sanctions in the case of non-compliance. The development of the EMU framework involved a central role for the Commission. Its president Jacques Delors chaired the committee that was in charge of studying and proposing institutional options for implementing EMU.[3] The Commission itself was fully involved in the relevant Intergovernmental Conference, and presented its own draft provisions.

Thus, the period of the run-up to the Maastricht Treaty and the Treaty itself can be understood to follow the logic of the classic community method. EU-level political authority was understood to be constituted by the formal transfer of ultimate legislative and executive decision-making powers and, thus, an intrinsic supranational element. Moreover, departing from and being triggered by the project of market integration, these developments marked the transition from an economic community to a political union following the well-known logic of European integration up to that point.[4] With the extension of legislative competence in the social policy field and the complete pooling of sovereignty in the field of monetary policy the integration process now comprised core areas of national sovereignty beyond the sphere of pure market integration. At the same time, the processes of market integration and supranational regulation were firmly anchored within EU law. How far-reaching these competences were (they included the powers of the Commission and the Court of Justice to monitor the application of and enforce EU

---

[3] This is of course not to say that the Delors committee was an instrument of the Commission. Delors found himself at the table together with some of the most outspoken sceptics of EMU. Yet the role assigned to him as chair reflected the—albeit slightly modified—role of the Commission as the prime initiator of institutional change (cf. Dyson and Featherstone 1999; Ross 1995; Verdun 1999).

[4] The Commission report 'One market, one money' (Commission of the European Communities 1990) is a historic example of the technocratic version of this argument.

law) had already become clear to all involved actors. Virtually all fields of domestic public policy were directly or indirectly affected by the single market agenda. A profound transformation of the way in which member states conducted their public policies was evident.[5] In this sense the Maastricht Treaty represented an important political step in consolidating and confirming this particular approach to European integration.

Nonetheless, the Maastricht Treaty constituted a paradoxical outcome. The above paragraphs portray Maastricht as the peak of legislative activism, including the far-reaching assignments of new formal decision-making competences to the EU level. Yet the Maastricht Treaty also marked, at least temporarily, the end of such an approach to integration. This is particularly obvious with regard to the field of foreign and security policy. This policy area was first constituted with the creation of the European Political Cooperation (EPC) mechanism in 1970. EPC was based on the principle of intergovernmental coordination, and was set up outside the treaty framework. Thus, in this policy area the community method did not apply. The EPC framework—although functional and operating in a technical sense—never developed the necessary political impetus needed for establishing a more assertive collective foreign and security policy. Instead of enhancing the EU's policy-making capacity in this field by delegating ultimate decision-making competences to the supranational level, the Maastricht Treaty sought to do this through further institutionalizing the model of intergovernmental policy coordination. The focus was on a reinforced declaration of political will and ambition, as well as a definition of institutional responsibilities and coordination instruments. Thus the Maastricht Treaty formally endorsed the original EPC formula that greater political integration was to be achieved only within an intergovernmental framework. As Nuttall (1992: 5) notes, this 'ambiguity has persisted to this day'.

Successful policy action was defined as the coordinated mobilization of decentralized national resources. The Maastricht Treaty emphasized the encompassing character of EU foreign and security policy coordination and included defence policy, which was also covered by other organizations such as the North Atlantic Treaty Organization (NATO). It underlined the importance of safeguarding the 'common values, fundamental interests and independence of the Union' (Article J.1.2, TEU Maastricht). The Treaty identified the Council as the central institution for collective decision-making in this policy field and established coordination procedures for devising common

---

[5] The scope of these developments is reflected not least in the European studies literature itself. The focus shifted increasingly in the second half of the 1990s, from the question of what moves integration forward to an interrelationship between domestic policy and integrated EU-level politics. Rather than 'integration', the term 'Europeanization' has become the focal point of debates (cf. among many others Cowles et al. 2001).

positions and joint actions. Except for procedural matters, the Council was to decide by unanimity (Article J.8.2, TEU Maastricht). The Council presidency was charged with the external representation of CFSP, and was made part of a troika group including the preceding and upcoming presidency. The Treaty also established the principle of diplomatic and consular cooperation. The European Council was put in charge of steering the coordination process, which involved establishing principles and guidelines for policy coordination. The Commission was not granted its traditional right of initiative under the new provisions, but instead was 'fully associated' (Article J.9, TEU Maastricht) with the coordination process. The Court of Justice was not granted jurisdiction over the substance of policy decisions adopted within the new coordination framework or their implementation.

The introduction of JHA cooperation as a new area of EU activity in the Maastricht Treaty followed almost the same logic. Like the EPC model, JHA cooperation had started to evolve from the mid-1970s onwards outside the formal community framework. Starting with the creation of the Trevi Group in 1975 a whole set of consultation groups covering various aspects of JHA policy were founded. The focus was on the constitution of networks of member state representatives from governments and law enforcement authorities, rather than the delegation of new decision-making competences to the supranational level. Again, the Maastricht Treaty focused on further institutionalizing JHA as a field of enhanced intergovernmental policy coordination. The Treaty brought JHA cooperation within the institutional framework of the EU without making it subject to community method decision-making. Most importantly, the relevant provision declared sensitive areas of national sovereignty as constituting 'matters of common interest' (Article K.1, TEU Maastricht). The list included asylum policy, the crossing of the EU's external borders, immigration policy, the fight against drug addiction and fraud, judicial cooperation on civil and criminal matters, and customs and police cooperation. The Council was defined as the central forum for policy coordination (Article K.3, TEU Maastricht). Policy initiative was shared between the member states and the Commission except for judicial cooperation in criminal matters, customs, and police cooperation. In these areas member states retained the exclusive right to initiate policy. As in the case of foreign, security, and defence policy the Court of Justice was not granted jurisdiction over the substance of policy decisions adopted within the new coordination framework or their implementation.

As indicated earlier the so-called second and third pillars—foreign, security, and defence policy and JHA cooperation—did not remain the only new areas of EU activity that followed the model of a new intergovernmentalism. EMU's economic governance arm—as opposed to EMU's monetary element around the independent and supranational ECB—was also built using a decentralized approach. Member states were considered to remain the prime movers in the field of economic policy, but were committed to 'regard their economic policies as a matter of common concern' (Article 103, TEC Maastricht). Again, the TEC identifies the Council as the central forum for policy coordination. As in the case of foreign, security, and defence policy the European Council is assigned an oversight function and establishes general policy guidelines based on input from the Council. The Council is also charged with monitoring compliance with EU policy guidelines in relation to national economic policy. Yet the Maastricht Treaty did not foresee sanctions beyond a reprimand mechanism. The Commission was not granted its traditional right of initiative, though it obtained a role in the process of the drafting of policy guidelines and the monitoring of the member states' economic policies. The relevant provisions of the Maastricht Treaty referred to Council action on the basis of so-called Commission 'recommendations' (Article 103, TEC Maastricht), which did not bind the Council and could be modified easily by ministers.

The Maastricht Treaty defined only one binding policy objective: the avoidance of excessive government deficits (Article 104c, TEC Maastricht). However, enforcement of this policy rule was not delegated to the Commission, as it would have been in areas of classic community method decision-making. The Commission rather was given the role of a watchdog. The Council was again declared to be the central decision-making authority. Only the Council could reprimand and eventually sanction individual member states for non-compliance with the deficit rule. The Maastricht provisions on economic governance did not foresee the possibility of regulating national economic policy through community legislation in a broader sense. The only areas in which legislative decision-making according to the classic community method was foreseen were the further definition of the so-called multilateral surveillance procedure (Article 103.5, TEC Maastricht), and the implementation of the excessive deficit procedure (Article 104c.14, TEC Maastricht). These legislative competences were used in connection with the adoption of the SGP in 1997 and its later amendments. In fact, only some aspects of the SGP were based on legislative acts. The other elements of the SGP were based on the declaration of political will and commitment to specific budgetary objectives on the part of the member states. As far as the legislative dimension of the SGP was concerned, the focus was on regulating decision-making procedures and defining the respective responsibilities of the different institutional actors within them. The SGP committed actors to act in a timely manner, to fulfil their obligations under the multilateral surveillance procedure and to prevent the occurrence of excessive deficits in the first place by aiming for a balanced or surplus budget over the medium term. As was the case with core treaty provisions on economic governance, the SGP was not based on the principle that authority to enforce common policy rules is delegated to the Commission. Similarly, the SGP arrangement implied that the role of the Court of Justice was defined as one that is focused on the question of whether the different institutional actors fulfilled their procedural obligations under the Treaty and the SGP.[6] The Court of Justice was not given jurisdiction over the question of whether a member state actually violated the excessive deficit rule, or any other coordination objective as specified by the Council and the European Council.

Finally, it is also necessary to revisit the field of social policy-making, which was dealt with at the beginning of this section. Despite the fact that the Maastricht Treaty provisions can be considered to mark a peak in a long series of transfers of legislative decision-making competences to the EU level in the social policy field, the Treaty de facto failed to give further and longer-lasting momentum to the process of expanding the legal EU social policy *acquis*. Apart from some legislative initiatives in the immediate aftermath of Treaty adoption, legislative innovation remained largely absent since the mid-1990s as far as it concerned the introduction of genuinely new elements to the existing social policy *acquis*. As one official described the situation:

> In terms of the legislative development there is no innovation anymore. In some areas we've even made a step backwards. There is no common idea of a European social policy. And the Commission has retreated [from the role of making new proposals].[7]

The focus of legislative activity in the social policy domain has been mainly on the reorganization and streamlining of existing provisions.[8] Political dynamism during the 1990s in the sphere of social policy-making was located elsewhere. Notably, the consequences of implementing the Maastricht EMU provisions against a background of high unemployment rates in many member states provoked a new push for initiatives in the areas of social and employment policy. The focus was on policy coordination rather than on legislative activity. The new policy agenda included policy issues that had so far not been dealt with by the EU or had been dealt with only in a very limited way. During an initial period in the second half of the 1990s coordination processes and new meeting formats were established by a series of European Council conclusions. Most importantly, employment policy was identified as an area of common concern by the Essen European Council in 1994 (European Council 1994). The EES was launched by the European Council at an 'employment summit' in Luxembourg in November 1997. It involved a

---

[6] For a rare example of such an intervention by the Court, see the ruling in Case C-27/04, *Commission of the European Communities v. Council of the European Union*.

[7] Interviewee PR-20/ECON, 4 November 2009. For further information on interview reference codes and the pool of interviewees, consult the list of interviewees at the end of this book.

[8] For an overview of the evolution of EU social policy instruments see Puetter (2009).

permanent coordination and monitoring mechanism directed by the Council under the supervision of the heads and assisted by the Commission (European Council 1997a). This mechanism was modelled on the Maastricht provisions on economic governance. Employment policy remained a national prerogative, but was declared a matter of common concern. Policy coordination was based on guidelines issued by the Council. The European Council assigned itself an oversight role. The Commission assisted in this process and was charged with monitoring the implementation of policy guidelines at the level of member states. Yet the Commission did not obtain any implementing powers or the right to sanction non-compliance. Instead, the emphasis was put on generating the commitment of member states, on peer review, and on multilateral surveillance. This approach became known as the open method of coordination (OMC) only a short time later, and was expanded to other domains (cf. Hodson and Maher 2001).

The above review of key institutional choices, as far as they were represented in the Maastricht provisions, confirms the earlier claim that the Maastricht Treaty marks a watershed in European integration. There is a clear pattern recognizable from the key provisions that refer to the new areas of EU activity. The key idea is to advance integration without delegating legislative competences and executive functions to the supranational level. This constitutes the integration paradox. The new intergovernmentalism contained in the Maastricht provisions is more than an institutional experiment. It is founded on a bold declaration of political will and ambition. The Council and the European Council are at the centre of these developments: they have been put in charge of steering the new areas of EU activity. In this sense the Maastricht Treaty also marks an important departure from the more experimental forms of foreign policy and JHA cooperation that existed earlier. The field of social policy reflects particularly well the transitory character of the Maastricht agreement. Though there is a push to develop the EU's social dimension further through the community method, the period immediately after the Treaty came into force reveals the early departure from this institutional model and the centrality of policy coordination.

The above reading of the Maastricht Treaty may be challenged with reference to a central controversy surrounding the agreement. The negotiations revealed a significant gap between the United Kingdom, on the one side, and almost all other member states, on the other side. The United Kingdom was fundamentally opposed to any of the competence transfers discussed at the beginning of this section. The country obtained opt-out clauses in the social policy field and with regard to EMU.[9] Denmark was also granted an opt-out

---

[9] The introduction of Title XI on social policy with the Amsterdam Treaty ended the British opt-out for this policy sector while the opt-out clause regarding EMU continued to apply. However,

from EMU, and the country obtained reassurance that it would not be bound to join defence-related cooperation activities in the field of foreign and security policy unless it wished to do so.[10] These controversies were caused not only by differences over specific policy decisions but reflected more fundamental divisions about the future of the integration project.

There is little doubt that these controversies imposed constraints on the further institutional development of the EU, and forced decision-makers to opt for more flexible and informal arrangements in order to avoid blockage of the decision-making process. Yet the crucial point here is that—at least in retrospect—Maastricht was much less about constituting a double- or even multi-speed EU than about constituting a Union that was essentially founded on an integration paradox. In the end there was broad agreement among the other member states not to opt for a centralization of decision-making powers within the new areas of EU activity, but rather to develop them following a model of decentralized but coordinated decision-making.

## 1.3 Three New Areas of EU Activity and the Expansion of Policy Coordination

The remaining chapters of this book analyse European Council and Council activity by making reference to three of the four new areas of EU activity highlighted above: economic governance; foreign, security, and defence policy; and social and employment policy coordination. The reasons for concentrating on these three areas rather than also making detailed reference to JHA cooperation are both methodological and pragmatic. Moreover, there are other established fields of EU activity that were developed mainly through community method decision-making prior to the Maastricht Treaty, but increasingly incorporated important coordination elements later, for example in environmental policy (cf. Sabel and Zeitlin 2008). Again, only occasional reference is made to these areas throughout this book for the same reasons. As briefly shown in the remainder of this section the three selected new areas of EU activity follow an almost identical institutional trajectory in the two decades of post-Maastricht EU policy-making, which is the reference time period of this study. Governance mechanisms and policy coordination instruments provide the basis for a most-similar-case study design. This best allows

legislative decision-making in the social policy field has been felt since then to be more difficult than it was before: this has become clear, for example, in the process of negotiating amendments to the working time directive, which was originally adopted when the British opt-out was still in place.

[10] Denmark also expressed reservations about policy areas besides those covered here. These reservations concerned the introduction of EU citizenship and aspects of JHA cooperation.

for the analysis of more specific variations in institutional design, notably when it comes to the study of institutional reform within the Council environment. Similarly, it promises a deeper understanding of how the suspected leadership role of the European Council within the context of new intergovernmentalism plays out in different policy domains and in relation to individual Council formations. Starting with the Amsterdam Treaty, the evolving institutional framework of JHA cooperation partially follows a different trajectory than the three selected policy domains. This would, at the very least, have made comparison more complex. Most importantly, with the Amsterdam Treaty, key aspects of JHA policy-making were based on legislative decision-making. However, the review of the three new selected areas of EU activity is focused primarily on revealing the consequences of the transition from legislative decision-making to policy coordination for the new roles of the European Council and the Council in post-Maastricht EU policy-making.

It can nevertheless be said that the development trajectory of JHA cooperation allows for the identification of most of the major institutional dynamics that are identified in this book as characterizing post-Maastricht new intergovernmentalism. The Amsterdam Treaty did not simply convert JHA coordination to the classic community method process. Instead, the Treaty offered a strongly modified version of community method decision-making. The relevant provisions stipulated that the right of initiative was shared between the Commission and the Council—a novel institutional arrangement in the history of European integration. The Lisbon Treaty formally ended this exceptionalism for most areas within the JHA cooperation domain, but stressed the leading role of the European Council in 'legislative and operational planning within the area of freedom, security and justice' (Article 68, TFEU). Such a role for the European Council is clearly incompatible with classic community method decision-making, but represents a key feature of the post-Maastricht new intergovernmentalism. Moreover, despite the legislative component of JHA decision-making, to which no equivalent exists in the areas of economic governance, foreign policy, or employment policy coordination, the coordinated use of decentralized resources under the control of member state governments remains a pivotal feature of contemporary JHA cooperation and, thus, can be considered as following similar institutional patterns to those observed in the other new areas of EU activity. As Emek M. Uçarer (2013: 293) remarks, 'the [JHA] policy remains intrinsically intergovernmental'.[11]

In order to substantiate further the argument that the selected three new areas of EU activity follow a very similar institutional development path and

---

[11] For an analysis of JHA decision-making practice in the light of arguments advanced by deliberative intergovernmentalism, see the chapter on JHA cooperation by Sarah Wolff in Bickerton et al. (2015).

that the Maastricht Treaty indeed marks the beginning of the new intergo-vernmentalism, the rest of this section offers a brief review of key institutional developments during the post-Maastricht period. What is striking about this period is that European integration continued as an extremely dynamic process. In particular the areas of economic governance and CFSP developed rapidly from the second half of the 1990s onwards. The decision to base them on the principle of intergovernmental policy coordination did not lead to abandonment of the relevant projects. Similarly, the field of social policy did not go out of focus despite the absence of legislative innovation. It became another subject of unprecedented coordination efforts. Within a period of about 15 years the EU saw three new treaties, a Convention on the Future of Europe drafting a Constitutional Treaty, and a series of European Council decisions resulting in the creation of a whole range of new coordination mechanisms and activities. This dynamism speaks to the post-Maastricht integration paradox. The absence of any major transfers of ultimate decision-making powers to the supranational level is not a sign of integration fatigue. Rather, the challenge has been to advance integration without, or with only strictly limited, delegation of power.

As foreseen by the Maastricht Treaty provisions, economic governance under EMU was developed gradually. Not only was the accession of individual member states to the single currency designed as a process of complying with a set of so-called convergence criteria, the provisions on EMU also foresaw the gradual development of its institutions and policies. With the irrevocable fixing of the exchange rates of the first EU currencies to be included in the monetary union by the end of the 1990s, the single currency became a reality. In 1997 the European Council created the Eurogroup as an informal forum for policy dialogue among euro-area finance ministers, the Commission, and the ECB (European Council 1997b). The group started to operate in addition to the ECOFIN Council with a schedule of monthly meetings, and evolved into the central forum for budgetary policy coordination under the SGP. A dedicated senior expert committee—the EFC, which was charged by the Treaty with supporting economic policy coordination—began to operate following the introduction of the single currency. The coordination agenda expanded rapidly. The process of budgetary surveillance became more complex and sophisticated over time. Issues such as structural reform, the long-term sustainability of public finances and external representation of the euro area, and the EU's representation on international financial and economic forums, were added to the coordination agenda. The Amsterdam and Nice Treaties left the provisions relating to economic governance unchanged. The European Convention reviewed the EMU institutional set-up within the context of a specific working group on economic governance; and it confirmed the decentralized framework of economic governance (European Convention

2002; Puetter 2007a). The Constitutional Treaty and the Lisbon Treaty also left the main institutional architecture unchanged. Instead both treaties introduced a number of additional provisions that were aimed at further refining the coordination set-up. The Eurogroup became recognized by the Treaty, and so did the fact that it was chaired by an elected president. The scope of decisions on which euro-area countries could decide among themselves was extended. The Commission's role in monitoring and publicly reprimanding member states for failure to comply with budgetary policy objectives was strengthened. Yet the Commission did not obtain any autonomous powers to reverse or dictate national policy.

From 2008 onwards the global economic and financial crisis triggered frenetic coordination activity covering a full range of crisis response policies including bank resolution, financial sector supervision, and financial assistance for member states facing the risk of bankruptcy. Yet again, the basic governance architecture remained largely unchanged (Hodson and Puetter 2013). Instead existing coordination procedures were tightened and expanded. The European Stability Mechanism (ESM), as the first-ever permanent EU rescue fund, was created on the basis of an intergovernmental treaty outside the framework of the EU budget, and put member states in full control of financial assistance processes to which they would have to agree unanimously. The main legislative changes brought forward during the crisis—also referred to as the so-called 'six-pack' and 'two-pack'—essentially follow the approach of earlier legislation on the SGP: multilateral surveillance and the excessive deficit procedure; coordination activity was regulated further and expanded in scope; and the procedural responsibilities of individual institutional actors were specified more clearly (cf. Armstrong 2013). The Commission's role as an independent watchdog was strengthened. Yet again these reforms did not involve the delegation of ultimate enforcement powers to the Commission. The Treaty on Stability, Coordination and Governance in EMU (TSCG)—the so-called Fiscal Treaty or Fiscal Compact—represented the most far-reaching attempt in this regard. In March 2012 the document was signed as an intergovernmental treaty outside EU law by all EU member states except the Czech Republic and the UK. It de facto modified and complemented the Treaty provisions on EMU. Demands for formal treaty change had been vetoed in the European Council by British Prime Minister David Cameron. The Fiscal Treaty amounts to a tightening of the excessive deficit procedure. The Commission's role within the process was strengthened in that the document stated that euro-area member states 'commit to supporting the proposals or recommendations submitted by the European Commission' (Article 7, TSCG), in case it considered a member state to be in breach of the deficit rule, unless a qualified majority emerged within the Council against such an assessment by the Commission. Originally a qualified majority was needed to pass a decision in the Council on the existence of an excessive deficit. For the first time the Fiscal Treaty gave the Court of Justice a role in deciding the question of whether a member state was complying with the corrective measures required of it in the context of the excessive deficit procedure. Yet the circumstances under which Court action could be triggered are noteworthy. The Fiscal Treaty stipulated that 'the matter will be brought to the Court of Justice of the European Union by one or more Contracting Parties' (Article 8, TSCG). It thus did not give this right to the Commission. Though these changes have undoubtedly tightened the excessive deficit procedure, they have not removed the Council's role as the central political decision-making forum; the Council can still exercise considerable political discretion on these matters. Perhaps most importantly, the trajectory of euro-area budgetary policy coordination since the late 1990s shows that the real challenge is to prevent member states from getting into the excessive deficit procedure in the first place. The crisis provided a drastic illustration of how limited the effects of the coercive elements of the excessive deficit procedure and the SGP can be in the midst of a spreading sovereign debt crisis. Though the coercive character of some of the crisis response measures—the conditionality attached to financial assistance packages—remained unprecedented, such measures are of limited effect if the very functioning of state authority at the domestic level is seriously threatened. Therefore the potential role of the Court of Justice in enforcing collective EU policy guidelines should not be overstated. As before, the system depends essentially on constant attempts at consensus formation around a set of commonly shared economic policy objectives, also and especially in economically easier times (cf. Hodson 2011). The Fiscal Treaty indeed reiterated earlier Euro Summit decisions to further expand the coordination infrastructure consisting of the European Council, the Euro Summit, the Eurogroup, and the specialized committees (see chapter 4). The constant quest for consensus generation, therefore, has remained a key characteristic of the EMU economic governance set-up.

A similar expansion of the coordination agenda can be observed in the field of foreign, security, and defence policy. Here too the enhancement of the related institutional infrastructure is clearly visible. The development of CFSP, especially in the period immediately after Maastricht, was by no means straightforward. However, instances of coordination failure did not lead to a standstill but rather triggered further institutional innovation. After the experiences of the 1990s, especially with the EU's difficulties in grappling with the disintegration of the former Yugoslavia, the Amsterdam Treaty confirmed the determination of EU member states to improve coordination and further develop the institutional set-up to this end. The Treaty abolished the troika leadership structure and created the position of High Representative (HR). The HR was charged with assisting the presidency in representing CFSP and was mandated to support the Council in formulating, preparing, and implementing policy, and could be authorized to conduct negotiations with external parties. The Amsterdam Treaty also backed up the coordination process by creating an administrative support structure. To this end the Policy Planning and Early Warning Unit—also referred to simply as the Policy Unit—was established and put under the supervision of the HR. Moreover, the Treaty highlighted the importance of the defence component of CFSP, and singled out humanitarian and rescue operations, peacekeeping missions, and the provision of combat forces in crisis situations. Finally, the Amsterdam Treaty created the instrument of common strategies by which the European Council could establish the overall direction of policy with regard to particular foreign policy issues. The Treaty of Nice further expanded the coordination infrastructure and set up the PSC as a senior expert committee in charge of supporting the Council in the process of policy definition and implementation.

This gradual build-up of the coordination infrastructure was continued with the Treaty of Lisbon, which added the EEAS as an EU diplomatic service and larger-scale administrative resource. The position of the HR was further strengthened. The office holder now supervised the EEAS, chaired the meetings of the FAC, and could initiate policy. The Lisbon Treaty represented the biggest step in the area of defence policy coordination so far. The Treaty emphasized the objective of establishing a common EU defence policy and authorized the European Council to finalize the transition to such a regime without a further change in the Treaty. The Treaty also explicitly required member states to support each other in case of aggression (Article 42.7, TFEU). The emphasis on operational capacity was expanded and now included reference to both civilian and military resources. Joint disarmament operations, the provision of military advice and assistance, and post-conflict stabilization were added to the existing catalogue of potential operational activities. A new mechanism of 'permanent structured cooperation' (Article 42.6, TFEU) implied more ambitious military cooperation arrangements of smaller groups of member states under the EU umbrella. The Lisbon Treaty also allowed the Council to charge particular groups of member states to carry out certain operational tasks. Finally, the Lisbon Treaty introduced the European Defence Agency (EDA), which was put in charge of coordinating the improvement of military capabilities and could be tasked by the Council to carry out managerial functions in this regard.

All of the above-listed institutional innovations expanded the scope of the coordination agenda and the institutional infrastructure for coordination. Yet they did not delegate ultimate decision-making powers to independent supranational actors. The EEAS does not fit the classic model of an independent supranational bureaucracy like the Commission, though the new service imported some of the Commission's external affairs resources. The EEAS instead has a crucial intergovernmental component too (see chapter 4.5).

The position of the HR is designed to forge consensus among member states, and to represent the EU's policy stance in relation to the outside world, it does not imply any independent enforcement powers vis-à-vis non-compliant member states. In fact, the Lisbon Treaty went farther than any other previous Treaty in emphasizing the distinct character of the field of foreign and security policy as an area based on intergovernmental policy coordination. Article 24.1, TEU stipulated that '[t]he adoption of legislative acts shall be excluded'. Moreover, the Lisbon Treaty reaffirmed that the Court of Justice 'shall not have jurisdiction' over CFSP and Common Security and Defence Policy (CSDP) policy decisions, or the implementation of such decisions on behalf of member state governments. As one external affairs official sought to explain the difference between CFSP agreements and community method decision-making:

Each agreement will be fragile but such agreement will be morally obligatory.[12]

Again it can be concluded that CFSP and CSDP coordination implies a constant quest for consensus formation among member states. As in the sphere of economic governance, formally stated policy guidelines remain 'fragile' by default, as member states can easily defect from earlier agreements.

The rapid expansion of coordination activity in the post-Maastricht period was also detectable in the field of employment and social policy coordination. Coordination activity in this domain also became increasingly integrated with the economic governance agenda. Shortly after the launch of the EES in 1997 the Cardiff European Council instituted a similar coordination arrangement in the field of domestic economic reform in 1998, including a focus on structural policy and the method of best practice comparisons between national policy approaches (European Council 1998). Only one year later the European Council established at its Cologne meeting the so-called macro-economic dialogue, which institutionalized the model of tripartite consultations at the EU level. These consultations included, besides the social partners, all relevant EU institutions: the Council, the Commission, and the ECB (European Council 1999b). The Lisbon European Council added further elements to the existing coordination agenda. The new coordination mechanisms were also to include, among other elements, poverty reduction and social inclusion as well as the future of social security systems. The so-called Lisbon agenda integrated the multiple coordination mechanism into a European reform agenda, and framed the new coordination approach of European Council supervision, regular Council-level coordination, and the new expert committee structure as the OMC (European Council 2000).

---

[12] Interviewee EU-13/EXT, 10 March 2009.

The coordination processes outlined above were gradually brought into the Treaty framework. As in the case of EMU economic policy and the CFSP, the Treaty provisions did not create new legislative competences at the EU level but focused on defining general patterns of coordination, related procedures, and the responsibilities of individual institutions. Close policy dialogue between member states was the main aim of the various processes. The Commission was assigned an important role in providing policy assessment and advice as well as general support to the coordination process, but it did not obtain its traditional right of initiative. The Commission was not authorized to sanction national policies except by expressing its position in the context of the specified procedures for policy dialogue. The Amsterdam Treaty incorporated employment policy coordination into the new Title VIII, TEC on employment. The new provisions were placed directly after those relating to EMU. The Nice Treaty provided for the creation of the Social Protection Committee (SPC) (Article 144, TEC Nice), thus underpinning the new emphasis on coordinating social inclusion and social protection matters. Finally, the Lisbon Treaty highlighted the link between economic governance and social and employment policy coordination by grouping these three areas under Article 5, TFEU, which defines, together with several other provisions, the core activities of the EU. The field of social and employment policy coordination also remains dependent on constant consensus generation. The failure to expand the EU's legislative *acquis* in this policy domain should not be conflated with the absence of salient policy issues. Both the processes preceding the Lisbon agenda and the more recent experience of the economic and financial crisis show the interrelatedness of this policy domain with the sphere of economic governance and monetary union. Member states might not agree to delegate legislative decision-making competences in this policy field to the EU level, but national governments are equally concerned that they may not be able to address the social dimension of European integration unilaterally.

## 1.4 Methods Matter

All these developments demonstrate the pervasiveness of the original Maastricht formula in its development of new areas of EU activity, mostly outside the sphere of classic community method decision-making. The post-Maastricht period by no means lacks dynamism. The rapid succession of Treaty changes and the related expansion of the coordination agenda and of the political and bureaucratic decision-making infrastructure demonstrate that the new intergovernmentalism is not a reflection of general integration fatigue. The proliferation of coordination mechanisms in the three selected new areas of EU activity outlined above follows a common institutional pattern. The Council is assigned the role of the central political decision-making institution. It is supervised by the European Council, which is endowed with the prerogative to determine the overall policy direction. The Commission is given an important role in all three new areas of EU activity—though its role is a modified one. The Commission contributes to policy formulation and supports implementation, but can neither exercise its traditional right of initiative nor does it have independent enforcement powers, which otherwise characterize its role as a guardian of the Treaties. The Court of Justice does not have jurisdiction over substantial policy decisions insofar as they are taken within the context of the main coordination procedures. It may only rule on matters arising from some of the procedural obligations of individual institutional actors within the coordination process. Even where the Court of Justice is given a limited role in reviewing issues related to the question of whether member states comply with specific policy guidelines, Court action needs to be triggered by member states rather than the Commission. In any case, the relevant clause within the Fiscal Treaty relating to the implementation of corrective measures under the excessive deficit procedure remains the only example in this regard.

The above review of key institutional decisions during the course of the first two decades after the adoption of the Maastricht Treaty in the three selected policy areas reveals the apparent rejection of further formal transfers of ultimate decision-making competence to the EU level. The emphasis on policy coordination and decentralized decision-making was, and still is, informed by a fundamental scepticism about the process of integration whereby inter-governmental decision-making is channelled into the adoption of legally binding policy decisions and the delegation of ultimate decision-making power—even in a limited way. Moreover, the procedural prerogative enjoyed by the Commission to propose legislation for approval by the Council and the EP as the two co-legislators has been called into question. Yet the above review of key institutional developments also shows that the new intergovernmentalism does not develop at the expense of previously created competences of the Union as far as specific policy domains are concerned. Rather, the new major areas of EU activity evolve in addition to the catalogue of existing EU policy domains, and the new intergovernmentalism prevails within these areas. There has not been a single major example of policy coordination replacing the previously established law-making competences of the Union.[13] With EMU's supranational monetary policy pillar and the Social Agreement,

---

[13] In the field of social policy there are instances in which new and revised legislation includes coordination elements and so-called soft law provisions, as no agreement in the Council could be found on other forthcoming legislative proposals. Yet in most of these cases coordination complements rather than replaces binding provisions.

the Maastricht Treaty had actually expanded the range of EU supranational competences. However, at that time the scope of EU-level policy action was expanded on the basis of a distinctively different approach.

This difference can be also characterized as a difference in methods of governance or—for that matter—of integration. The community method links EU-level decision-making with legislative decision-making, and insists on the binding character of policy decisions. Thus, it is fundamentally different from a predominantly intergovernmental method of decision-making. This was highlighted by the discussion about the so-called Lisbon agenda, which subsumed a number of intergovernmental policy coordination processes under the OMC. The much-quoted White Paper on European Governance (European Commission 2001) described the community method as having the Commission at the core of EU-level policy-making. The Commission alone initiates legislation and policy. By doing so, it acts independently and in the general interest of the Union. The Council and the EP act as 'the Union's legislature', and provide democratic representation of member states and European citizens respectively. The Commission hails the use of qualified majority decision-making in the Council as 'an essential element in ensuring the effectiveness of the [community] method' (European Commission 2001: 8). Both the Commission and national authorities may assume the task and competence of executing policies decided at the EU level. The Commission also acts as the guardian of the Treaty and is responsible for external representation. Finally, the Court of Justice assumes the role of guaranteeing 'respect for the rule of law' (European Commission 2001: 8). In the view of the Commission these elements of the community method also contribute to 'fair treatment' (European Commission 2001: 8) of all members of the Union and allow for arbitration between rival interests.

Although none of the different treaties since Maastricht have ever made reference to the term 'community method', the elements highlighted by the Commission's White Paper are clearly identifiable. Interestingly, the Lisbon Treaty has offered the strongest endorsement so far of the community method as the EU's core legislative mechanism. The Lisbon Treaty introduced the term 'ordinary legislative procedure' (Article 289.1, TFEU), which involves joint legislative decision-making by the Council and the EP based on proposals by the Commission (Article 294, TFEU). Although the Lisbon Treaty did anything but abandon entirely the diversity of legislative and non-legislative decision-making procedures, it lent moral authority to the community method in the sense that this method was characterized as the legislative decision-making procedure that ought to be the 'ordinary' one. The Lisbon Treaty also brought the greatest expansion of the principle of co-decision by the Council and the EP thus far, as well as the use of QMV as the main procedure for legislative decision-making within the Council. The Lisbon Treaty's focus on methodology, however, was equally apparent with regard to the new spheres of intergovernmental policy coordination. There was an equally strong endorsement of intergovernmental policy coordination as the main governance method with regard to the three areas of EU activity referred to in this book. The Lisbon Treaty contained new provisions and new language in this regard. As highlighted earlier in this chapter the acknowledgement of the Eurogroup and new reference to the distinct character of CFSP and CSDP coordination make clear the difference between the governance method applied within the new areas of EU activity and the community method.

There is little doubt about the ongoing political contestation related to the issue of what constitutes the right balance between the community method and intergovernmental policy coordination in EU governance. In particular the Commission and the EP are at times vocal proponents of expanding the community method to areas governed by intergovernmental policy coordination. Their view is essentially that the struggle for closer EU integration is about expanding the use of the community method. There is no shortage of statements by representatives from the two institutions. In April 2012, particular symbolism was added to such calls on the occasion of the EP president Martin Schulz's participation in a regular Commission meeting—a new practice aimed at underpinning closer ties between the two bodies. Commission president José Manuel Barroso was quoted emphasizing that:

> [T]he strong commitment of our two institutions to the Community method is the best way of helping the EU to make progress and to make it prosperous . . . The Community method is the only way of guaranteeing fairness and commitment to the general European interest.[14]

And the EP president seconded this as follows:

> We want to pursue European integration; there is no question of going backwards . . . We want more integration but some countries are talking about renationalization; the European institutions have to work hand-in-hand to avoid that.[15]

Member state governments countered these calls by insisting that the Union was based on the coexistence and at times the combination of the two alternative methods. As documented by subsequent rounds of treaty negotiations since Maastricht, member state governments were unanimous in repeatedly rejecting calls for an expansion of the community method. Moreover, the duality of the current system of governance was stressed repeatedly. In a speech at the College of Europe in Bruges in November 2010, which received considerable attention, the German chancellor Angela Merkel set

---

[14] As quoted by Agence Europe, 25 April 2012.
[15] As quoted by Agence Europe, 25 April 2012.

out her view of the Lisbon Treaty. She argued that the Treaty in fact provided for a clear distribution of competences between the different EU institutions, including a reinforced European Council. Merkel differentiated between the 'intergovernmental method' and the 'community method', emphasizing that the former could lead as easily to a common European position as the latter method.[16] In her view EU policy-making was about combining the two methods, so that legislative action under the community method supported the coordinated action of the member states, and vice versa. Merkel labelled such a symbiosis 'the new "Union method"'.[17] Somewhat cryptically the German chancellor also emphasized that the 'Community Method was not intended to transfer competences to Europe but is a method of applying already transferred competences in a good, reasonable and efficient way'.[18] Again, this interpretation confirmed the emphasis on a dual governance structure. Within this structure the realm of community method decision-making has proved to be fairly stable ever since Maastricht. Accordingly, any new dynamism in the evolution and expansion of EU policy activities should be located elsewhere—namely in the intergovernmental realm.

Speaking at the same venue as Merkel earlier the same year, the first elected European Council president Herman Van Rompuy had advanced a similar argument by making reference to the example of EU foreign policy—one of the new areas of EU activity:

> As you have learned here at the Collège, Europe started as a market, with a unique working method. We can be proud of what it achieved. However, building a market is different from being a power. 'L'Europe-puissance', as the French like to call it. I should like to mention two, somewhat sensitive, consequences.
>
> First: the decision method. In foreign policy you need quick decision and action, whereas our original working method was devised, and works well, as a rule making procedure. Progress in European foreign policy has relied largely on the impulse and the authority of the Heads of State or Government. That's why some analysts have described the European Council, operating in foreign policy, as 'a collective head of state'.[19]

How politically charged the discussion around the new intergovernmentalism was, was illustrated further by former French president Sarkozy. He was quoted hailing the basic agreement at the December 2011 European Council meeting on the Fiscal Treaty as a progressive step, as it located collective political authority outside the established supranational institutions:

> The fact that the governance reverts to heads of state and governments marks an incontestable democratic process compared with the previous situation in which

---

[16] Merkel (2010).      [17] Merkel (2010: 7).      [18] Merkel (2010: 6).
[19] Herman Van Rompuy (2010b: 6).

everything revolved around the European Central Bank, the European Commission and the stability pact[.][20]

That for many of the heads of state or government who are represented in the European Council similar considerations are pivotal was also confirmed by a senior member state official working as one of the personal officials of a European head of state or government. The civil servant explained that the heads would always get into the game of directly deciding matters related to policy coordination by themselves as soon as they noticed that the de facto level of integration and the potential implications for domestic policy-making were high:

> The level of integration matters when it comes to the heads deciding whether something is politically important or not.[21]

## 1.5 Conclusions

By making reference to key institutional choices at Maastricht and beyond, this chapter has demonstrated that integration can no longer primarily be conceptualized as a process of *delegating legislative powers and ultimate executive decision-making competences* to the EU level. Rather, further integration is pursued through the *closer coordination of domestic policies at the EU level* and the targeted pooling of national resources for achieving collective ambitions. The Maastricht Treaty indeed marks a watershed in EU integration, as the document embodies both the peak and the end of legislative activism as the main driving force of EU integration. Never before had member states committed themselves so clearly to an additional and distinctive approach to integration. The Maastricht Treaty not only placed EMU economic governance, as well as CFSP and CSDP coordination, under a distinct institutional framework outside the community method: it also assigned to these policy domains a central role in EU integration. It is this combination of political prioritization and the specification of a distinct governance method that characterizes the Maastricht Treaty and the subsequent development of other new areas of EU activity. In contemporary EU policy-making the conviction that stronger EU-level action is the precondition for resolving today's fundamental policy challenges clashes increasingly with insistence on ultimate national sovereignty. This institutional dilemma is referred to here as the *integration paradox*.

---

[20] As quoted by the *Financial Times*, 12 December 2011.
[21] Interviewee MS-06/GEN, 3 July 2009.

The argument throughout this book takes this integration paradox seriously when studying the role of the European Council and the Council as key forums for representing member state governments in contemporary EU decision-making. The salient and unprecedented role of intergovernmental decision-making is a consequence of the integration paradox. As the option of transferring further powers to the EU level is ruled out, member state governments need to compensate for the lack of supranational steering power by developing new intergovernmental decision-making structures. Methods indeed matter in the way the integration process evolves. It would, therefore, be wrong to take the normative debate about which method the EU ultimately should follow as the answer to an analytical question, namely what the role of the European Council and the Council in EU decision-making actually is and how both institutions have developed over time. Reference to methods of governance—whether in the Treaty or made by leading representatives of EU institutions and member state governments—is not merely a rhetorical exercise but a reflection of the fact that methods indeed matter enormously in the question of how the EU is currently governed.

The core institutional logic of post-Maastricht new intergovernmentalism, which has been outlined in this chapter, implies a particular challenge for EU decision-making: member states need to reach consensus within the European Council and the Council each and every time they want to level genuine collective EU action. Moreover, policy consensus needs to be broad and to involve all, or almost all, actors. In the absence of automatic sanctioning mechanisms it is easy for individual actors to defect from commonly adopted policy guidelines. Yet even where such sanctioning mechanisms exist—as in the case of the excessive deficit rule—it cannot be taken for granted that their application solves the problem or is actually possible. The reason for this is that many policy issues imply serious repercussions on domestic policy and politics. It is far from certain that a potentially more rigid enforcement of common policy objectives by a central EU authority would find acceptance at the domestic level. Difficult budgetary decisions or the sending of troops as part of an EU military mission, let alone guidelines on how to reform national pension systems, could hardly be ultimately enforced against the will of member state governments.

This is not to say that the balance between centralized supranational authority and member state authority has not always been a fundamental problem of EU integration in general. There is no shortage of examples showing, for instance, that the exercise of existing regulatory competences by Brussels has sometimes been considered as intrusive interference with national autonomy. Yet overall the existing framework of single market governance through the community method is respected. The main difference as regards the development of the new areas of EU activity is that reservations about further centralization, which have arisen in connection with the expansion of single market governance, have led to a set of specific institutional choices at Maastricht and beyond, all of which have kept increased delegation of ultimate enforcement powers to an absolute minimum. Wherever the EU exercises political authority in new areas of activity it prefers to do so by coordinating national policies and the use of national resources within collective bodies for joint member state decision-making: the European Council and the Council.

This arrangement does not mean that the EU remains inactive with regard to its new areas of activity. No matter how opposed individual member states might be in relation to particular decisions, there is very little opposition to the idea that the EU in general plays a greater role in the three new areas of EU activity. Quite to the contrary, and as demonstrated throughout this chapter, member states have repeatedly expressed their desire to develop these policy domains further as areas of common concern. Member state governments since Maastricht have been unanimous in their analysis that ever-growing policy interdependencies and new policy challenges have required more EU-level activity rather than unilateral policy action. Post-Maastricht, new intergovernmentalism has been characterized by a permanent quest for consensus. As member states generally aspire to collective policy responses, divergences over policy have therefore led to a renewed quest for consensus, rather than to abandoning the decision-making process. In other words, consensus and deliberation have become ends in themselves (Bickerton et al. 2015).

The above review of key institutional decisions on new areas of EU activity shows the reiterated commitment to coordination and problem-solving. Commitment to the coordination process has thus become the guiding procedural norm of the new intergovernmentalism, ranking even before and above any commitment to particular policy objectives. Such reasoning is also detectable in the following statement by European Council president Herman Van Rompuy:

> All member states can, and do, have particular requests and needs that are always taken into consideration as part of our deliberations. I do not expect any member state to seek to undermine the fundamentals of our co-operative system in Europe.[22]

The rise of new intergovernmentalism and the dependency on ongoing consensus generation affects the way EU institutions operate. The focus of intergovernmental activity in EU politics is now to a much lesser extent a function of the supranational legislative process. Thus it is to be expected that the core EU arenas for intergovernmental decision-making and member state representation—the European Council and the Council—are undergoing a process of profound institutional change.

---

[22] Herman Van Rompuy, interview, *The Guardian*, 27 December 2012.

# 2

# Deliberative Intergovernmentalism and Institutional Change

This chapter introduces deliberative intergovernmentalism as an analytical framework, which focuses on understanding a particular institutional dynamic that dominates the post-Maastricht European Union (EU): new intergovernmentalism and the centrality of European Council and Council of the European Union decision-making in the governance of the new areas of EU activity. The previous chapter revealed that pivotal decisions about the EU's institutional architecture in the post-Maastricht era have been triggered by the *integration paradox*. Member states have been reluctant to commit to further transfers of ultimate decision-making powers, but have remained eager to act collectively as regards core areas of state sovereignty.

This dilemma could be addressed only by organizing collective policy action outside the EU's previously established framework of community method decision-making. Moreover, as the delegation of enforcement powers and policy-making resources to independent supranational institutions is ruled out, policy development and implementation depend on the structured pooling of national resources and existing EU-level capacities. The threshold for defecting from commonly agreed policy objectives is relatively low, as the European Commission and the Court of Justice are usually banned from acting, according to the same legal principles that govern policies adopted under the community method. This has had a major impact on EU decision-making practice: the member states constantly need to aim for consensus among themselves and with the Commission over collective policy action—far more so than has been the case in the domain of classic community method decision-making.

The trajectory of institutional development from Maastricht to Lisbon documents the quest for consensus. Member states have repeatedly committed themselves to expanding the coordination agenda and the related institutional infrastructure. Consensual agreement on common policy guidelines is the basis for exercising political authority in the three new areas of EU activity. Deliberative intergovernmentalism holds that this quest for consensus *triggers permanent attempts at institutional engineering that are aimed at increasing the consensus generation potential* of the EU's main forums for member state representation: the European Council and the Council of the European Union ('the Council'). The two bodies cannot relate to the new areas of EU activity, which are organized outside the framework of the community method, as they relate to established fields of community method decision-making. Instead, the newintergovernmentalism requires—to a considerable extent—a different approach to collective decision-making. The main analytical aim of deliberative intergovernmentalism is to provide criteria for tracing and assessing these changes in intergovernmental decision-making practice.

This chapter develops this theoretical argument further. To this end it first seeks to establish a clearer understanding of what distinguishes classic community method decision-making from the new intergovernmentalism in EU politics. The community method is identified as establishing some form of independent though limited supranational authority. Similarly, the juxtaposition of supranationalism and intergovernmentalism as the two most prominent opposing concepts in the literature on EU decision-making and governance is discussed. In a second step this chapter explores the relationship between the analytical framework of deliberative intergovernmentalism and existing research on new governance and literature on decision-making within the European Council and the Council. Finally and most importantly, this chapter provides a set of theoretically informed propositions on post-Maastricht institutional change in relation to the European Council and the Council. These propositions entail specific criteria for analysing institutional change and represent the main reference frame for reviewing the processes of institutional engineering that have occurred in the European Council and Council environment since the second half of the 1990s, when the two bodies came to lead the development of the EU's new areas of activity.

## 2.1 The Community Method and New Intergovernmentalism

The terms community method, intergovernmentalism and supranationalism belong to the alphabet of European integration studies. However, they each acquire different connotations depending on who uses them and in what context. In the following, each concept is considered briefly in relation to the underlying argument of deliberative intergovernmentalism that post-Maastricht EU institutional choice is informed by the integration paradox and that collective decision-making outside the framework of the classic community method requires the constant generation of consensus among member state governments on specific policy moves. The point here is not to settle differences in terminology once and for all or to offer an encompassing review of the vast EU studies literature. but rather to provide guidance on how each concept is understood and applied in the context of this study.

### 2.1.1 The Community Method and the Constitution of Supranational Authority

Giandomenico Majone (2005: 51) sees 'the zenith of the Community method' reached with the Single European Act (SEA)—the legal basis for the relaunch of the single market in the 1980s. In his view the shift of attention towards regulatory governance instead of so-called positive integration was the precondition for the rise of the community method. Regulatory governance through community method decision-making was an adequate mechanism for advancing integration against the background of member states' reluctance to pool budgetary resources at the European level, so as to sustain a 'positive state' (Majone 1997). This speaks to the idea that was advanced in the previous chapter: that with the Maastricht Treaty the EU saw the peak and the end of legislative activism. Deliberative intergovernmentalism also follows Majone's idea that it should not be surprising that the empowerment of supranational actors—notably the Commission and the Court of Justice—was challenged by member states at a later stage. Majone (2005: 74) also considers that such scepticism about the community method is not necessarily an indication of a lack of commitment to the integration process.

For Fritz Scharpf, community method decision-making can be conceptualized according to two main ideas: its problem-solving capacity and the balance between negative and positive integration. Scharpf (2003) emphasizes that the community method implies that national governments have to accept EU-level decisions without being able to correct them should these decisions prove not to be opportune in the domestic context later. Under the community method, intergovernmental decision-making among member states is the basis for empowering certain supranational actors and adopting binding policy decisions. The procedure through which member states agree and the role of supranational actors in it determine the problem-solving capacity of a given EU governance set-up. For Scharpf, all forms of intergovernmental decision-making face a fundamental dilemma: the joint-decision trap. In Scharpf's (1988) original conception of the joint-decision trap hypothesis, the reduced problem-solving capacity of European decision-making was caused by the dependency on unanimous decisions. Member states found it very difficult to escape from this situation. None of them wanted to be the first to give away authority to institutions that enjoyed enough autonomy to distance themselves from the redistributional conflicts among member states. According to

Scharpf such autonomy is required for producing effective policy decisions. Empowering supranational actors to devise and execute policies independently may be the most extreme way of insulating EU decision-making from the joint decision-making trap. Thus, the Commission's right of initiative and qualified majority decision-making are important institutional features that have the potential to increase the problem-solving capacity of the multilevel governance setting (Scharpf 2006).

This conceptualization of the community method also confirms the juxtaposition by deliberative intergovernmentalism of community method decision-making, which involves the delegation of ultimate decision-making authority, on the one hand, and intergovernmental policy coordination, or intergovernmental agreement, as Scharpf calls it, on the other hand. Scharpf's scepticism about the problem-solving capacity of intergovernmental decision-making in general and decision-making outside the framework of the community method in particular almost amounts to a complete rejection of post-Maastricht new intergovernmentalism as a significant form of integration.

Such interpretation is further reinforced by Scharpf's argument about the 'asymmetric political economy of European integration' (Scharpf 2001). As a consequence of the process of market integration—or 'negative integration', in Scharpf's terminology—the policy-making capacity of member states in areas that are not also formally subject to EU decision-making competences is heavily constrained. Such lack of capacity could only be compensated for by reconstituting political authority, notably core welfare functions, at the EU level (cf. Leibfried and Pierson 1992). For Scharpf, the emergence of such political authority would constitute a case of positive integration. However, Scharpf concludes that 'under the constraint of the joint-decision trap, the EU will not be able to do much, if anything, about filling the problem-solving gap through European measures of positive integration' (Scharpf 2006: 856).

Deliberative intergovernmentalism does not deny Scharpf's argument that federal or multilevel political systems are prone to joint-decision trap scenarios. Neither is the point here to deny the obvious failures of some of the open method of coordination (OMC) initiatives that were launched in the late 1990s as part of the Lisbon agenda. Yet deliberative intergovernmentalism follows Armstrong (2010: 189–90), who rejects Scharpf's scepticism that policy coordination by default cannot trigger positive integration. If this were true the EU would be a static construct. This is not what can be observed in the post-Maastricht era (see chapter 1). The new areas of EU activity all involve aspects of positive integration. Deliberative intergovernmentalism seeks to respond to the puzzle of how the EU can further integrate, in the absence of an omnipotent supranational authority at its centre. Moreover, there is no a priori defined limit as regards the scope of intergovernmental policy coordination. The joint-decision trap is essentially an institutional dilemma. As long as there is a general quest for policy consensus and collective action, this dilemma may be addressed in different ways. Each route may lead to imperfect solutions. The community method represents no exception in this regard: any expectation that the community method must do better on this front may be unrealistic. Rather than postulating that only community method procedures may enhance the problem-solving potential of EU decision-making, deliberative intergovernmentalism expects to find evidence of attempts at institutional engineering that are aimed at improving the EU's problem-solving capacities by developing specific routines and procedures for policy deliberation within the core intergovernmental forums for EU policy coordination, i.e. the European Council, the Council, and the coordination committees.

The following definition of the community method can serve as an analytical reference point throughout this book. The community method deals with the constitution of independent—though limited—supranational capacity to act autonomously. An extreme form of such supranational capacity may be defined by what Scharpf (2003) refers to as the 'supranational centralization mode', or what Wallace (2000: 28–32) calls the 'distinct community method'. Generally, community method decision-making aims to establish some form of supranational authority. The massive expansion of the EU's regulatory policy *acquis* in connection with the implementation of the single market may serve as the key reference case here. The role of EU law is crucial in this regard. There is a formal procedure, which regulates the process of aggregating member states' interests. Collective decision-making is framed as legislative decision-making. The community method codifies the result of this process and defines a mechanism for controlling the implementation and application of EU law. This definition of the community method is also sufficiently close to the one offered by the European Commission's (2001) White Paper on European Governance, and it accommodates the notion of the ordinary legislative procedure that was established by the Lisbon Treaty.

The fact that the community method is invariably tied to the EU legislative process (Joerges and Rödl 2009) requires further inspection. EU legislative decision-making implies that procedures are in place for executing and implementing policy and for settling disagreements between the various actors. The fact that the Court of Justice operates as a constitutional court in this context can be considered as a further expression of supranational authority (cf. Hinarejos 2009). However, this supranational legal order is peculiar. EU law scholars emphasize the difference in the way public authority is exercised at the EU and member state levels respectively. As Armin von Bogdandy (2010: 30) points out, the EU 'is (only) a community of law and not also a community of coercion'. Through the community method the process of European integration has been tied to the principle of the rule of law. Accomplishing integration can in many ways be understood as creating legal unity. According to von Bogdandy (2010: 33) this process 'transformed, federalised and constitutionalised the relationship between Union and Member States'.

Given the absence of a monopoly of coercion, integration through law under the community method can also be considered as the combined use of decentralized resources. The assignation of supranational competences to the EU level implies the authority to initiate legislation, to define policy more or less independently in a given area, and to represent the Union internally and externally. Yet the most important supranational resource—the body of EU law or the *acquis*—relies on decentralized resources, i.e. the member states, when it comes to enforcement. The EU supervises the implementation of the legal order but lacks the resources to enforce it independently of the member states. Following this line of thought Philipp Dann (2010: 243) conceptualizes the EU's political system as 'executive federalism', which is characterized by a 'vertical structure of interwoven competences' that requires constant cooperation. This logic finds its expression in the central role of the Council in EU governance, which in Dann's (2010: 244) words is the 'institutional complement of the system of competences'. Moreover, because the overall system depends so much on cooperation, Dann considers consensual decision-making to be a key characteristic of the Council's work.

Christian Joerges and colleagues argue that the consensus orientation of the legislative process can be traced empirically, and that it leads to particular institutional features (Joerges and Neyer 1997; Joerges 2002; Joerges and Rödl 2009). The decision-making process cannot rely purely on formal decision-making rules such as unanimity or qualified majority voting (QMV), but needs to engage member state representatives into a deliberative process during the policy formation phase. Only where agreement is reached that a given EU policy can serve to resolve policy deficiencies stemming from the inadequacy of national-level solutions will EU legislation carry the relevant legitimacy. Such legitimacy is required to ensure policy implementation and the overall acceptance of the legislative process. This institutional dynamic is referred to by Joerges and colleagues as deliberative supranationalism. Joerges and Neyer (1997) applied this concept empirically with regard to community method comitology. What is important here is that deliberation is recognized as an inherent feature of EU decision-making. Deliberative intergovernmentalism indeed owes its name to this argument of deliberative supranationalism. The original idea was to define the strong focus of post-Maastricht intergovernmentalism on policy deliberation, in analogy to a core feature of the community method system.[1] Yet the institutional dynamics are also inherently

---

[1] Cf. Puetter (2006, 2012b). It is also important to note that Christian Joerges' reasoning behind the concept of deliberative supranationalism is explicitly motivated by normative considerations (see chapter 5.2).

different. In the context of the community method, final decisions become codified as EU law. This is not so in the sphere of intergovernmental policy coordination outside the community method.

Deliberative intergovernmentalism is sympathetic to approaches that have investigated and highlighted the role of consensus in community method decision-making. It follows for example Elgström and Jönsson (2000: 701), who argue that the historic expansion of the EU's regulatory *acquis* was possible only on the basis of a 'normative consensus around the European common market'. Deliberative intergovernmentalism, however, shifts the focus towards understanding the particular role of consensus building within the context of the new intergovernmentalism and the consequences for institutional design. In the new areas of EU activity, policy deliberation needs to flank collective action at all stages of the policy process. For example, the implementation of Stability and Growth Pact (SGP) rules requires as much effort engaging in policy deliberation as the adoption of these rules or the formulation of annual or multi-annual policy guidelines. Moreover, policy deliberation is not essentially confined to the sphere of technocratic governance but spreads to all levels of decision-making. The community method emphasizes technocratic consensus, as Joerges and Neyer demonstrate, as well as broader political consensus, as Elgström and Jönsson argue and as expressed, for example, in historic decisions of the European Council (see section 2.2.2). Deliberative intergovernmentalism expects these distinctions to become blurred in the context of new intergovernmentalism, and operational aspects of policy-making to play out more strongly at all levels of decision-making. This largely determines how the European Council, the Council, and the relevant committees operate.

Finally, a key question linked to the rise of new intergovernmentalism concerns the relative importance of the community method and alternative governance procedures, and whether the latter constitute only a temporary phenomenon or are there to stay, at least for the foreseeable future. Chapter 1 provided no indication that the major amendments of the EU's core institutional framework at Maastricht and beyond changed the centrality of the community method in those areas for which it had previously been identified as the main governance mechanism. Dehousse and colleagues analyse EU legislative activity by the Commission, the Council, and the European Parliament (EP) since the beginning of the new millennium, and cannot find evidence of a decline in such activity (Dehousse et al. 2010). The number of Court of Justice and Court of First Instance rulings has actually increased due to enlargement. These findings are not in conflict with deliberative intergovernmentalism and the claim that since Maastricht the EU has massively expanded its policy-making agenda by establishing new areas of activity outside the classic community method. Deliberative intergovernmentalism thus does not deny the importance of the community method for understanding EU governance. Quite to the contrary, the point of departure for analysing institutional change within the European Council and Council environment is that studying institutional change requires attention to modifications of decision-making practices that originally evolved in relation to EU legislative activity.

However, deliberative intergovernmentalism does not infer from the historical and present importance of the community method that the community method represents what Renaud Dehousse (2013) pointedly calls the 'Union's operating system by default'. The point here is to take seriously post-Maastricht efforts to govern outside the community method and to understand the consequences of these institutional choices. Deliberative intergovernmentalism follows Armstrong (1998), who criticizes political scientists in particular for too easily treating EU law as an instrument of integration. He attests a 'displacement or decentring of the classic "Community Method"' (Armstrong 2010: 9–10), and stresses the consequences for EU integration theory more generally. For him, approaches that understand 'the EU as dominated by forms of "regulatory politics" in which legislation and litigation are foregrounded as key drivers of European integration' seem out of touch with the new reality. Suggesting that sooner or later all collective decision-making will be brought under the community method risks devaluing the phenomenon of post-Maastricht intergovernmentalism as something short-lived and temporary, which may be analysed only to the extent that research distinguishes between different degrees of approximation to the classic community method but treats any interest in understanding the inherent logic of new intergovernmentalism as something secondary or a priori problematic on normative grounds.

### 2.1.2 Supranationalism and Intergovernmentalism

The concepts of supranationalism and intergovernmentalism obtain a central role in this study, and both feature prominently in the EU studies literature. Yet they have different connotations. The point here is not to offer the ultimate explanation of each concept but rather to clarify how they are understood in this study and to show how communication with other scholarly perspectives can be established. The term supranationalism is normally understood to refer to the EU's institutional capacities for autonomous action. It can, however, be understood differently. For example, the Commission, the EP, the Court of Justice, and the European Central Bank (ECB) are supranational institutions in the sense that they have the political and bureaucratic capacity to act independently within their mandate. Such independence is generally seen as a guarantee that these institutions act in the general interest of the EU, rather than that they function as bodies in which national interests are represented. Supranationalism is above all considered to imply emancipation from national interests.

However, the story is more complicated. In addition, the EU's main intergovernmental forums, the European Council, the Council, and the numerous expert committees, are obliged to act in the general interest of the EU.[2] What is difficult to say is whether and how specific institutional actors can develop a capacity to act in the general interest of the Union in a given decision-making scenario. For those who believe that only the Commission can represent the general interest, the terminological distinction is relatively clear: supranationalism is a state of affairs in which an independent supranational authority rules, while acting in the general interest of the Union (cf. e.g. Ponzano 2011). The EU's capacity to act independently is constituted through the formal transfer of decision-making powers. Intergovernmentalism thus becomes a sphere of dispute and the representation of narrow national interests, which need to be tamed by supranational actors and the threat of QMV.

For many scholars the two concepts thus cannot be treated separately from each other. Collective decision-making in the EU has tended to be conceptualized as a particular form of intergovernmentalism (Keohane and Hoffmann 1991). Andrew Moravcsik's (1991, 1993, 1998) concept of liberal intergovernmentalism is the prime example in this regard. The emphasis is on the role of national governments in controlling EU policy-making in the context of the community method or in relation to major historical decisions on Treaty change. The role of supranational actors is generally acknowledged, but the EU is primarily understood 'as a successful intergovernmental regime designed to manage economic interdependence through negotiated policy-coordination' (Moravcsik 1993: 474). For Moravcsik community method decision-making is 'policy-coordination'—not the opposite of it. The dispute with other approaches is about what role supranational institutions play once they have been created, i.e. whether they fulfil a functional role in the process or develop an independent capacity to act and attract political loyalty and legitimacy independently of national governments (see the seminal collections Sandholtz and Stone Sweet 1998; Stone Sweet et al. 2001). Similarly, studies of the interaction of governments within the Council tend to focus on the strategic dimension—notably on voting within the Council (Hosli 1996). Tsebelis' and Garrett's (2001) much-cited attempt to unravel the interrelation between supranational and intergovernmental elements in the EU's governance architecture similarly focuses on understanding the relative importance

---

[2] See Article 13.1, TFEU, as well as individual provisions in the work of the relevant decision-making bodies. Reference to the 'general interest' is often also made in the rules of procedures of the respective bodies.

of these elements in the context of community method decision-making. For them the reconfiguration of the respective roles of the Commission, the Court of Justice, the Council, and the EP in EU governance is connected to key instances in the evolution of community method decision-making, such as the Luxembourg Compromise, the introduction of qualified majority decision-making and, eventually, the emergence of the EP as a co-legislator.

In short, notions of intergovernmentalism, which originally emerged at the time or in the immediate aftermath of the Maastricht Treaty, are closely tied to the process of community method decision-making. The intergovernmental dimension of EU politics is understood very much in terms of the EU's legislative process. Increasingly, contributions to the EU studies literature have challenged this understanding. In his analysis of the role of law within the context of the EU's foreign, security, and defence policy, Rames A. Wessel (2007) invokes Pernice's (1999) argument of a European 'multilevel constitution', which 'treats European integration as a dynamic process of constitution-making instead of a sequence of international treaties which establish and develop an organization of international cooperation'.[3] Wessel concludes that it would be misleading to organize different areas of EU activity according to the terms 'supranationalism' and 'intergovernmentalism'. For him it is more accurate to say that 'competences related to these areas are allocated between the different levels of decision-making' (Wessel 2007: 166). Jakob Lempp and Janko Altenschmidt (2008) opt to refer to the emergence of informal practices among government representatives, which aim to promote the general EU interest, as a process of supranationalization. Jolyon Howorth (2011) proposes the term 'supranational intergovernmentalism' to conceptualize the dense policy network of expert committees in the Common Security and Defence Policy (CSDP). The term 'supranational' also indicates a modification of EU intergovernmental practice, which previously tended to be seen as competitive and based on clear national preferences. Howorth remarks that the CSDP has by now probably moved on to the next stage—'intergovernmental supranationalism' (Howorth 2011: 24). This means that certain intergovernmental networks and contexts are seen as pivotal in advancing integration, as opposed to a situation in which these actors are seen as preventing further integration and defending the status quo. Bickerton (2011: 174) argues that '[s]upranationalism is therefore as much about the *subjective orientation of national political elites towards consensus* as it is the creation of new pan-European institutions'.[4] Daniel Thym (2011) proposes the term 'legal intergovernmentalism' for conceptualizing the Common Foreign and Security Policy

---

[3] Pernice as quoted in Wessel 2007, p. 166.    [4] Emphasis as in the original text.

(CFSP) and CSDP domains as areas in which no legislation is produced, but for which the Treaty defines specific decision-making procedures.

What is clear from these more recent accounts is the rejection of the old dichotomy of supranationalism and intergovernmentalism, understood as embodying the progressive and the destructive elements of European integration respectively. The terminology used above also implies a challenge to a particular stream of thought within EU studies that for a long time saw this dichotomy as the compass for studying the EU. The analytical concept of deliberative intergovernmentalism, which was first developed in the context of the study of the informal Eurogroup (Puetter 2006), thus shares common ground with several of the more recent contributions listed above. Analogous to Joerges' concept of deliberative supranationalism, the term 'deliberative' is chosen to indicate a particular quality of the new intergovernmentalism that is central to its analysis. Whatever terminology is used, the EU policy process is likely to involve both a constitutive element, which consists of defining and propagating collective policy objectives and thus the EU's general interest, and equally an element that accounts for the representation of diverging national interests. The key question is how these two elements are combined and mediated in a given context.

In order to avoid misinterpretations and to facilitate discussion with other approaches the use of the terms 'supranational' and 'intergovernmental' throughout this book follows a process-oriented and narrow definition, which characterizes an institutional context rather than a specific disposition towards integration. *Supranational institutions* are based on a particular mandate, which grants them a certain degree of institutional independence from the member states. This involves the competence to take decisions and command over autonomous bureaucratic resources. Thus, the Commission, the EP, the Court of Justice, and the ECB are referred to as supranational decision-making bodies. *Intergovernmental institutions*, in turn, are populated by member state representatives and take decisions—formal or informal—on the basis of agreement among these representatives. The European Council, the Council, and the Eurogroup fall within this category. High-level expert committees such as the Economic and Financial Committee (EFC), the Political and Security Committee (PSC), and the Employment Committee (EMCO) are referred to as intergovernmental bodies. The point is that decisions are based on the consent of member state representatives. How this consent is expressed—whether through nodded agreement or QMV—does not matter.[5] Such a process-oriented definition of supranationalism and intergovernmentalism allows for

---

[5] Beyers and Dierickx (1998) distinguish between supranational and intergovernmental negotiation networks within the Council environment. Their definition captures similar aspects but is slightly different.

the attribution of specific qualities to the respective processes and contexts, such as the term 'deliberative'.[6]

## 2.2 The Study of New Governance, the European Council, and the Council So Far

The analysis of the European Council and the Council within the analytical framework of deliberative intergovernmentalism connects in particular with two broader streams of literature. First, it connects with the literature on the EU's so-called new modes of governance. This literature offered the first attempt to conceptualize post-Maastricht decision-making practices outside the community method. Yet most contributions have concentrated on OMC comitology and the supposedly participatory dimension of the OMC. The changing roles of the European Council and the Council have been mostly ignored, and not become subject to further empirical and theoretical investigation. Second, deliberative intergovernmentalism relates to previous research on the European Council and the Council. This body of literature—although quite diverse in its theoretical and empirical foundations—offers important insights into the role of the two forums in EU decision-making. However, it also largely fails to pick up more explicitly on the changing roles of the European Council and the Council in EU policy-making, as well as the process of their internal transformation. This section discusses what can be learned from the debate so far and what obstacles would need be overcome to offer a better understanding of the EU's new intergovernmentalism and of the roles the European Council and the Council play within it.

### 2.2.1 *The Debate about New Modes of Governance*

The literature on new modes of governance emerged in relation to the OMC. The phenomenon of policy coordination as an alternative to the community method received systematic attention for the first time (cf. among many others Borrás and Jacobsson 2004; Hodson and Maher 2001; Pochet 2004). The rapidly growing interest in the new modes of governance was originally motivated by frustration with the apparent lack of innovative potential in community method decision-making (see chapter 1.2). Since the resignation of the Santer Commission in 1999 little hope has been invested in

---

[6] Referring to the provisions of the Treaties of Nice and Lisbon on foreign, security, and defence policy Wolfgang Wessels and colleagues use the term 'rationalized intergovernmentalism' (Wessels 2001; Wessels and Bopp 2008)—though this term is not underpinned by a particular conceptual framework. Deliberative intergovernmentalism seeks to provide such a framework for the study of new intergovernmentalism.

policy initiatives coming from the supranational bureaucracy. Contributions on new governance thus rest on the assumption that 'the EU is today in crisis, and will likely remain so for several years to come' (Sabel and Zeitlin 2008: 272). New modes of governance are seen as instruments for increasing the EU's role in governing 'sensitive policy areas' (De la Porte 2002)—especially those linked to welfare state politics. The start of employment policy coordination and the adoption of the Lisbon agenda represent reference events in this regard. The Commission's White Paper on European Governance (European Commission 2001) is also seen by many authors as a strong indication that a two-tier system of community method decision-making and new governance mechanisms exists.

Lawyers are among the most influential and active contributors to the debate about new governance. In reaction to emerging forms of new policy coordination mechanisms several authors have sought to conceptualize the difference between the new modes of governance and the community method by making reference to the concept of 'soft law', as opposed to 'hard law' generated by legislative decision-making under the community method—a distinction that is also developing within international relations literature (Abbott and Snidal 2000; Snyder 1994; Trubek and Mosher 2003). The emergence of alternative forms of governance challenges established notions of law and policy-making. As Armstrong (2008: 416) argues, the 'new forms of governance simply pose a challenge to EU constitutionalism: they occupy an unsettled constitutional space'.

The literature on new modes of governance puts particular emphasis on interaction among member state representatives. Policy learning, benchmarking, the focus on best practices (Trubek and Mosher 2003), and the key role of expert committees and epistemic communities (Cross 2011 and 2013; Grosche and Puetter 2008; Horvath 2008; Jacobsson and Vilfell 2007) are studied as key features of new governance. The new policy-making context is identified as being distinctively different from established procedures for joint decision-making. Moreover, these new institutional contexts are not understood as negotiation processes based on predefined preferences. For example, Sabel and Zeitlin (2008: 272) characterize decision-making in the new areas of EU activity as 'at least in part deliberative: actors' initial preferences are transformed through discussion by the force of the better argument'. They also find the committee system to be conducive to the linking of 'national administrations with each other and the EU without establishing a hierarchy between them' (Sabel and Zeitlin 2008: 273). For most contributors to the literature on new modes of governance the constitutive character of policy discourse for processes of policy change is a central theme (Schmidt and Radaelli 2004).

There is also a distinctive focus on participatory elements, including the question of how non-governmental actors and stakeholders become more closely involved in EU-level decision-making. Yet on closer inspection the reality of the participatory dimension of new governance mechanisms has not been found to be as pronounced as propagated by the Commission (Smismans 2004, 2008). Nevertheless, there was wide agreement that the EU was applying a new and 'experimentalist' (Sabel and Zeitlin 2008) type of governance, which enabled actors to engage with competing policy ideas—a precondition for avoiding stalemate. The debate about the new modes of governance also identified the link between informal structures and formal procedures or—to be more precise—between informality and law (Sabel and Zeitlin 2008). Informality is crucial in an area where either no tangible negotiation outcome exists, or this outcome does not take the form of a legislative act that formally binds those who have adopted it.

Though the term 'new modes of governance' is much less fashionable with those who study foreign, security, and defence policy, there are obvious parallels between the two literatures. For the latter group of researchers too the key question is what constitutes the new quality of CFSP and CSDP coordination. Policy learning and the role of epistemic communities are identified as central elements of the new context. Processes of group social-ization and the orientation of decision-making routines and committee pro-cesses towards problem solving are analysed through elaborate case studies, which combine theoretically ambitious frameworks with in-depth qualitative research (Cross 2011; Meyer 2006). This implies that member state adminis-trations become increasingly intertwined and geared towards identifying col-lective policy responses. For example, Paul James Cardwell (2009: 5) argues that 'CFSP creates an institutional environment in which the EU Member States become used to dealing collectively with the outside world through a common frame'. Again, the interaction of member state representatives in key coordination forums is identified as constituting the definition of policy options (cf. e.g. Thomas 2009, 2011).

The academic debate on new modes of governance provides an important basis for developing the central claim of deliberative intergovernmentalism: that a key feature of the new intergovernmentalism is a permanent process of consensus generation among member states representatives. The new govern-ance literature has treated the new institutional arrangements as a clear alter-native to the community method. Yet for analysing the central role of the European Council and the Council in the EU's new intergovernmentalism it is important to revisit and develop further some of the other key arguments on new governance that are outlined here.

First, deliberative intergovernmentalism puts a stronger emphasis on link-ing the study of micro-institutional contexts for intergovernmental policy coordination with an argument on the systemic dimension of the proliferation of policy coordination mechanisms in the post-Maastricht EU. The integration paradox is seen to explain the simultaneous occurrence of a broad set of institutional choices at Maastricht and beyond. Deliberative intergovernmentalism emphasizes the wider repercussions of the new governance mechanisms for the overall EU architecture, and shifts the focus to the European Council and the Council. In this sense deliberative intergovernmentalism moves beyond the notion of the new modes of governance as 'experimentalist governance' (Sabel and Zeitlin 2008). Though deliberative intergovernmentalism stresses the importance of informal arrangements and of a flexible approach to agenda-setting that help to test the expansion of coordination to new policy domains, it considers the phenomenon of new intergovernmentalism to be based on a powerful institutional trend. This is expressed in the deep institutionalization of coordination procedures over time—beyond the point of experimentation. The codification of all major coordination routines through Treaty law speak to this point.

Second, with only a few exceptions (cf. especially Hodson and Maher 2001), the empirical focus of new governance studies has been mainly on social and employment policy coordination and the Lisbon agenda. Yet this field represents only a small portion of the rapidly expanding EU coordination *acquis* in the post-Maastricht era. Economic and Monetary Union (EMU) governance and CFSP policy coordination represent the other two major new areas of EU activity that have quickly come to dominate European Council and Council decision-making (see chapter 3.4), and account for the biggest share in increased comitology activity (see chapter 4.5). Unfortunately, there is very little communication between the new governance literature and research on CFSP, and CSDP decision-making. This limitation is addressed by deliberative intergovernmentalism, which offers a comparative perspective on the new areas of EU activity.

Third, the concentration on specific episodes of OMC decision-making may have prevented a broader understanding of policy coordination as encompassing various aspects of decision-making, including guidelines for medium- and long-term policy reform as much as ad-hoc executive decisions or coordinated national-level legislative action in response to crisis situations. This implies that it may be misleading to conceptualize the outcome of policy coordination processes as soft law. Kenneth Armstrong (2010) argues for adopting such a broader perspective on policy coordination in relation to his study of social inclusion policy, and points to the limitations of earlier contributions to the literature on new governance in this regard. This argument is taken up by deliberative intergovernmentalism.

Fourth, though the key role of the European Council and the Council, as well as the limitations to the traditional role of the Commission, have been recognized in principle (cf. the helpful mapping exercise by Borrás and

Jacobsson 2004), most of the empirical research so far has focused on micro-institutional contexts, notably the committee structure. This has made sense insofar as policy learning and deliberation are related to the emergence of expert networks. The focus of many OMCs on benchmarking and indicators certainly suggests an important role for technocrats. Yet this implies that the new governance literature has not sufficiently addressed the question of how and to what extent policy coordination generates political support at the highest level of decision-making. Though the lack of such support has been repeatedly noted as a problem of OMC processes, few contributions allow deeper insights into Council and European Council processes. Deliberative intergovernmentalism therefore emphasizes the importance of consensus generation through policy deliberation all the way up from comitology to European Council decision-making.

Finally, the introduction of new governance mechanisms has triggered the emergence of numerous contributions with a distinctively normative focus. The link between law and new governance as well as the focus on new partici-patory elements received most of the attention. Yet economic governance as well as governance of foreign and security policy are essentially consultation-free zones as regards the involvement of actors outside the sphere of executive decision-making. Governments and EU institutions are essentially talking among themselves. Apart from the so-called macroeconomic dialogue process in the field of EMU and the privileged role the social partners enjoy in some areas of social and employment policy coordination, there are few traces of the involvement of non-governmental actors. Moreover, the experience of the EU's reactions to the global economic and financial crisis shows that political conflict over EU policy decisions erupts predominantly in domestic arenas of decision-making, thus exacerbating the central role of national governments in EU-level policy-making. This observation by no means vindicates the exist-ing context of new intergovernmentalism as unproblematic on democratic grounds. It just highlights that the institutional dynamic that has led to the proliferation of policy coordination mechanisms in the post-Maastricht era is focused on the intergovernmental level, as it is mainly triggered by a reaction on the part of member state governments to the system of community method decision-making. Deliberative intergovernmentalism avoids making norma-tive claims in this regard but focuses on understanding the underlying logic of institutional change behind these processes.

### 2.2.2 *The European Council and the Council as Forums of Intergovernmental Decision-making*

Simon Bulmer's (1996) conceptualization of the European Council and the Council as the 'shapers of a European confederation' provides an important starting point for outlining a more complex argument about the changing role of the two EU forums for intergovernmental decision-making. Bulmer emphasizes the key role of the two forums within a confederal European order. For him, the potential of the two institutions to forge consensus among member states is pivotal to the functioning of the EU's political system. This highlights the constitutive element in the work of these two institutions and their role in the wider integration process. Bulmer's argument was developed against the background of the experience of accelerating single market integration under the community method, and it links up with arguments from the beginning of this chapter on the consensus-dependency of the community method. Deliberative intergovernmentalism follows this argument. Yet the aim is to explain the transformation of European Council and Council decision-making during the post-Maastricht era and its link with the new areas of EU activity. This requires connecting the general argument about the consensus-dependency of the EU's political system with an analysis of the particular processes of institutional change and policy-making dynamics within the relevant policy areas. Unfortunately, there are very few attempts to theorize in a more general sense the role of the European Council and the Council in EU policy-making, or the interrelationship of the two bodies. Jonas Tallberg (2008: 686) has already lamented the lack of theoretically grounded research on the European Council.[7] A similar complaint has been put forward by Philippa Sherrington (2000: 70), who points to the conceptual difficulties scholars are confronted with when they try to theorize Council activity, and criticizes integration theory for lacking the necessary analytical tools.[8]

Simon Bulmer's and Wolfgang Wessels' (1987) monograph on the European Council, which dates back a quarter of a century, takes up Bulmer's concept of the European Council and the Council as key forums for consensus building within a European confederation, quoted above. The two authors conclude from their study of the first decade of European Council activity that the forum 'was not created to provide the EC heads of government with a thrice-yearly opportunity to bang the table in defence of national interests' (Bulmer and Wessels 1987: 134–5). Moreover, Bulmer and Wessels stress that it is a defining feature of the European Council that 'each participating head of

[7] Tallberg counts altogether five monographs that appeared during the 1980s and 1990s and follow a mainly descriptive approach. The 2008 monograph on the European Council by the journalist Jan Werts (2008) provides the only recent and comprehensive empirical account for several years on the European Council. It follows the descriptive approach of Werts' (1992) original study from the 1990s.

[8] The number of monographs on the Council is limited too, though there are comprehensive and fairly recent works that seek to understand the Council as a complex institution with various administrative levels. A more descriptive perspective is offered by Galloway and Westlake (2004). In the academic field, the most authoritative account on the Council has undoubtedly emerged from the work of Fiona Hayes-Renshaw and Helen Wallace (2006).

government must be prepared to engage in some shared problem solving, whether in the specific context of the EC's competences or in a looser framework of mutual adjustment between the policies of the member state governments' (Bulmer and Wessels 1987: 134–5).

Wolfgang Wessels, who continued to follow the work of the European Council closely,[9] argued later that the role of the European Council evolved in much the same way as the roles of other core EU institutions. The institution is seen 'as both actor and indicator of a fundamental logic of evolution of the EU system' (Wessels 2008: 19). Applying his fusion thesis, Wessels sees an expansion of European Council activity, as member states are trying to compensate for their inability to deal with global challenges unilaterally. Similarly, the event of the 2004 enlargement is seen as reconfirming the role of the European Council rather than changing it fundamentally. Though this argument captures the overall increase in EU activity and related political decision-making, it cannot explain the changing role of the European Council and the Council in relation to other actors in EU politics, and does not account for the decline in community method decision-making. The explanation for such changes therefore has to be found elsewhere.

Helen Wallace (2002) was first in pointing more explicitly to the multifaceted nature of Council decision-making, and alerted scholars to its consequences for analytical work on the Council. Given the very different activities the Council is engaged in, different analytical tools may be required. Wallace distinguishes five different 'images' of the Council. This categorization is not underpinned by a particular theoretical framework, but points to the diverging potential of different scholarly perspectives with regard to individual areas of Council decision-making. The first image is that of a Council–Commission tandem. It reflects the classic division of labour under the community method, and casts the Council as an authorizing forum. The rise of the EP as a co-legislator challenges the central role of this tandem in EU politics. The second image is that of a club of governments. National executives unite in the Council in order to pass decisions that lock in domestic actors. They share a mutual interest in keeping others out of their club. The third image captures the exact opposite dynamic, which is the competition of member states over which can best influence EU politics according to its own interests. The fourth image portrays the Council as a network and as only one among multiple venues for intergovernmental decision-making in EU politics. The fifth image is that of 'intensive transgovernmentalism' (Wallace 2002: 339–441). It is an image not just of the Council, but also of a new mode of governance, which represents an alternative to the classic community

---

[9] At the time of writing Wolfgang Wessels was preparing a new book on the European Council. See Wessels (2014).

method. Wallace identifies this mode of decision-making with the fields of EMU, CFSP, and justice and home affairs (JHA). She also sees a concentration of activities around the responsible Council formations. Wallace proposes the term transgovernmentalism instead of intergovernmentalism, in order to emphasize the high degree of commitment on the part of the member states to act jointly in these areas. For Wallace, the latter dimension cannot be found in contexts normally identified as intergovernmental.

Hayes-Renshaw and Wallace (2006: 165–85) also offer a hint as to what might constitute the particular division of labour between the European Council and the Council. They associate the Council with a decision-making agenda that is dominated by 'issues largely subject to the so-called "Community method"'. The European Council, on the other hand, is identified as 'a much more obviously intergovernmental setting' (Hayes-Renshaw and Wallace 2006: 165). Yet this observation is not backed up by further theorization. Deliberative intergovernmentalism follows Wallace's (2002) call for more academic research on the occurrence of distinct institutional dynamics within the new areas of EU activity. Moreover, deliberative intergovernmentalism also seeks to underpin this analysis with theoretical argument on institutional change in the post-Maastricht era.

While broader conceptualizations of European Council and Council decision-making remain rare, the study of individual aspects of the work of the two bodies have triggered research that is focused more explicitly on theoretical arguments. Two broader theoretical perspectives deserve particular attention: rational choice institutionalism and constructivist–institutionalist perspectives. On the rationalist end of the spectrum the focus is on the question of why specific institutional arrangements have been adopted, and what they imply for different actors. What connects the overwhelming majority of rationalist perspectives is that they see the Council as a highly formalized and regulated institutional environment.[10] Within this environment, member states compete for influence over EU policies while being constrained by certain decision-making rules (Hosli 1996). In particular the historic 2004 enlargement and the debates about the post-Maastricht Treaty reforms have all provided a boost for rationalist approaches focusing on the Council. Formal decision-making procedures have received increased attention as policymakers and academics have worried about the capacity of the enlarged EU to take decisions, and have feared the formation of blocking minorities. Accordingly, studies have emphasized potential patterns of conflict and alignment,

---

[10] This is not to say that rational choice institutionalists ignore informal practice and norms by default. For example, Héritier, in her research (2007: 46), provides a definition for informal rules, and operationalizes the concept (cf. Farrell and Héritier 2003, 2007). Yet in this context informal practices are understood predominantly as modifications of formal decision-making rules, and thus may not be considered to influence institutional life in other ways.

including left–right party competition, the potential division between old and new member states, the grouping into pro- and anti-integration governments, the division of the EU into poorer and more solvent countries, or (as others believe) into North and South (cf. among others Mattila 2004; Zimmer et al. 2005). As regards the study of institutional change the focus has been on how decision-making rules can enhance the decision-making capacity of the Council. Notably the expanded use of qualified majority decision-making is at the centre of interest (Carrubba and Volden 2001).

However, this literature is of limited use when it comes to the study of the EU's new intergovernmentalism. The empirical focus on formal decision-making implies a bias towards community method decision-making. This methodological choice might well be justified depending on the issue under investigation. It implies a research design that aims to identify member state preferences in terms of 'ideal points' (Zimmer et al. 2005: 408). Even if the interaction between the Council and other institutions such as the Commission and the EP is included (see for example König and Proksch 2006), this literature misses essential aspects of the practice of decision-making within the Council.[11] Finally, as situations of 'explicitly contested voting' (Hayes-Renshaw et al. 2006) still remain very rare and occur in the domain of community method decision-making, not much can be derived from this research for analysing core aspects of the EU's new intergovernmentalism.

Jonas Tallberg's (2006) seminal work on the rotating Council presidency is also based on a rational choice institutionalist perspective, and is explicitly positioned against sociological institutionalist accounts. His work, however, differs from the rationalist accounts mentioned above, which rely primarily on data reflecting decision-making outcomes, on official minutes and on the simulation of decision-making activity based on formally defined voting procedures. Instead Tallberg's work is based on comprehensive qualitative enquiry, including in-depth and process-oriented interview research that also traces decision-making practices beyond formally defined decision-making rules and during specific policy-making episodes. The central role of the Council presidency as a key intergovernmental element of the EU's institutional architecture is identified as a functional response to the autonomy enjoyed by the Commission. Yet the presidency is required to solve 'collective-action problems in decentralised bargaining' (2006: 206), and is therefore endowed with procedural privileges by the member states, which accept, and even demand, formal leadership in this regard. This argument gains particular importance with regard to the analysis of the changes away from the principle

---

[11] Gerald Schneider (2008) provides one of the most radical defences of the concentration on a quantitative and outcome-based methodological perspective on the Council, and denounces alternative ways of studying the Council altogether as unscientific.

of rotation to a permanent chair in the presidency regimes of the European Council, the Foreign Affairs Council (FAC), and the Eurogroup (see chapters 3.7 and 4.1–3).

In later contributions Tallberg has somewhat modified the juxtaposition of theoretical perspectives, thus indicating the need to accommodate different theoretical perspectives in order to understand particular aspects of Council decision-making—an argument that overlaps with Helen Wallace's call for an understanding of the Council as a multifaceted environment (cf. Tallberg 2008, 2010). Blom-Hansen and Brandsma (2009) contrast deliberative supra-nationalism and intergovernmental bargaining as two coexisting modes of interaction within the comitology environment, and thus bring together different conceptualizations in one research design. Yet it is also clear that most research is still far from providing convincing and sufficiently precise definitions of the scope conditions of specific approaches (Wrantjen 2010).[12] Here, deliberative intergovernmentalism suggests the integration of a broader conceptual perspective on the European Council and the Council, with a clearly defined empirical focus on the EU's new intergovernmentalism as a particular institutional dynamic. Though deliberative intergovernmentalism takes issue with rationalist approaches that have sought to explain institutional change in the European Council and Council environment, especially in relation to the Lisbon Treaty, the intention is not to deny altogether the relevance of research on the role of formal leadership.

This shifts the focus to the constructivist–institutionalist end of the spectrum. Constructivists tend to focus on the Council as an informal environment, which is structured through practice and routine. They emphasize the dual quality of the decision-making process.[13] Member state representatives rework and alter the normative structure of the Council environment, inasmuch as their own work within the Council is structured through existing formal and informal procedural and behavioural rules. A variety of perspectives fall into this category. Sociological institutionalism is one of the most influential ones, and it is thriving especially in relation to the analysis of Council comitology and working groups (Beyers and Dierickx 1998; Beyers 2005; A. Juncos and Reynolds 2007; Lewis 1998, 2010). A prominent example is the notion of 'coordination reflex' used in the European Political Cooperation (EPC) and CFSP studies literature to characterize how much member

---

[12] In particular the study of Council comitology has inspired more systematic research into the multi-faceted nature of Council negotiations. Elgström and Jönsson (2000) provide one of the best critical reviews of the literature on EU negotiations in this regard, including an excellent synthesis of related literatures on international negotiation and cooperation.

[13] Constructivism is understood as a meta-theoretical frame that enables researchers to establish a middle ground between rationalist and reflectivist approaches. The key point is its understanding of social behaviour as being both structured through and at the same time constitutive of social norms and institutions (Christiansen et al. 2001; Wiener 2007).

state diplomats have internalized the overall commitment to consensus seeking in that particular policy domain (cf. Juncos and Pomorska 2006). Also, approaches that focus on policy learning, epistemic communities, and informal policy deliberation share the constructivist perspective on social behaviour. They typically go beyond the socialization argument and emphasize interactionist dynamics within the Council, i.e. the constitutive element of collective decision-making processes (Cross 2011; Horvath 2008; Joerges and Neyer 1997; Neyer 2006; Puetter 2006, 2007b). Most importantly, the focus on policy learning and deliberation provides theoretical insights as to why certain decision-making practices are particularly conducive to consensus generation, i.e. they mobilize commitment to commonly agreed policy objectives because the involved actors converge on the question of what constitutes an appropriate policy response. Again, the comitology environment is typically considered to be particularly conducive to such processes as it features an important epistemic element (Adler and Haas 1992; Verdun 1999). In this regard the constructivist–institutionalist literature on the Council overlaps with the literature on new modes of governance.

The focus on explaining consensus generation and the constitutive element of collective decision-making within the EU's intergovernmental forums make approaches located at the intersection of constructivist and institutionalist research particularly suited for studying policy-making within the context of the EU's new intergovernmentalism. Moreover, there is a notable proximity between constructivist–institutionalist research on the Council environment and arguments on policy formation emerging within the literature on new modes of governance (cf. Schmidt and Radaelli 2004 as a prominent example). What is missing, however, is an analytical framework that allows connections between the insights of such contributions, which are predominantly focused on the study of individual micro-level institutional contexts, with a broader argument about institutional change in the post-Maastricht era.[14] Deliberative intergovernmentalism, therefore, seeks to integrate knowledge about micro-level institutional contexts such as the Committee of Permanent Representatives (COREPER), the PSC, the Eurogroup, or Council working groups with an explanation about the proliferation of a particular decision-making practice and the related processes of institutional engineering. Moreover, deliberative intergovernmentalism transfers insights from the field of comitology to higher and more political levels of decision-making: the relevant Council formations and the European Council.

---

[14] The term 'micro-level institutional context' refers to a contained decision-making setting, such as a particular expert committee, a Council working group, or the Committee of Permanent Representatives (COREPER). For example, Beyers and Dierickx (1998: 295) refer to their analysis of Council working group decision-making as being focused on the micro-level.

## 2.3 A New Analytical Framework

Deliberative intergovernmentalism as a novel analytical framework focuses on understanding a particular institutional dynamic in the post-Maastricht EU. Its central theoretical claim is that because of the post-Maastricht integration paradox, major new areas of EU activity are developed outside the classic community method. The refusal to frame collective decision-making in these areas as EU legislative decision-making gives rise to a new intergovernmentalism in EU politics. The proliferation of novel coordination mechanisms is accompanied by a constant quest for consensus generation among member state governments in day-to-day policy-making. This quest for consensus, which is detectable at all stages of the policy process and all levels of decision-making, causes a transformation of intergovernmental decision-making practice, and thus changes the way the European Council, the Council and the related comitology processes in the new areas of EU activity function. The scarce literature on the European Council and the Council has so far addressed individual examples of new practices in intergovernmental decision-making, yet a broader analysis of the transformative character of the EU's new intergovernmentalism is still lacking. By building on the discussion so far, this section develops a detailed set of propositions on how the constant quest for consensus generation, which characterizes the EU's new intergovernmentalism, translates into a demand for specific institutional choices. In short, deliberative intergovernmentalism expects the roles of the European Council and the Council in post-Maastricht EU decision-making to be heavily affected by the rise of new intergovernmentalism.

It is important to revisit established notions of the role of the European Council and the Council in EU politics, and of the internal functioning of these two bodies against the background of the specific institutional design of the new areas of EU activity. The experience of community method decision-making, especially in the field of regulatory governance, has very much shaped the scholarly understanding of EU governance so far. Because of this, there may be a temptation not to engage with the new areas of EU activity more systematically. Most importantly, it would be wrong to consider policy-making episodes in these domains simply as cases of non-legislative decision-making in the 'shadow of hierarchy' (Börzel 2010). That this 'shadow' is not cast over the new areas of EU activity as it might be in policy areas that are closely related to core aspects of community method decision-making is rather the defining feature of these new areas.

Thus the key point of deliberative intergovernmentalism is to move beyond an understanding of the European Council and the Council as the main forums for member state decision-making, which is informed by a notion of the community method as the default EU decision-making mode. Rather, deliberative intergovernmentalism expects to identify a series of attempts at institutional engineering that are aimed at modifying established decision-making routines which originally evolved in the context of community method decision-making. The main aim is to trace and explain these attempts at institutional engineering and the resulting new practices of intergovernmental decision-making in relation to the functioning of the European Council and the Council.

The conviction of member state governments that stronger EU-level action is a precondition for resolving fundamental issues in contemporary public policy-making clashes with their insistence on ultimate national sovereignty. This *integration paradox* is associated with the post-Maastricht EU, which has extended integration to all core areas of national sovereignty, and is integrated to a degree that makes it almost impossible to ignore interdependencies in any public policy domain. There is strong evidence that member states are willing to expand and further develop the EU's policy agenda. Yet the formal transfer of competences to the EU's supranational institutions is not an option, or is allowed only in exceptional circumstances and only if member states retain political discretion and influence over policy initiatives in the concerned field. The unprecedented role of intergovernmental decision-making in EU politics is a direct consequence of the integration paradox. As the transfer of further powers to the EU level is ruled out, member state governments need to compensate for the lack of supranational steering power by developing new intergovernmental decision-making structures.

National governments insist that key resources of public policy-making, including fiscal, judicial and military powers as well as core aspects of welfare state governance, remain formally under their control, i.e. that legislative powers in these areas are not delegated to the supranational level. The point here is to recognize the process-oriented character of the definition of national sovereignty applied in contemporary EU decision-making practice: member state governments insist first and foremost on a specific format of decision-making which grants them a final say. This has led to a scenario in which any specific EU-level activity requires prior authorization from the European Council or the Council. Member state governments may be under little illusion that their de facto power to implement preferred policy options unilaterally is increasingly limited but this procedural distinction matters enormously in the context of governing the new areas of EU activity. Deliberative intergovernmentalism acknowledges that the notion of ultimate sovereignty that prevails in contemporary EU policy-making has little in common with outdated notions of sovereignty—an aspect that is highlighted by Chris Bickerton (2011).

To be clear, this book does not advance a normative argument on what direction European integration should eventually take. The identification of the integration paradox is based on the observation of a particular attitude of member state governments towards integration, which was identified in chapter 1. Thus, the insistence on ultimate nation state sovereignty is one assumption on which deliberative intergovernmentalism as an analytical framework is based.[15] As demonstrated earlier, there is no evidence that this attitude will change in the foreseeable future. Yet this does not imply postulating teleology of integration. Political integration is a contested political process by default. Moreover, and this is the other assumption made here, there is no sign of integration fatigue. Member state governments subscribe to the idea that key aspects of public policy can be managed successfully only on the basis of EU involvement. Were member states to retreat from the integration project altogether, there would be no integration paradox.

### 2.3.1 The Underlying Institutional Dynamic

Under the condition that the post-Maastricht integration paradox persists it is possible to derive a set of theoretically informed propositions. These propositions build on the review of key institutional decisions concerning the new areas of EU activity in chapter 1 and are theoretically grounded in the critical discussion of existing research perspectives in the earlier parts of this chapter. Each of these propositions can be translated into hypotheses for empirical research, thus constituting deliberative intergovernmentalism as an analytical framework for the study of the European Council and the Council, to which the remaining chapters of this book relate. The first subset of propositions entails conceptualizations of the main institutional features of new intergovernmentalism as an underlying institutional dynamic that largely determines the changing roles of the European Council and Council in contemporary EU governance. The second subset of propositions, which is listed in the following section 2.3.2, features the main conceptualizations of post-Maastricht attempts at institutional engineering that occur in the European Council and Council environment. Key propositions are highlighted in italic.

In the post-Maastricht EU there is considerably *less scope for new major legislative activities* under the classic community method, though the community method is not challenged in those areas to which it already applies—

---

[15] The term 'assumption' is used here to emphasize that the analytical framework of deliberative intergovernmentalism is not without preconditions, i.e. it responds and applies to a particular phase of the integration process. This does not imply that there is no empirical basis for the assumption. The observation is made that member states insist on ultimate national sovereignty. Deliberative intergovernmentalism itself does not hypothesize about whether member states are going to change this stance or not. It simply holds that there is currently no evidence for such a change in attitude.

notably the field of market integration. Of the three new areas of EU activity that serve as reference cases throughout this book, the domain of social policy coordination is most closely related to an earlier and existing trajectory of classic community decision-making. Yet legislative activity in the post-Maastricht EU relating to the field of social policy is concerned mainly with *reacting to case law and consolidating the existing body of secondary legislation* and, thus, leaves policy innovation in this area to the context of novel coordination procedures. Economic governance and CFSP coordination *see very little or no legislative decision-making at all.* Where legislative decision-making occurs it is mainly aimed at *codifying or regulating coordination routines including the responsibilities of individual actors within these contexts.* The codification of coordination mechanisms in primary law is the most visible form of this trend. The SGP framework constitutes an example that also involves secondary legislation.

There is *little scope for the formal delegation of policy initiative* and leadership functions to the supranational level. Where this occurs, member states are expected to establish strong oversight powers for the European Council and the Council. The *Commission and the Court of Justice can no longer play their historical roles* as drivers of European integration as they did in the context of the development of the single market. Finally, and related to the above points, the EU is not expected to acquire major new material resources—financial, administrative, diplomatic, or military—over which supranational actors can exercise direct and immediate control. Outside the field of its core regulatory competences and the common agricultural policy as well as its regional policy instruments, the EU continues to rely on the direct and indirect command of decentralized national resources for policy implementation and execution. Thus control over new resources for policy-making is invariably attached to the EU's new intergovernmentalism. In short, *collective political authority in the new areas of EU activity is constituted predominantly through the coordinated use of decentralized resources.* Given that there is no evidence of integration fatigue, an expansion of these activities and the proliferation of predominantly intergovernmental governance mechanisms are expected to go hand-in-hand. Moreover, as the early discussion in this chapter demonstrated, deliberative intergovernmentalism does not expect to find intergovernmental policy coordination processes to be a priori limited in scope.

The challenge of coordinating and controlling the use of decentralized resources so as to achieve commonly defined EU policy objectives informs a constant quest for consensus. As cooperation arrangements are in most cases non-binding and feature coercive elements that carry little weight, successful policy implementation depends on the commitment of national governments. In other words, consensus becomes an end in itself, and a norm that informs institutional design and actor behaviour.[16] Thus, the new intergovernmentalism differs considerably from earlier instances of either loose intergovernmental cooperation or intergovernmental competition in the context of legislative decision-making under the community method. The notion that *the new intergovernmentalism centres on an important deliberative core* is the starting point for formulating more specific expectations about the evolution of decision-making practices and structures within the European Council and Council environment.

Member states need to routinize and intensify their efforts to find acceptable solutions among them. They *need to reach consensus at all stages of the policy process*—including the initiation and development of policy, the agreement of specific guidelines and objectives, and the collective monitoring of policy implementation—as opportunities to delegate particular functions to supranational decision-making are limited. Deliberative intergovernmentalism thus predicts an *ongoing search for consensus*. Whereas the community method allowed the codification of agreements in the form of legislative acts, and channelled political competition into formal decision-making mechanisms such as the allocation of the right of initiative to the Commission and the definition of QMV rules, deliberative intergovernmentalism expects consensus seeking to be a permanent feature of day-to-day policy-making in the new areas of EU activity.

Deliberative intergovernmentalism thus offers an alternative perspective for studying the European Council and the Council. It counters the preoccupation of rationalist accounts of Council decision-making with the community method and challenges their understanding of the Council as a highly formalized environment.

The emphasis on policy deliberation within the context of the EU's new intergovernmentalism is not expected to imply an a priori harmonious relationship between member state governments. However, it is expected that member states *show a high degree of commitment to consensus seeking* processes as they overwhelmingly share the general conviction that collective EU action is required in the relevant policy fields. Such bias towards consensus orientation and pragmatism has not only been evident in the past two decades of post-Maastricht decision-making, but can be further explained by the underlying transformation of nation states into member states, as Chris Bickerton (2011, 2012) argues. Bickerton emphasizes that, especially within the new areas of EU activity, national policy-making elites do not consider unilateral action a viable option and have a predisposition towards investigating the possibility of collective action. Coordination processes are thus expected to be

---

[16] See chapter 1 and Bickerton et al. (2015). The author owes the notion of consensus as an end in itself to collaborative work with Chris Bickerton and Dermot Hodson.

characterized by a high degree of continuity and procedural stability. In other words, member states agree that they have to argue it out even if this process proves cumbersome.

Deliberative intergovernmentalism is based on a constructivist–institutionalist framework for studying the emergence and impact of institutional settings on decision-making in a particular context of EU policy-making. Constructivism here is not understood in a narrow sense as a particular theory of decision-making. It rather serves as a meta-theoretical perspective, which draws attention to the constitutive character of social interaction and, in this case, the processes of collective decision-making. Deliberative intergovernmentalism is a form of applied constructivist research as it identifies particular features of the institutional environment that are both enacted and transformed by those operating within this environment. At a methodological level, deliberative intergovernmentalism calls for process-oriented qualitative research. The focus on policy deliberation in contemporary intergovernmentalism is derived from a particular governance problem or paradox. The intention is not to deny or ignore the competitive dimension of intergovernmental decision-making. Yet deliberative intergovernmentalism is about identifying specific formal and informal mechanisms for dealing with and taming potential conflict so as to avoid decision-making deadlock and lowest common denominator solutions. Deliberative intergovernmentalism does not provide its own analytical tools for determining conflict and relative gains. It is focused on identifying and tracing the evolution of consensus-generating features at all hierarchical levels of intergovernmental decision-making. The scope for conflict and disagreement as well as the forms this may take are well outlined in the existing EU studies literature and have been studied in the context of Council decision-making under the community method. Yet deliberative intergovernmentalism devotes attention to conceptualizing disagreement in forums for policy deliberation. Diverging views on appropriate policy options are an essential aspect of consensus formation. Contesting core policy norms and diverging interpretations of these norms in particular decision-making episodes are considered to be the norm rather than the exception in transnational policy-making (Wiener 2008). A key question therefore is how particular decision-making forums can function as 'venues for contestation' (Puetter 2007b) and allow for addressing divergence rather than ignoring it.

It is important to acknowledge that deliberative intergovernmentalism as an analytical framework does not constitute a particular theory of policy deliberation nor does it speak to the normative literature on deliberative democracy (cf. Puetter 2012b: 164). It shares common ground with democratic theory perspectives (Elster 1998; Eriksen 2000; Habermas 1995) to the extent that these perspectives understand political decisions to be appropriate and legitimate because they were derived from reasoned consensus and argumentation. However, deliberative intergovernmentalism focuses on consensus generation among government representatives. Legitimacy and appropriateness matter in this context too—a key insight shared with the framework of deliberative supranationalism (Joerges 2002). Yet such decisions have not necessarily acquired popular legitimacy. Quite to the contrary, decisions taken in the EU's intergovernmental arenas are frequently challenged and contested domestically and at the level of supranational representative democracy within the EP.[17]

### 2.3.2 Institutional Engineering

As a consequence of the permanent quest for consensus generation, which characterizes policy coordination processes within the new areas of EU activity, deliberative intergovernmentalism expects important *transformations in intergovernmental decision-making practice* and thus *changes in the way the European Council, the Council and the related comitology processes function*. The commitment to consensus seeking, as well as the further expansion of EU activity, translates into a powerful institutional dynamic. Key processes and forums for collective EU decision-making are being constantly transformed and adapted. A *process of complex institutional engineering*[18] is required so as to enable the relevant processes and decision-making bodies *to enhance the consensus generation potential and to overtake policy initiation and implementation functions* that were previously not associated with them. The European Council, the Council, and the top-level expert committees in which the member states and the EU institutions are represented are at the centre of such attempts at institutional engineering.

The Maastricht Treaty has provided a watershed for EU decision-making in the sense that it both establishes commitment towards developing new areas of EU activity and provides the institutional context of a new system of decentralized authority. Deliberative intergovernmentalism expects these changes in the EU's policy agenda to be key to understanding which direction institutional engineering takes. The shift in focus away from legislative decision-making to policy coordination and intergovernmental agreement implies both a *quantitative and a qualitative dimension of institutional change*. In quantitative terms the expansion of the EU's policy agenda needs to be

---

[17] Risse and Kleine provide an example in which 'deliberative institutions' (Risse and Kleine 2010: 721) can be based at the nexus between executive and parliamentary decision-making with the model of EU Treaty reform and the convention approach being examples. Yet this does not apply to the standard model of European Council and Council decision-making.

[18] The concept of institutional engineering is borrowed from and used by analogy with Giovanni Sartori's (1994) famous work on constitutional engineering.

absorbed through an intensification of related decision-making and policy dialogue processes at the level of the European Council and the Council. Thus, this type of institutional change should be traceable both in terms of the growing relative importance of decision-making and policy dialogue, which is focused on the new areas of EU activity, in comparison to pre-established roles of the European Council and the Council, as well as in terms of absolute increases in European Council and Council activity. In qualitative terms the shift in focus towards policy coordination should be detectable in the way the European Council and the Council operate more specifically. So far, the specific features of community method decision-making—the focus on legislation and formalized decision-making routines—have served as the main reference points, especially for rationalist studies on the Council (see section 2.2). Deliberative intergovernmentalism derives its expectations towards contemporary processes of institutional change from the previously outlined features of post-Maastricht new intergovernmental-ism. Decision-making procedures and routines are expected to adapt so as to reflect the new emphasis on consensus generation and decentralized policy resources. Moreover, as many decisions concern core aspects of domestic politics and are often considered to affect national sovereignty, *policy deliberation spreads to and is detectable at the highest levels of decision-making*—thus involving ministers and heads of state and government. Without the consent and, in fact, the active backing of the most senior government representatives, policy coordination on macroeconomic policy issues, foreign policy and security matters, and welfare state-related policies is doomed to failure.

It is thus expected that the European Council and the relevant Council formations and committees that are involved in the initiation, negotiation and implementation of policy witness *a sustained increase in the frequency of meetings, longer sessions as well as more intensive deliberations over policy among senior government representatives*. The European Council assumes a particular role in the new policy-making environment because of the salience of the relevant policy issues in the domestic arena and increasing concerns about sovereignty. Deliberative intergovernmentalism identifies the *European Council as the political centre of new intergovernmentalism*. Only the heads of state and government command the necessary political authority domestically to engage in such processes. As some of the policy issues need to be resolved on the spot, delegation to the Council or specialized committees is not always an option. Thus, the *European Council is expected to deal increasingly with day-to-day policy issues* rather than only long-term decision-making and the definition of broad policy guidelines. As the *new areas of EU activity* are the ones most dependent on non-legislative decision-making and as they reveal a great potential for conflict over sovereignty concerns they are expected to *dominate the European Council agenda*. The relative importance of other functions previously associated with the European Council is declining. Council formations dealing with the new areas of EU activity assume a crucial role and are convened more frequently than others. It is expected that the *relationship between the European Council and the relevant Council formations will become increasingly hierarchical*, with the latter being tasked with preparing specific items for decision-making by the 'heads'. Moreover, as executive decisions are not delegated to the Commission but require the consent of member state governments each and every time they occur, the *meeting schedule becomes more and more event-driven*. Instead of following a predefined schedule, which is mainly determined by the EU's legislative agenda, the number of ad-hoc meetings of the European Council and relevant Council formations increases.

The new decision-making agenda does not only have repercussions on how often and under what conditions European Council and Council sessions take place but also on the way the internal functioning of the relevant decision-making bodies is organized and how their work is prepared. Thus, *new working methods and meeting formats* are introduced and a *novel organizational and administrative infrastructure* develops. The focus on achieving agreement, which centres on the personal commitment of individual policy-makers to advocate and/or implement the relevant decisions at home as well as the focus on policy development and initiation, implies an *emphasis on face-to-face debate* between top-level decision-makers. It is therefore expected that *informal working formats will gain in importance*. Following the initial study of the Eurogroup (Puetter 2006) it is also expected that *decision-making under uncertainty is a crucial feature* of the new intergovernmentalism as the EU faces so far unknown policy challenges for which no specific templates exist at the national level. This too encourages the formation of informal working methods. These formats focus on a *reduction in the number of participants* by using individual representatives rather than national delegations. Moreover, informal working formats allow for greater procedural flexibility and are not always aimed at orchestrating a particular decision-making result—which is crucial in the context of policy development and under conditions of uncertainty.[19] It is expected that the deliberative potential of a forum for policy dialogue increases with the introduction of a greater flexibility of the decision-making

[19] Elgström and Jönsson (2000: 687) quote Fearon, who argues that EU negotiations will lead to confrontational behaviour, particularly if negotiators feel that they are involved in making a deal that will bind them for a long time to come. This in turn implies that negotiations not involving formal decision-making or more short-term practical arrangements are less threatening to negotiators.

agenda. Policy deliberations that are issue-driven promise a higher potential for consensus generation.[20]

Unlike legislative decision-making under the community method, new intergovernmentalism does not always produce tangible results in the form of written agreements, nor do policy documents that are being adopted and issued by the relevant institutions have the status of formal EU decision-making acts. However, as policy coordination processes become more complex and rely increasingly on the communication of specific policy decisions, alternative forms of written communication are expected to gain much greater significance. The so-called European Council conclusions and Council press releases issued after meetings are becoming increasingly relevant as an instrument for exercising leadership primarily within the EU's own apparatus and member state administrations. Moreover, the *role of the chair therefore gains in importance* too as it also involves summarizing and communicating the informal consensus of a particular meeting or a series of meetings. The chair is also required to facilitate consensus seeking. As expectations of the role of the chair grow and meetings become more frequent and complex, a *'professionalization' of the chair function* is expected. Individual chairs are increasingly likely to be appointed outside the system of the rotating EU Council presidency.

The scope and complexity of the new system of continuous and intensive intergovernmental policy dialogue also has repercussions on the preparatory administrative structures supporting the work of the European Council and Council formations. Deliberative intergovernmentalism expects the *evolution and growing importance of a system of senior expert committees* to underpin the process of decision-making among the ministers and heads. This comitology system differs from comitology under the community method, although some features are similar. The task to develop legislative proposals becomes less important while the development, implementation, and operational oversight of coordination processes and particular executive functions assume priority and become dominant agenda items of committee work. Moreover, the nexus between high-level EU committees and the senior leadership of national line ministries is likely to be a central aspect in designing specific bodies and processes. A key feature of new intergovernmentalism is that the institutionalization of policy deliberation processes is not confined to technocratic settings, though there may be a distinct quality to such processes. The role of committees also needs to reflect the importance of policy deliberation at higher levels. *Committees are designed to assist such processes, and there is a*

---

[20] This baseline argument on informal working methods was first introduced and applied in relation to the informal Eurogroup of euro area finance ministers (Puetter 2006).

*high degree of proximity between top-level technocrats and the prime political representatives* in the European Council and the Council.

Moreover, committees are at the core of an increasingly integrated intergovernmental bureaucratic space. In the relevant policy areas the *work of national administrations is structured increasingly by the requirements of EU-level coordination processes.* It is also expected that the dominant position of the European Council is reflected domestically in the way the personal administrations of the heads of state and government are involved in the process of preparing EU-level coordination. More specifically, deliberative intergovernmentalism seeks to add to and partially builds on constructivist–institutionalist scholarship on Council comitology (see section 2.2). In particular, deliberative intergovernmentalism links existing analysis of micro-institutional contexts with a wider institutional dynamic, and integrates insights gained in relation to different policy areas and spheres of decision-making within one research design.

As member states seek to avoid the delegation of formal decision-making competences to supranational bodies the *administrative support of the Commission is taking new forms* and/or is being replaced by *new bureaucratic structures that centre on the use of existing national administrative resources.* As key aspects of economic governance and external affairs combine intergovernmental coordination and existing supranational resources, in some cases the status and role of supranational actors in the relevant forums will resemble more the role of individual member state governments, rather than one of a *primus inter pares.*

Given that the intergovernmental policy coordination process depends above all on continuity and functioning of the process, it is expected that the *new routines and practices of intergovernmental decision-making will become increasingly structured and proceduralized, although not in the sense of community method decision-making.* Thus, a *formalization of the informal* may be observed. This leads, not to a transfer of ultimate decision-making competences to the EU level, but rather to a definition of the particular roles of individual actors or processes. Formally non-binding documents, such as the conclusions issued after European Council and Council meetings, are of particular importance in this regard. In some cases, increasing formalization may indeed come at the expense of the functional integrity of informal working formats, and may thus imply a reduced institutional capacity to trigger policy deliberation in a specific field of decision-making (cf. Hodson 2011, as discussed in chapter 4.2).

## 2.4 Conclusions

This chapter has established deliberative intergovernmentalism as an analytical framework for the study of the European Council and the Council. It has set the scene for the subsequent chapters, which respond to and substantiate the set of propositions introduced above. Deliberative intergovernmentalism follows Bulmer's (1996) argument conceiving of the European Council and the Council as venues through which member states develop and substantiate integration. Its analytical focus and scope make deliberative intergovernmentalism compatible with other perspectives on Council decision-making, which subscribe to the notion of the Council as a multifaceted environment. Deliberative intergovernmentalism thus takes some aspects of European Council and Council decision-making, which fall outside its own theoretical framework, for granted. The approach pursued here in particular responds to Wallace's (2002) call for new research into non-community-method decision-making within the Council. Deliberative intergovernmentalism departs from existing scholarship on the European Council and the Council by introducing an explicitly theoretical argument on the specific context of post-Maastricht new intergovernmentalism. The key point is to link changes in the EU policy agenda with post-Maastricht institutional change. This way deliberative intergovernmentalism particularly challenges rationalist accounts on post-Maastricht and, most importantly, post-Lisbon institutional change in relation to the European Council and the Council.

Deliberative intergovernmentalism shares common ground with other approaches that emphasize the role of consensus-oriented practices in EU decision-making. As such the occurrence of consensus-oriented decision-making is not a new phenomenon in Council and European Council decision-making. Yet the procedural difference between community method decision-making and the new intergovernmentalism prevailing in the new areas of EU activity matters. Even though the community method requires an underlying political consensus it allows de facto and procedurally the creation of limited supranational authority. The insistence of member states on strictly limiting the expansion of community method decision-making since Maastricht reflects how far-reaching the consequences of such authority can be.

Philippe de Schoutheete (2011: 3) emphasizes that both the community method and the intergovernmental method have changed, compared to the way they were in the early decades of European integration. Yet it is important to distinguish between them when it comes to decision-making in the Council. He accuses contemporary research of conflating the two methods by terming all decision-making in the Council 'intergovernmental':

> That is clearly wrong: the Community method involves a final decision by the Council, which is comprised of ministers. And those with experience know that sitting at an institutional table or at an occasional meeting does make a difference on the debate and on the interlocutors' positions.

As deliberative intergovernmentalism is based on the assumption that there is no general integration fatigue but that the intention to (re-)organize core areas of national sovereignty within the EU context prevails, further explanation is needed of how this political agenda translates into concrete institutional structures for collective decision-making. Given that the EU already has a complex institutional framework, change is occurring within existing structures and is linked to the complex processes of institutional engineering.

# 3

# The European Council: the New Centre of Political Gravity

*The European Council will be the power centre [of EU policy-making].*[1]

The European Council has emerged as the new centre of political gravity in European Union (EU) policy-making. It embodies the new intergovernmentalism in post-Maastricht EU integration: this is the key claim of the present chapter. While the overall importance of the European Council to the functioning of the EU is not new to students of European integration (see chapter 2.2), the claim that the European Council assumes centrality in the day-to-day policy-making process does not necessarily accord with the standard image of EU decision-making to date. Only a few accounts speak of the growing importance of the institution in this regard. In the mid-2000s Borrás and Jacobsson (2004) highlighted the lead role assigned to the European Council and the Council of the European Union ('the Council') in the context of the open method of coordination (OMC), and noted a shift in the inter-institutional balance of power in relation to the European Commission ('the Commission'). Only more recently have the provisions relating to the European Council in the Lisbon Treaty, together with the economic and financial crisis, triggered more pronounced comments in the scholarly community on the growing importance of the institution (Devuyst 2008, 2012; Dinan 2012; Nederlof et al. 2012).

However, the EU's attempts to manage the consequences of the global economic and financial crisis, which occurred from 2008 onwards, are interpreted in this chapter as revealing a much more fundamental shift in the role of the European Council in EU decision-making. The crisis has essentially amplified an underlying institutional trend, which can in fact be traced

---

[1] Interviewee EU-07/ECON, 30 March 2010.

back to the second half of the 1990s. This trend is a consequence of the way major new areas of EU activity were designed at Maastricht and later. This chapter shows that the emergence of new intergovernmentalism and the dependency of this governance mode on policy deliberation have led to the growing importance of the European Council as well as to the changes in its relationship with other key EU bodies. As discussed in chapter 1, the areas of economic governance and foreign, security, and defence policy, and the field of social and employment policy coordination are central to this process. This chapter traces how the role of the European Council in EU policy-making has changed over time and demonstrates how the European Council and its operation have been transformed through a constant process of institutional engineering, which has aimed to improve the consensus-generating capacity of the top-level EU forum. Moreover, the chapter analyses how the European Council exercises leadership in relation to other EU bodies and member states without relying on legislative instruments of classic community method decision-making.

## 3.1 Acquiring a New Role in the Policy-making Process

The discussion of the integration paradox in chapter 1 provides the basis for understanding the new centrality of the European Council in EU decision-making. Some decisions can only be taken by heads of state and government. This is vital for ensuring commitment to common EU policy objectives in the absence of legislative arrangements, and for governing within policy areas that are at the heart of national sovereignty and domestic politics. The following statements from interviewees who have close familiarity with European Council decision-making from either a Brussels- or a capital-based perspective illustrate how much importance policy-makers attach to the changing role of the European Council in EU policy-making.

The extent to which the European Council is by now seen as a pace-maker in EU policy-making in general is well reflected in the following quote:

> What has changed is that now we speak about handing over really big political issues [to the European Council], which are not part of the legislative calendar. Only the European Council matters—not the EU [Council] presidencies—this was in the past.[2]

This illustrates the pertinence of policy issues that are being addressed within one of the new areas of EU activity. EU legislative activity is perceived to tick along as before, but it does not make the headlines in contemporary EU

---

[2] Interviewee EU-06/GEN, 3 June 2010.

policy-making. Thus, the overall role of the European Council is thought to be different. As one official put it:

> The heads got much more involved because of the importance of these issues for coalitions and domestic politics.[3]

And another official explained:

> All sovereignty-related topics go up to the European Council. This can't be decided by the Council.[4]

Such views are echoed in the capitals. For example, a senior line ministry official confirmed that the prime minister intervenes increasingly in the relevant portfolio, and that these interventions are linked to the European Council agenda:

> EU politics are domestic politics—not some external matter—and they require tight control by the Prime Minister. If you want to govern nowadays bring it first to the EU agenda—European Council and Council—and see what happens. Then go through the process at home.[5]

The same official thought that his/her prime minister devoted 'quite a bit of his personal attention to the EU file', in order to ensure a consistent position and to instruct the line ministries to follow up on individual points. The official also believed that the national model of internal EU coordination mattered with regard to a country's ability to bring topics to the European Council agenda and to detect strategic issues at an early stage.—A diplomat in one of the permanent representations had a similar view, and attributed the growing involvement of the heads to the complexity of decision-making in the EU following Lisbon:

> It is simply because there are new members and it gets more and more complicated and the interest of Prime Ministers' offices in key policy issues has increased. Take fiscal policy, bank guarantees and then elections matter. There is now a lot of internal coordination [of EU-related issues] between our Prime Minister and the finance ministry.[6]

A capital-based official working in a personal administration office of a head of government believed that dynamics in the domestic sphere had changed considerably over recent years because of European Council decision-making. The administration would intervene in individual dossiers much earlier than previously. Moreover, the official believed that the head of government and the head of the personal administration office 'tend to take up portfolios at a

---

[3] Interviewee EU-09/ECON, 4 July 2011.     [4] Interviewee EU-07/ECON, 7 April 2009.
[5] Interviewee MS-05/ECON, 9 December 2009.
[6] Interviewee PR-11/ECON, 5 November 2009.

very early stage—even before a line ministry was in a position to make a [final] decision. We are monitoring instructions for COREPER[7] very closely'.[8]

The trend for more decisions related to specific policy issues in the areas of economic governance, Common Foreign and Security Policy (CFSP), Common Security and Defence Policy (CSDP), and social and employment policy coordination to be referred to the European Council is widely noted among interviewees. The European Council frequently claims direct responsibility for decisions over policy, and the Council increasingly refers decisions to the European Council for final approval. It is understood that there are no limits to the European Council's concentration on policy detail:

> Decisions concerning details become more and more important for the heads. This can even involve the financing of specific projects—be they worth 0.5 billion or 5 billion EUR.[9]

This also implies changes in the way the European Council works. This is reflected not least in the outcome of European Council meetings, as it becomes manifest in the conclusions (see section 3.9), and in the form of informal agreement among the heads. One official describes these developments as follows:

> The European Council has changed due to the increased focus on detailed issues. The heads want to see concrete deliverables and are no longer happy with philosophical statements of the kind that Europe needs to grow together and that we are supporting a free market economy.[10]

The same official sees the European Council's ambition to exercise stronger leadership and its attention to technical detail as inevitable consequences. This might even involve more focus on complicated legal issues, which otherwise would have been sorted out by the Council and the Commission.[11] The growing involvement of the European Council in day-to-day policy decisions is linked to the growing complexity of the coordination agendas in the new areas of EU activity, which have evolved from nascent fields of policy-making into areas of crucial importance for both member states and EU institutions:

> The tendency of policy decisions going from the Council to the European Council is true because we are more ambitious now than ever before.[12]

Moreover, almost all interviewees expect an ongoing intensification of the existing coordination processes. Some believe that even more radical changes to the role of the European Council in EU policy-making are possible in the

---

[7] Committee of Permanent Representatives.      [8] Interviewee MS-06/GEN, 3 July 2009.
[9] Interviewee MS-06/GEN, 3 July 2009.      [10] Interviewee EU-07/ECON, 7 April 2009.
[11] Interviewee EU-07/ECON, 30 March 2010.
[12] Interviewee PR-01/ECON, 4 November 2009.

not-so-distant future. As one senior official pointed out just ahead of the Lisbon Treaty reforms of the European Council presidency:

> Under a strong president the European Council could even develop further into a central decision-making body that meets frequently and decides on all overarching topics. This would imply that the European Council would partially replace the Council.[13]

Three years later, ahead of a European Council meeting in October 2012, the French president François Hollande criticized the practice of compensating for the rising workload of the European Council by holding additional non-regular ad-hoc meetings and demanded that at least the heads of the euro area should follow a schedule of more regular meetings:

> I am equally in favour of monthly meetings of the heads of state and government of this [euro] zone. Let us finish with these summits which are called at the last moment, these historical meetings, these exceptional gatherings—which only lead to transitory successes. [ ... ] Europe cannot be late anymore![14]

In post-Maastricht EU policy-making the European Council has come to intervene increasingly in the Council's work in relation to aspects of day-to-day decision-making. All indications are that it will do so even more frequently in the future. As at the national level, where heads of state and government preside over the work of their respective ministerial cabinets, the European Council now presides over the work of the Council—at least in those areas of EU activity that are governed through intergovernmental policy coordination.[15]

The growing importance of the European Council, and its interference with a full range of policy issues that were previously dealt with mostly at the level of the Council and the Commission, has thus not been without friction. The new role played by the heads challenges established patterns of inter-institutional relations and political control. The Commission and the European Parliament (EP) are directly affected by these developments, as one senior diplomat with long-term experience in Brussels makes clear:

> There is still fighting between Barroso and Van Rompuy. There is a fear of creeping intergovernmentalism, which is mainly criticized by the European Parliament because they don't control the European Council.[16]

---

[13] Interviewee MS-06/GEN, 3 July 2009.
[14] Interview with *Le Monde*, 17 October 2012, own translation.
[15] In her research on the Council presidency Ana Mar Fernández (2008: 624) has also interpreted the leading role of the European Council as 'the extension of the founding principles of the Presidency—representativeness and equality—to the top of the institutional architecture'.
[16] Interviewee PR-16/GEN, 3 June 2010.

The European Council's role as the political centre of the EU's new intergovernmentalism implies that it has established a distinct decision-making
mode outside the community method that is not primarily focused on creating new EU legislation. While the European Council—at least according to its
treaty mandate (see section 3.3)—cannot overtake the legislative functions of
other EU institutions, there is nothing to prevent the institution from interfering directly with non-legislative policy decisions prepared by the Council
and the Commission. This type of decision-making is referred to as 'policy
dialogue', or 'political' decision-making as opposed to legislative decision-
making. As one official explains:

> The differentiation between policy dialogue and legislation is not surprising
> because [legislation] is not the European Council's business.[17]

Another official tried to explain the difference between European Council
activity and decisions taken within the Council using a new terminological
distinction, which in the view of this official reflected that the European
Council, according to EU procedures, does not often take final decisions[18]
but only agrees that other EU bodies or national governments can take certain
executive or legislative decisions:

> The European Council is an institution for decision-coordination rather than
> decision-making. [ ... ] The most important thing for the European Council to
> do is to create support for something among the heads. Later the ministers will
> come in and do the actual decision-making. But it is important that everyone
> knows this comes from the heads. Then it is difficult to do something else.[19]

Yet another official offers the term 'political' to describe the character of European Council decisions, and explains the difference by the way of an example:

> The G-20 coordination by the European Council is a good example of taking
> 'political' and not 'legal' decisions.[20]

The European Council is seen to play a superior role in relation to the Council
and the Commission, whose work in the relevant areas of decision-making it
closely monitors. The heads instruct the relevant Council formations and also
the Commission to work towards specific objectives, to provide input for
European Council meetings, and also to revise proposals. The following official offered this succinct definition of the European Council's superior role:

> It sets strategic guidelines and deals with crises.[21]

---

[17] Interviewee EU-09/ECON, 4 July 2011.
[18] For a discussion of the formal status of European Council decisions, see section 3.9.
[19] Interviewee EU-25/GEN, 4 March 2013.     [20] Interviewee EU-07/ECON, 30 March 2010.
[21] Interviewee EU-02/GEN, 4 July 2011.

## 3.2 The Matrix of European Council Decision-making

Studying institutional change requires comparisons of European Council decision-making over time. The focus of this book is on the first two decades of the post-Maastricht era. The claim is that the European Council has gradually become the political centre of Europe's new intergovernmentalism and has thus assumed a new role in EU policy-making. Moreover, this shift in focus in European Council activity has triggered profound changes in the way the European Council operates and how it relates to other institutions. The focus is on permanent consensus seeking among the most senior government executives representing EU member states. The policy fields of socio-economic governance and external affairs are the new items on the European Council agenda. Yet the European Council was created much earlier. It assumed specific functions and roles in European governance (cf. in particular Bulmer and Wessels 1987; Werts 2008), which it still carries out. Partially, these roles and functions overlap with what the European Council does in the EU's new areas of activity. Partially, they differ.[22]

In order to facilitate analysis of the changing mandate and decision-making agenda of the European Council this section provides for a matrix of European Council decision-making. To this end 16 core areas of European Council activity are identified (see Table 3.1). These areas have been selected on the basis of research on previous periods of European Council decision-making, reference to European Council decision-making in the treaties since the Single European Act (SEA) and, following the author's own analysis of the European Council agenda since 1992, on the basis of European Council conclusions, press reports, and expert interviews. Each activity area represents a recurring item on the European Council's agenda that is further defined through a procedure, a competence as specified in the treaties, or a decision by the European Council to deal with a particular policy issue on a regular basis. Each category belongs to one of four broader categories of European Council activity.

The **new areas of EU activity** constitute the first broad category of European Council activity. Though the European Council was active on some of these policy issues before the Maastricht Treaty entered into force, this category came to represent a comprehensive set of European Council responsibilities and activities that, in terms of scope and depth, had not existed before. It is in this area that the dynamics of deliberative intergovernmentalism are most pronounced. Within this first broad category five subcategories are

---

[22] The existing literature on the European Council covers its traditional functions very well. Reference to earlier phases of European Council decision-making is therefore kept to a minimum here. See chapter 2.2 for a discussion of existing literature on the European Council.

distinguished. The area of *economic governance* ('ECON') includes all activities related to broader economic policy coordination involving all member states, including reform processes such as the Lisbon agenda and EU2020 (the EU's growth strategy for the decade, 2011–20), as well as all aspects of euro-area governance. The area of *foreign, security, and defence policy* ('FP') includes all external affairs activities that fall under the CFSP and CSDP frameworks. *Employment and social policy coordination* ('EMSOC') includes the various coordination procedures and routines in this field. *Justice and home affairs policy* ('JHA') is also part of this first broad category, though this aspect of European Council activity is not analysed in greater detail within this book. Finally, the European Council's growing role in coordinating common EU positions in *global decision-making forums* ('GLOBAL'), such as climate negotiations and G7, G8, and G20 meetings belongs here. Reference to individual European Council sessions may include combinations of subcategories such as ECON/EMSOC for the so-called spring meetings of the European Council in March each year or ECON/GLOBAL for a European Council meeting focusing on the preparation of a G20 meeting on the global economic and financial crisis.

The second broad category comprises **major institutional decisions**. It is one of the historical roles of the European Council to have paved the way for all major institutional reforms and competence changes since the mid-1970s.[23] The European Council dealt and deals with issues that have a constitutional dimension. It is paving the way for treaty reform—indicated by the category 'CON' for *constitutional decision-making*. The European Council also decides about issues that were left open during previous rounds of treaty reforms. The Lisbon Treaty, for example, foresees a number of European Council decisions on aspects that otherwise would have required a treaty change. The composition of core EU institutions, such as the Commission and the EP, is a good example. Yet it is well known that the European Council is also a forum in which major institutional reforms are agreed that change the way the EU operates, though this is not mentioned in the Treaty. Such decisions might resemble decisions on treaty reform in their relevance and scope, but they could lead instead to an *intergovernmental agreement or an intergovernmental treaty concluded outside the EU treaties*. The decision to create the European Monetary System (EMS) is a case in point. The Fiscal Treaty is the most recent example of such an activity. This category is referred to as 'CON\*'. Moreover, in the post-Maastricht era the European Council has repeatedly taken decisions that can be best characterized as de facto constitutional decisions (see section 3.9), but which are neither related to the process of treaty

---

[23] John Peterson (1995) refers to these decisions as 'history-making' and 'super-systemic' decisions.

reform nor an intergovernmental agreement outside the EU treaties. Such decisions are communicated via the presidency conclusions, and have the power to modify existing treaty provisions and/or to establish rules and procedures like those found in the treaties. The creation of the Eurogroup in 1997, which effectively modified the mandate of the Economic and Financial Affairs Council (ECOFIN) as stipulated in the Treaty, is an example of this. The European Employment Strategy (EES), which devised a procedure for inter-governmental policy coordination including the definition of responsibilities and obligations of the different EU institutions and the member states, con-stitutes another case, and so did the original establishment of Euro Summits (see section 3.8). Such activities are referred to here as *informal constitutional decisions* ('INF-CON'). In a way the European Council's own constitution as an informal forum for high-level political dialogue through the Paris declaration of the heads in December 1974 (Hayes-Renshaw and Wallace 2006: 166–7) can be considered as the archetype of such decision-making. Finally, the European Council plays a crucial role in *enlargement* of the Union ('ENLG'). The historic process of the EU's eastward enlargement following the fall of the Iron Curtain is a recent and powerful example of this role. Not only does the decision to accept a country into the Union matter in this context, but the constitutional dimension of the enlargement process also matters, as it involves setting standards for accession, and a political appreciation of the perceived consequences of the process for the Union as a whole. The Lisbon Treaty also added a procedure for exiting the EU. It implies a central role for the European Council and falls into this subcategory.

The third broad category of European Council activity identified here refers to the European Council's direct or indirect involvement in **formal EU decision-making**. This implies that the European Council has final deci-sion-making competences on particular issues, or agrees how the Council should decide on issues on which ministers cannot (or are not allowed to) reach a decision among themselves. Some of these decisions may have the status of 'grand bargains', and correspond to notions of top-level intergovern-mental decision-making highlighted especially in the context of the process of market integration (Moravcsik 1998; Scharpf 1988). This includes the recur-ring negotiation of the multi-annual *EU budget* ('BUD'), which cannot be concluded without the direct involvement of the European Council and is fraught with historical legacies. Though the European Council is not one of the core decision-making institutions under the classic community method, the Treaty grants it the power to make a number of key *personnel decisions* ('PD') that are final and do not require a further decision by the Council. The selection of presidents of the Commission and the European Central Bank (ECB), as well as the appointment of the High Representative (HR), belongs to this subcategory.

In some cases the European Council may also make a de facto decision that is then implemented by the Council or through another procedure. The appointment of the Eurogroup president is a case in point.[24] The European Council also intervenes from time to time in *legislative decision-making under the classic community method* ('LEGS'). This happens when there is deadlock in the Council or a slowdown in important legislative processes. In such cases the European Council acts as a steering committee; it is the final arbiter and at times also coordinates the legislative work of the Council horizontally (cf. Dann 2010: 261–5). The European Council is also involved in negotiating acts that are not legislative acts under EU law but have a similar status or function ('LEGS*'). Such action recently occurred in the context of establishing the European Financial Stability Facility (EFSF) and the European Stability Mechanism (ESM)—a matter that was dealt with primarily at the level of ministers but was reviewed and partially negotiated by the European Council.

The fourth and final broad category comprises any **other activities** that do not acquire the status of the sub-fields of activity mentioned above. This category includes activities that do not occur on a regular basis and account for only a very small share of the work of the body if assessed over a longer period of time. This is not to say that these activities are not important. For example, before the office of a full-time European Council president was created, many governments that took up the rotating presidency used the European Council as a forum for initiating high-level debates about priority projects that they championed. However, the relevance of such activities to analysing the processes of institutional change is considered to be low. There are only two further fields of European Council activity to which reference is made in analysing the European Council agenda below: *environmental policy* ('ENV') and *energy policy* ('ENER'). These policy areas constitute recurrent items on the European Council's agenda though they are not dealt with as regularly as the new areas of EU activity. The reason they are mentioned here is that they involve a mix of intergovernmental policy coordination and classic community method decision-making. Existing research, especially on environmental policy, suggests that both the introduction of novel coordination mechanisms and European Council involvement are key to the further developments in these policy areas (Lenschow 2002; Sabel and Zeitlin 2008). Moreover, environmental policy in particular requires the coordination of common EU positions for international forums—the climate negotiations being a case in point. European Council *activity in other areas* ('OTHER') is not specified further but is highlighted in the presentation of European Council agenda data in the remaining parts of this chapter so as to help in explaining the relative importance of the individual fields of activity.

---

[24] See chapter 4.2 on the appointment of the Eurogroup president.

**Table 3.1.** Core areas of European Council activity

| | | |
|---|---|---|
| New areas of activity | ECON | Economic governance, all member states and euro area (EMU[25]) |
| | FP | Foreign, security, and defence policy (CFSP and CSDP) |
| | EMSOC | Social and employment policy coordination |
| | JHA | Justice and home affairs |
| | GLOBAL | Positions for international forums (climate, G7/8/20) |
| Major institutional decisions | CON | Treaty reform (preparation, ratification, failure) |
| | CON* | Intergovernmental agreement outside the Treaties of similar scope |
| | INF-CON | De facto CON decisions that are not formally codified in the Treaties or an international treaty outside the Treaties |
| | ENLG | Enlargement |
| Formal EU decision-making | BUD | EU budget |
| | PD | Personnel decisions |
| | LEGS | Resolving deadlock over legislative decisions in the Council |
| | LEGS* | Implementing acts outside EU legislation (EFSF and ESM) |
| Other activities | ENV | Environmental policy and climate change |
| | ENER | Energy policy |
| | OTHER | Other policy areas |

## 3.3 Codifying Change: from Maastricht to Lisbon

The new role of the European Council in EU policy-making can be traced both with regard to changes in the formal institutional framework and by studying the practice of European Council decision-making. The practice dimension is analysed in detail in later sections of this chapter. This section reviews how the role of the European Council is defined within the treaties. The Lisbon Treaty is widely considered to constitute the most important change so far in the European Council's formal mandate, as well as its modes of operation (Devuyst 2008; Nederlof et al. 2012; Wessels 2008). This makes the Lisbon Treaty an important reference document for studying the European Council's role in contemporary decision-making. This section offers a particular perspective on the Lisbon Treaty and views the new provisions on the European Council as manifestations of a longer-term process. By reviewing the way the European Council is referred to in past and present treaties, it interprets the Lisbon Treaty as the latest in a series of attempts at institutional engineering (Puetter 2012a).

Moreover, as it is argued throughout this chapter, the story of the European Council is one of many repeated attempts to define and reshape the forum's role in EU policy-making through practice. The formal mandate of the institution as it is enshrined in various treaty provisions has changed over time. Often these changes only codify practices that were already established prior to the act of treaty reform. Moreover, many provisions remain fairly general. Reviewing the treaty provisions hardly suffices for understanding the body's

---

[25] Economic and Monetary Union.

role in EU governance. This exercise provides only the starting point for analysing further the relation between formal and informal mechanisms of institutional change.

Early European Community summitry, which was chiefly triggered by French president Charles de Gaulle, was intended to limit the autonomous powers of the Commission (Devuyst 2008: 267). Yet this is hardly the main reason that the heads thought it important to involve themselves more closely with European-level policy-making. The initiative of the later French president Valéry Giscard d'Estaing and German chancellor Helmut Schmidt to institutionalize summit meetings as regular informal consultations on key issues in European integration from December 1974 onwards revealed that the original community method system of decision-making could not create sufficient political impetus for further integration, but required additional top-level impetus to move integration forward (cf. Bulmer and Wessels 1987). The development of the Community relied on a broader political consensus, which had to be generated outside the context of specific legislative initiatives. Though Giscard d'Estaing and Schmidt were very clear that they considered regular political dialogue among the most senior decision-makers a precondition for running the integration project, the European Council was constituted as a political forum outside the treaties that existed at that time. The 1989 SEA was the first treaty amendment to acknowledge the existence of the European Council. This move came 15 years after the forum was constituted as a venue for top-level informal debate. Yet the SEA did little more than mention the name of the new body. It specified only that the European Council convene at least twice a year (Title I, Article 2, SEA).

The Maastricht Treaty introduced the European Council as an institution of the new Treaty on European Union (TEU) and mandated it to 'provide the Union with the necessary impetus for its development'. Explicit reference was made to the European Council's prerogative to 'define the general political guidelines thereof' (Article D, TEU, Maastricht; Article 4, TEU, Nice). Again, this new provision can be read as codifying a practice that already existed at the time. In particular the period starting shortly before the SEA entered into force and continuing until the ratification of the Maastricht Treaty can be characterized as one during which the European Council developed into an institution that would provide impetus for the integration process, both in terms of preparing major institutional reforms and ultimately by anchoring the policy process by resolving decision-making deadlock. Without the European Council's direct involvement, neither the implementation of the single market agenda nor the development of the Economic and Monetary Union (EMU) would have been possible (De Schoutheete 2011: 184–5).

Like the SEA, the Maastricht Treaty defined the European Council as composed by the heads of state or government and the president of the Commission, the foreign ministers, and a further member of the Commission (Article D, TEU, Maastricht). The ministers and the commissioner were considered to act as assistants to their relevant bosses. The role of president of the European Council was attributed to 'the Head of State or of Government of the Member State which holds the Presidency of the Council' (Article D, TEU, Maastricht). This rather short description of the European Council mandate and its internal functioning remained unchanged until the Lisbon Treaty entered into force. Moreover, by placing this provision on the European Council in the TEU rather than in the TEC, it was made clear that the high-level forum was not part of the community's core institutional triangle—the Council, the Commission, and the EP. From the beginning the European Council was thus not constituted as a formal decision-making organ as understood within the context of the classic community method.

Though there was little doubt that the European Council de facto took important decisions, the overall role of the European Council in EU governance as outlined in the Maastricht TEU remained ambiguous. The Maastricht Treaty provided for a more specific definition of the role of the European Council with regard to only two policy areas: economic policy coordination and CFSP. In both cases the European Council obtained a policy-making role that was more clearly defined than the general mandate to provide 'impetus' to the development of the EU. In the case of the TEC provisions on economic policy coordination, the European Council's role was defined in the context of a novel policy coordination procedure, which followed an annually approved set of written, though non-binding, policy guidelines. The adoption of these guidelines by the Council required prior approval from the European Council. In this way the European Council was formally given the mandate to review and actively take decisions over specific policy-making issues. Devising concrete policies was seen previously as an exclusive domain of the Council, the Commission, and to some extent the EP. Moreover, the procedure on adopting broad economic policy guidelines established a clear hierarchy between the European Council on the one hand, and the Council and the Commission on the other. The Council and the Commission were asked to submit work to the European Council for review. The somewhat obscure wording of the relevant provision in the Maastricht Treaty and the complicated procedure it described reveal how difficult the idea of giving final decision-making powers to the European Council proved, at least with some of the Treaty's authors:

> The European Council shall, acting on the basis of the report from the Council, discuss a conclusion on the broad guidelines of the economic policies of the Member States and of the Community.

On the basis of this conclusion, the Council shall, acting by a qualified majority, adopt a recommendation setting out these broad guidelines.[26]

Moreover, the Maastricht Treaty left open the issue of what type of policy instructions the guidelines had to cover. This gave the European Council an extremely important role, as it could steer the coordination process in different directions and assign different roles and responsibilities to the Council, the Commission, and national governments. In a similar fashion the Maastricht TEU provisions on the CFSP assigned to the European Council the role of providing the Council with 'general guidelines' (Article J.3.1, TEU Maastricht), whenever it decided on so-called 'joint actions', i.e. instances of collective and coordinated foreign policy action by the member states and, where applicable, the Commission. As in the case of economic policy coordination, the procedure established a clear hierarchy between the European Council and the Council.

The Amsterdam Treaty kept the references to the overall role and mandate of the European Council, which were established by the Maastricht version of the TEU, unchanged. Rather it expanded the definition of the new roles of the European Council through policy area-specific provisions. The provisions on foreign, security, and defence policy coordination were slightly revised and complemented. The European Council was assigned the role of 'defin[ing] the principles of and general guidelines for' foreign and security policy-making as well as 'common strategies' (Article 13, TEU Amsterdam). The Council was charged with preparing such decisions by the European Council and with ensuring their implementation. In addition, the Amsterdam Treaty expanded the use of European Council-led procedures for intergovernmental policy coordination to include the field of employment policy. Again, the European Council was assigned an oversight role in relation to the Council and the Commission. The latter two bodies were charged with drafting and implementing specific coordination objectives (Article 128, TEC Amsterdam). With these new provisions, the Treaty codified a coordination procedure that had been previously put in place by a European Council conclusion (see section 3.9).

While the general provisions relating to the European Council remain short and ambiguous, the policy area-specific provisions in the Maastricht and Amsterdam Treaties can be read as a catalogue of tasks and competences reserved for the European Council. This catalogue is not contained in a single provision or title, but consists of numerous provisions relating to the European Council's role within the new areas of EU activity. Moreover, while there is no reference to a role for the European Council in legislative

---

[26] Article 103.2, TEC Maastricht.

decision-making, the three new areas of EU activity are all founded on the principle of direct political oversight by the European Council. The Nice Treaty confirmed this basic approach without introducing further modifications.

At first sight, many affirmative reactions to the new Lisbon Treaty provisions relating to the European Council might suggest that this original approach was actually modified. Indeed, the vast majority of interviewees believe that the Treaty added to the importance of the institution. As one senior official put it:

> The European Council has gained enormously in terms of importance through the Lisbon Treaty.[27]

In fact, the Lisbon Treaty offers a double approach. First and foremost, it reproduces and in some cases further clarifies the existing catalogue of policy area-related provisions on the European Council. Thus, the Lisbon Treaty confirms the approach pursued by all treaties since Maastricht, namely of making the European Council the veritable centre of political gravity in the context of the EU's new intergovernmentalism. No single provision or title defines the decision-making competences of the forum: this is done by the catalogue of various policy area-related provisions (see Tables 3.2 and 3.3). Before the Lisbon Treaty entered into force this catalogue had already received endorsement by the Convention process and the signed but never ratified Constitutional Treaty (cf. Puetter 2007a). Thus the Lisbon Treaty can be interpreted as a deliberate move to reassert the role of the already established system of intergovernmental policy coordination and the role of the European Council within it. The second important element of the Lisbon Treaty's approach to the European Council is the introduction of the most comprehensive set of general provisions relating to the decision-making forum so far, including modifications to the way the European Council operates. Closer inspection of these provisions reveals that they are not meant to change the focus on the new areas of EU activity discussed above. Rather, the new provisions react to the growing demand for decision-making capacity in the new areas of EU activity. Thus the relevant provisions can be best interpreted as a renewed attempt at institutional engineering. They are aimed at modifying the operation of the European Council so that it can better adapt to a changing decision-making context.

In terms of language and scope, reference to the European Council now resembles reference to the other core EU institutions. For the first time, the Lisbon Treaty incorporates the European Council among the 'Union's institutions' (Article 13.1, TEU) together with the EP, the Council, the Commission, the Court of Justice of the European Union ('the Court of Justice'), the

---

[27] Interviewee EU-07/ECON, 30 March 2010.

ECB, and the Court of Auditors. As for the other EU institutions there is a separate article in the TEU defining the general role of the European Council and its composition (Article 15, TEU). A special section in the Treaty on the Functioning of the European Union (TFEU) details decision-making rules and stipulates that the European Council is supported by the Council's General Secretariat and that its president can be heard by the EP (Article 235, TFEU). Moreover, Article 10.2, TEU identifies the European Council, next to the Council, as the central forum for representing member states in EU decision-making:

> Member States are represented in the European Council by their Heads of State or Government and in the Council by their governments, themselves democratically accountable either to their national Parliaments, or to their citizens.[28]

The main general article in the Lisbon Treaty on the European Council (Article 15.1, TEU) repeats the Maastricht formula that the European Council provides impetus for the Union's development and sets political directions and priorities, but now also clarifies:

> It shall not exercise legislative functions.

Thus, the Lisbon Treaty underlines that the European Council is not part of the institutional triangle of classic community method decision-making.[29] Again, this can be read as codifying the already existing practice of governing the EU through two distinct governance mechanisms. The emphasis on the European Council not legislating reflects its de facto engagement in detailed policy decisions and implementation in areas subject to policy coordination. Because the European Council's relation with the Council and the Commission in these fields is changing, it is more relevant than ever before to guard established prerogatives in inter-institutional relations. Yet these prerogatives are granted only in the sphere of legislative decision-making.

The fact that the European Council is not a legislative body, however, does not imply that it is immune to the principle of legality. As any other EU institution, European Council action may be subject to review by the Court of Justice if a member state so requests (Article 269, TFEU). It may also be subject to infringement proceedings (Article 265, TFEU). Moreover, the Treaty acknowledges that European Council action may have 'legal effects *vis-à-vis*

---

[28] Article 10.2, TEU.

[29] This provision does not rule out, however, that European Council focusing on issues decided under the community method. It could do so by providing 'impetus' or 'general political direction'. Yet the European Council has no operational role in the legislative process. The provisions on JHA matters come closest to giving the European Council a formal role in legislative decision-making. The heads provide 'strategic guidelines' (Article 68, TFEU), which effectively bind the Commission in the exercise of its right of initiative (cf. also Devuyst 2008: 271).

third parties' (Article 263, TFEU). Accordingly such acts of the European Council can be subject to review by the Court of Justice.

The remainder of Article 15, TEU is devoted to the internal functioning of the European Council. The relevant provisions most clearly reflect the new focus on institutional engineering. The provisions stipulate the introduction of a new membership regime that excludes ministers from most European Council meetings. They highlight the increased frequency of meetings and foresee the possibility of convening special meetings. Article 15, TEU creates the office of a full-time elected president. All these aspects are discussed in detail in the following sections. Apart from creating the post of an elected European Council president, these provisions again mainly codify practices that were already constituted before the Lisbon Treaty came into force. Yet the fact that they have acquired the status of treaty rules constitutes in itself an important statement. As one official stressed:

> The Lisbon Treaty formalized a role the European Council already had in practice.[30]

The new focus on the internal functioning of the European Council is also reflected in another provision hidden in the institutional provisions title of the TFEU. Article 235.3, TFEU stipulates that the European Council establishes its own rules of procedure. For the first time in its history the forum has obtained a formal set of rules of procedure. This set of rules came into force together with the Lisbon Treaty.[31]

As indicated above, an analysis of how the Treaty defines the European Council's role cannot be limited to the general provisions of Article 15, TEU, but requires a review of the various policy area-specific provisions relating to the top-level forum. Tables 3.2 and 3.3 provide a detailed overview of how the Lisbon Treaty refers to the European Council and how it defines the process of European Council decision-making in relation to specific fields of activity. Analysed this way, the formal mandate of the European Council emerges more clearly. In order to facilitate assessment of the scope and type of European Council decision-making, individual treaty provisions are categorized according to the matrix of European Council decision-making that was introduced in the previous section. Table 3.2 assembles all TEU provisions relating to the European Council. The provisions of Article 15, TEU that define the general role of the European Council and its internal functioning are excluded, as they were dealt with in detail in earlier paragraphs and are reviewed further later in this chapter. Table 3.3 refers to the relevant provisions in the TFEU.

---

[30] Interviewee EU-02/GEN, 4 July 2011.
[31] See European Council Decision 2009/882/EU adopting its Rules of Procedure, published in OJ L315/51.

**Table 3.2.** European Council decision-making as specified in the TEU (except Article 15)

| Treaty provision | Policy area/scope (where applicable) | Decision-making mode[a] | |
| --- | --- | --- | --- |
| | | Majority decision | Consensus/ unanimity |
| Article 7.2, TEU *Determination of a serious and persistent breach of EU values* | CON | | X |
| Article 10.2, TEU *Representation of member states at the level of heads* | | | X |
| Article 14.2, TEU *Decision on EP composition* | CON | | X |
| Article 16.6, TEU *Strategic guidelines on external action for Council* | FP | | X |
| Article 17.5, TEU *Decision on changing the number of Commission members after 1 November 2014* | CON | | X |
| Article 17.5, TEU *Decision on system of equal rotation of Commission members among member states* | CON | | X |
| Article 17.7, TEU *Proposing a candidate for the office of Commission president* | PD | X (QMV[32]) | |
| Article 17.7, TEU *Appointment of the Commission* | PD | X (QMV) | |
| Article 18.1, TEU *Appointment and dismissal of the HR* | PD | X (QMV) | |
| Article 22.1, TEU *Identification of EU strategic interests and objectives* | FP | | X |
| Article 24.1, TEU *Definition and implementation of the CFSP (with the Council)* | FP | | X |
| Article 26.1, TEU *Identification of EU strategic interests, objectives and general guidelines incl. defence matters* | FP | | X |
| Article 31.2, TEU *Decision on solving impasse related to concerns that CFSP policy is conflict with vital national policy* | FP | | X |

*(continued)*

**Table 3.2.** Continued

| Treaty provision | Policy area/scope (where applicable) | Decision-making mode[a] | |
|---|---|---|---|
| | | Majority decision | Consensus/ unanimity |
| Article 31.3, TEU *Extension of the scope of Council QMV decisions on CFSP* | FP | | X |
| Article 32, TEU *Consultation on national foreign and security policy action* | FP | | |
| Article 42.2, TEU *Transition to a system of common defence* | FP | | X |
| Article 48.3, TEU *Decision on examining Treaty amendments by a Convention or a conference of government representatives only* | CON | X (simple) | |
| Article 48.6, TEU *Decision to amend provisions of Part III of the TFEU—simplified revision (requires ratification)* | CON | | X |
| Article 48.7, TEU *Decision to change Council voting procedures to QMV for TFEU and Title V, TEU provisions (requires EP approval)* | CON | | X |
| Article 49, TEU *Specification of conditions of eligibility for EU member states* | ENLG | | X |
| Article 50.2, TEU *Provision of guidelines to the Council for the negotiation of an agreement on a member state withdrawing from the EU* | ENLG | | X |
| Article 50.3, TEU *Extension of period before termination of membership* | ENLG | | X |

Note: [a] An empty line indicates that no specific decision needs to be taken.

[32] Qualified majority voting.

**Table 3.3** European Council decision-making as specified in the TFEU

| Treaty provision | Policy area/scope (where applicable) | Decision-making mode | |
|---|---|---|---|
| | | Majority decision | Consensus/ unanimity |
| Article 48, TFEU<br>*Reactivation of blocked ordinary legislation procedure regarding social security arrangements related to free movement or request of new Commission proposal* | LEGS | — | X |
| Article 68, TFEU<br>*Definition of strategic guidelines for legislative and operational planning in the area of freedom, security and justice* | JHA | — | X |
| Article 82.3, TFEU<br>*Review of contested draft directives on mutual recognition of judicial decisions and cooperation in criminal matters* | JHA | — | X |
| Article 83.3, TFEU<br>*Review of contested draft directives on minimum rules for defining criminal offences and sanctions* | JHA | — | X |
| Article 86.1, TFEU<br>*Review of contested draft regulations on the establishment of a European Public Prosecutor's Office* | JHA | — | X |
| Article 86.4, TFEU<br>*Extension of the powers of the European Public Prosecutor's Office* | JHA | — | X |
| Article 87.3, TFEU<br>*Review of contested Council decisions on operational cooperation* | JHA | — | X |
| Article 121.2, TFEU<br>*Conclusion on the broad economic policy guidelines* | ECON | — | X |
| Article 140, TFEU<br>*Discussion on convergence status of a member state seeking accession to the euro area* | ECON | — | X |
| Article 148, TFEU<br>*Adoption of conclusions on the employment situation on the basis of the annual Council and Commission report* | EMSOC | — | X |
| Article 222.4, TFEU<br>*Regular threat assessment under the EU solidarity clause* | FP/OTHER | — | X |

*(continued)*

**Table 3.3** Continued

| Treaty provision | Policy area/scope (where applicable) | Decision-making mode | |
|---|---|---|---|
| | | Majority decision | Consensus/ unanimity |
| Article 230, TFEU<br>*Right to be heard in the EP as defined in the European Council's rules of procedure* | — | — | — |
| Article 235.3, TFEU<br>*Decision on procedural issues and own rules of procedure* | — | X (simple) | — |
| Article 236(a), TFEU<br>*Decision on establishing Council configurations* | CON | X (QMV) | — |
| Article 236(b), TFEU<br>*Decision on the presidency of Council configurations* | CON | X (QMV) | — |
| Article 244, TFEU<br>*Decision on a system of rotation for the Commission* | CON | — | X |
| Article 283.2, TFEU<br>*Appointment of ECB executive board members* | PD | X (QMV) | — |
| Article 312.2, TFEU<br>*Authorization of the Council to apply QMV to the multi-annual financial framework regulation* | BUD | — | X |
| Article 355.6, TFEU<br>*Amending EU status of Danish, French and Netherlands territories* | CON | — | X |

The two tables show the distribution of European Council activity and the specific roles assigned to the European Council by the Treaty. In addition they list the decision-making mode as defined in the relevant treaty provision. Apart from the specific decision-making arrangements listed in the two tables, the Lisbon Treaty establishes the principle of consensus in European Council decision-making as the general mode of decision-making (Article 15.4, TEU). This was standard practice before, but the unwritten rule has now been formalized. The policy area-specific provisions of the Treaty confirm this general rule and define only a limited set of exceptions.

The Treaty grants the European Council the right to decide a number of fundamental issues that have a constitutional dimension ('CON'). Thus, the Treaty's provisions substantiate the European Council's role as the most senior decision-making body holding the ultimate power to trigger decisions about the Union's constitutional character and to resolve conflict that might threaten the coherence and existence of the Union. In this respect also the crucial role of the European Council in any enlargement or the potential secession of a member state from the Union should be considered ('ENLG'). Moreover, the European Council is endowed with the power to decide a number of major institutional questions without triggering another process of formal treaty change. Competences to decide about the composition of the EP and the Commission are the most prominent examples. In this sphere of decision-making the European Council obtains not only de facto but also procedurally a superior role in the overall system of EU decision-making, no matter which policy sphere or governance method is concerned—the classic community method or new intergovernmentalism. Though not all these provisions were first introduced by the Lisbon Treaty, it is fair to say that no other treaty has gone so far in formalizing the de facto role of the European Council, which ultimately holds the Union together, as a political forum for decision-making. The Lisbon Treaty reveals an inevitable flaw in both the community method and new intergovernmentalism, namely that political integration within the EU relies on voluntary commitment on the part of member states to complying with EU-level decisions. As the EU is not a state, it lacks the power of coercion.

The European Council's role in constitutional matters and the question of EU expansion are products of this dilemma and key characteristics of EU governance. This dimension of the European Council's role in EU policy-making was detected early on (cf. especially Bulmer and Wessels 1987; Bulmer 1996). The Lisbon Treaty is much more explicit about this function than any previous treaty. Given that there is no higher authority than the European Council it is not surprising that the forum decides by consensus. The decision to call a Convention or a conference of government representatives to review potential treaty amendments, however, is a notable exception.

Yet national governments have a privileged role in both procedures, and unanimity is also required here. Decisions about the establishment of Council configurations and about modifications of the Council's presidency regime remain the only exceptions from the unanimity rule. In other words, achieving consensus is the very function of the European Council when it comes to deciding constitutional issues or the question of EU enlargement.

The European Council is also mandated to take a number of key personnel decisions ('PD'). These decisions are taken by qualified majority voting (QMV). This may not surprise, as the European Council's decision on the Commission in any case requires cooperation with the EP. Parliament also needs to be consulted regarding ECB personnel. Finally, the Lisbon Treaty makes only brief reference to the European Council's role in the negotiation of the EU budget. The relevant provision does not refer to the European Council's de facto role as a forum for resolving deadlock during the final phase of budget negotiations, but is limited to an authorization clause relating to Council decision-making.

As regards the policy area-specific treaty provisions relating to the European Council that are listed in Tables 3.2 and 3.3, a clear picture emerges. Article 48, TFEU contains the only example of a formal European Council mandate to intervene in a policy-making process that is related to a traditional area of community method decision-making. By contrast, the European Council has obtained a prominent role in *all* new areas of EU activity. In each field it devises the major policy guidelines and defines the overall orientation and strategic focus of EU-level policy-making. The key mechanisms for policy coordination are all centred on the European Council. In all cases unanimity is required. Again the key function of the European Council is to generate consensus—a requirement best explained by the post-Maastricht integration paradox (see chapter 1). The field of JHA constitutes a hybrid case, as it involves legislative decision-making. Though a closer analysis of this particular policy field is beyond the scope of this book, it is noteworthy that the relevant provisions constitute an important modification of legislative decision-making under the classic community method as they grant the European Council a right to initiate policy and to intervene in legislative processes or matters of competence allocation.

The above review of Treaty provisions offers two major insights. The European Council is a forum for generating consensus over the overall direction and character of the integration process. The forum holds the key to resolving issues that have a constitutional dimension and impact on the overall coherence and functioning of the Union. There is little to suggest that this function of the European Council is less important today than it was at the time the SEA was concluded. The other insight relates to the importance of European Council intervention in processes of day-to-day policy-making in all new areas of EU activity. What is less clear from the Treaty provisions is how important each of the different areas listed in Tables 3.2 and 3.3 is in relation to the others and in how far they shape the internal dynamics of European Council decision-making. This question can only be answered through a closer review of European Council decision-making practice, to which the next section turns.

## 3.4 The Agenda

In order to better understand the relative importance of individual agenda items this section, based on the matrix of European Council decision-making (section 3.2), reviews the first 21 years of post-Maastricht European Council activity. Starting with the Lisbon European Council in June 1992, the first meeting after the December 1991 Maastricht European Council, which reached agreement on the Maastricht Treaty, and ending with the Brussels European Council in December 2013, the agenda review covers altogether 118 European Council meetings including informal gatherings and the so-called Euro Summits.[33] In a first round of analysis the total number of occurrences per agenda item was recorded. In addition, the distribution of occurrences per agenda item over time was logged. From these data, however, it might still be difficult to conclude how much time the European Council actually devoted to discussing a particular agenda item. Therefore this exercise was comple-mented by a closer inspection of individual presidency conclusions and the review of media reports. Moreover, extraordinary or informal meetings were not necessarily followed up by the usual set of official European Council conclusions. In such cases, press reports and interview data were used as the primary source in order to reconstruct the agenda. Finally, the research accounted for the fact that there might be discrepancies between the text of the presidency conclusions and the actual proceedings during a particular meeting. For example, an agenda item that received ample attention in the presidency conclusions might not have been discussed at great length at the relevant meeting, as the heads simply adopted a Council or Commission report or did not find time to engage in a more profound debate. Therefore, the results of the agenda review were triangulated with the author's own interview data on agenda composition and time management. Figure 3.1 provides an overview of the dominant agenda items in European Council

---

[33] Euro Summits, or informal meetings of the euro-area heads of state and government, are treated as separate events, even though during the context of the economic and financial crisis several of them took place ahead of full European Council meetings. This accounts for the fact that Euro Summits constitute a distinct meeting format, and add to regular European Council meeting activity (see section 3.8).

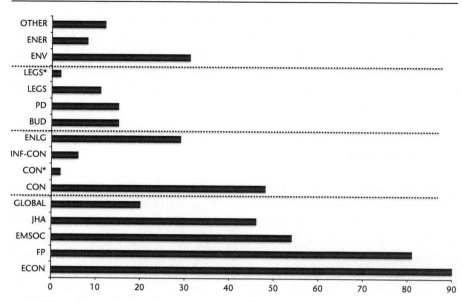

**Figure 3.1.** European Council agenda items (total number of occurrences)

debates by showing the total number of occurrences of each item for the period of 1992–2013.

The overwhelming majority of European Council agenda items are related to the new areas of EU activity. Economic governance (ECON) and foreign affairs matters (FP) dominate the agenda like no other topic. Except for a number of special issue or crisis summit meetings, almost all European Council gatherings feature discussion related to these two issue areas. Moreover, the broader category of agenda items linked to the new areas of EU activity ('ECON', 'FP', 'EMSOC', 'JHA', 'GLOBAL') accounts for almost two-thirds of the overall number of agenda items. Within this block, the relative importance of economic governance and foreign affairs issues requires further qualification. Though the total number of occurrences is almost identical, the actual discussion time allocated to each of the two policy areas typically differs, with economic governance taking up considerably more time than foreign affairs issues. As one interviewee very familiar with European Council proceedings summarized the situation:

> Economic governance takes up 50–65% of the time during European Council meetings. Then come G20 coordination and foreign affairs [as the other major agenda items].[34]

[34] Interviewee EU-09/ECON, 4 July 2011.

This assessment is endorsed by other interviewees, and also matches the findings drawn from the analysis of Agence Europe and media reports. Asked about the role of the European Council in economic governance, another senior official pointed to the fact that policy-making depends entirely on coordination endorsed by the European Council:

> In economic governance you are talking about coordinating national policies, the role of the EU [itself; its budget] is negligible, and [the European Council has] a role in system changes.[35]

Moreover, especially in the period from 2008 onwards, the economic crisis was seen as the major reason that prevented the European Council from spending more time debating foreign affairs issues. As another interviewee with close familiarity of European Council proceedings explained:

> External relations account for less of 20% of the time of the European Council but the debt crisis currently distorts the picture.[36]

This was also confirmed by another official, who thought that the euro crisis had prevented a greater focus on foreign affairs more recently. Yet this official was convinced that there had been general agreement among the heads on strengthening the focus on foreign affairs. The official also believed that the reorganization of the European Council after the Lisbon Treaty came into force, and the increased frequency of meetings do allow room for this (on the frequency of meetings see also section 3.6).[37] Devuyst (2012), who reviewed the European Council's more recent involvement in foreign affairs decision-making, points to the lack of a more substantial involvement of the heads, including their failure to engage in defining a more ambitious strategic perspective on external action by the EU. Yet seen over the entire period of the last two decades there is little doubt that foreign policy is the second most important agenda item for the European Council, and that it is one of the key functions of the forum that deals with day-to-day policy decisions related to CFSP and CSDP matters. In most cases this involves the endorsement of a common EU position in relation to a particular foreign policy scenario or to the international situation. Even though it may be questioned whether the EU has succeeded in asserting itself more forcefully on the international scene in relation to recent major foreign policy crises, there is little doubt that the European Council has acted as ultimate decision-maker on foreign affairs issues—even if only to make a decision that the EU as a whole would not engage more forcefully with a particular conflict or situation. As the above-quoted official explained:

[35] Interviewee EU-02/GEN, 4 July 2011.     [36] Interviewee EU-10/EXT, 8 July 2011.
[37] Interviewee EU-24/EXT, 17 November 2011.

> The European Council brings together all the stakeholders. [...] The focal points of consensus building [on foreign affairs] have always been the European Council meetings. See for example Libya. Before [the European Council got together], it could not be resolved. We always managed—even when there was disagreement as with Libya—to agree on a declaration and a way forward.[38]

As shown in greater detail below, both economic governance and foreign affairs require constant engagement of the heads with day-to-day policy issues, not only with long-term decisions. Meetings almost always involve discussions on a number of policy issues falling under one of the two subcategories of economic governance and foreign affairs. There is much to suggest that the CFSP and CSDP portfolio ('FP') will receive more attention as the EU exits from the most heated period of economic crisis management. For example, the European Council meeting of 13–14 December 2012 adopted a comprehensive set of conclusions on the further development of CSDP.[39] Similarly, the European Council of 19–20 December 2013 focused attention on this matter.

Employment and social policy coordination ('EMSOC') is the third most frequently occurring agenda item. Interview data and presidency conclusions suggest that discussion in this field is more proceduralized and less event-driven than economic governance and foreign affairs. The large number of occurrences demonstrates how much EU policy-making in this field relies on constant European Council intervention and oversight. At almost every second meeting the European Council deals with issues falling under this subcategory—especially if one deducts emergency meetings. JHA issues follow closely. Here again, the data suggest that regular oversight by the European Council is a precondition for governing this policy field. For example, issues related to the operation of the Schengen system of visa-free travel between the participating member states requires constant consensus seeking within the European Council. This was not only the case during the establishment of the system and its later integration into the EU's institutional framework, but, as interviewees have highlighted, was also the case more recently.[40]

Finally, the European Council is frequently engaged in coordinating common EU positions for negotiations in international forums ('GLOBAL'). Efforts to reach a common EU position in global climate change negotiations fall under this category as much as the coordination of a single EU position ahead of G20 and G8 meetings. As one interviewee stressed:

> G8/20 coordination is very prominent on the agenda.[41]

---

[38] Interviewee EU-10/EXT, 8 July 2011.
[40] Interviewee EU-02/GEN, 4 July 2011.
[39] See European Council (2012a), paras 20–25.
[41] Interviewee EU-02/GEN, 4 July 2011.

The second most important issue area in European Council debates is the field of major institutional decisions. The preparation, execution, and ratification of formal Treaty changes in particular require the involvement of the European Council ('CON'). Enlargement too is a major issue on the European Council agenda ('ENLG'), featuring on the agenda of about one-quarter of all the sessions analysed here. Yet this implies that major institutional issues and questions related to EU enlargement occur much less often than agenda items from the broad category of the new areas of EU activity. Even debate on employment and social policy coordination occurs almost as often as discussion on constitutional issues. Yet there are many more meetings of the European Council at which such issues are not debated. Occasionally the European Council has taken de facto constitutional decisions that have lacked the status of formal treaty changes ('INF-CON').

The third and next broadest category—formal EU decision-making—accounts for only a very small share of European Council activity. Intervention in legislative decision-making in areas traditionally governed by the community is marginal if compared with the overall agenda. Though European Council intervention may have been crucially important in resolving deadlock in specific situations, this aspect of European Council decision-making is not dominant. This observation is key, as it confirms the critical distinction, made throughout this book, between the new areas of EU activity and traditional fields of community method governance, which are managed chiefly by the Commission, Council, and EP triangle. The number of occurrences of agenda items related to decisions on personnel and on the EU budget does not seem to suggest a massive engagement with such issues either. This is not to say that negotiations of a new multi-annual financial framework do not rely on European Council intervention, but it has become clear that references to such European Council activity help little in understanding the overall expansion in European Council decision-making in the post-Maastricht period. Indeed, the figures on agenda composition reveal that the European Council's role in governing the new areas of EU activity is an additional responsibility of the forum that cannot be understood within the context of the pre-Maastricht framework of EU decision-making and the European Council's role within it. This was one of the key arguments behind the analytical framework of deliberative intergovernmentalism. The above findings thus also reject the notion advanced by the competing theory of liberal intergovernmentalism that EU decision-making is characterized by so-called 'grand bargains'. At least during the post-Maastricht period the European Council's role in EU decision-making is essentially characterized by regular involvement in managing the new areas of EU activity rather than by a focus on finalizing deals on limited formal power transfers to the supranational level.

Finally, it should be noted that environmental policy is the single policy issue dealt with most frequently by the European Council outside the category of the new areas of EU activity. Agenda data indeed support the interpretation, which was offered earlier, that the repeated occurrence of this policy area on the European Council agenda is based on an expanding environmental policy coordination agenda, which has developed in addition to community method-based governance in that policy domain. This expanding agenda has involved coordination in response to global environmental policy-making initiatives such as those that are focused on sustainable development and climate change. Moreover, in June 2001 the Gothenburg European Council decided to add an environmental policy dimension to the Lisbon agenda. This has prompted regular follow-up activity similar to what could be found in the domains of economic governance as well as social and employment policy. For example, the European Council has reviewed the environmental situation and adopted policy on annual basis.

In order to illustrate this point further and to substantiate the findings in the earlier parts of this section, Figure 3.2 shows the distribution of individual agenda items over time according to the aggregate number of occurrences per year.

Debate on the new areas of EU activity clearly gathered momentum from the second half of the 1990s onwards. This confirms the earlier argument in

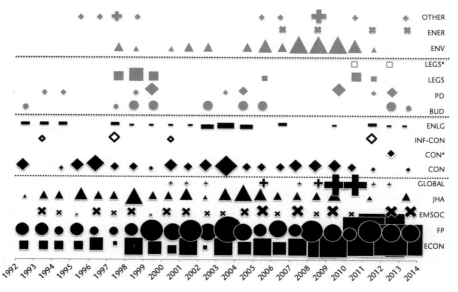

**Figure 3.2.** European Council agenda items (distribution over time)

Note: The size of the shapes indicates the number of occurrences per year. Bigger shapes indicate a large number of occurrences. The minimum number of occurrences per year is one and the maximum number of occurrences is 11.

chapter 1 that the expansion of EU coordination processes following the implementation of EMU, the reinforcement of CFSP and CSDP coordination structures by the Amsterdam Treaty, and enhanced employment and social policy coordination functioned as the main trigger of expanding European Council activity. The global economic and financial crisis in 2008 undoubtedly provided a major boost to the European Council's work on economic governance issues. Yet it is also clear that the crisis by no means constituted the beginning of European Council intervention. It rather reinforced an underlying institutional trend. Related to the crisis was also the increased focus on the coordination of common EU positions for the G8 and, even more so, the G20 (cf. Hodson 2011). What is particularly interesting is to see how European Council involvement with the coordination of employment and social policy issues developed over time. Activity related to employment policy and social issues can be clearly related to major institutional changes in this area (see chapter 1). However, European Council activity in economic and social policy coordination suffered markedly from a lack of attention during the period of most frenetic crisis management. The activation of the Lisbon process successor scheme EU2020 did not prevent this. Interviews with officials who have close familiarity with this policy area indeed suggest that the European Council paid less attention to social and employment issues. As one of them explained:

> The role of the European Council [in coordinating social and employment policies] is less important today than it was in 1997 but this is ok. The process has become much more routinized.[42]

More attention to this policy portfolio is only detectable again in 2012 and 2013 (see section 3.7). The European Council's engagement with questions concerning major institutional reforms clearly followed the calendar of treaty reform. The failed ratification of the Constitutional Treaty caused recurring European Council activity until the Lisbon Treaty eventually entered into force. The data also show the impact of enlargement on agenda composition. Preparations for the historic 2004 eastward enlargement caused regular European Council intervention. This activity culminated with the run-up to the 2004 accession date. After this date, enlargement became an occasional agenda item—far from having the status of a dominant subject. There is little to suggest that future enlargement will trigger a level of European Council activity comparable in scope and intensity to pre-2004 activity levels.

Occurrences under the category of informal constitutionalism ('INF-CON') are worth mentioning, not because of the time they occupy in European Council decision-making, but because of the consequences of this type of

---

[42] Interviewee EU-21/ECON, 11 November 2009.

European Council decision-making. The 1993 Copenhagen criteria are the first example to mention here, as by defining the conditions for all following enlargements they implied that a de facto constitutional decision had not been made at the Maastricht Treaty. The European Council established a general accession rule by the simple act of an agreement among the heads. The same method was used in 1997 when the European Council created the Eurogroup (cf. Puetter 2006: 54–62). The launch of the OMC under the Lisbon agenda can be considered as constituting a similar act. The further decision to create a euro-area European Council formation—the Euro Summit—is another far-reaching institutional decision that de facto modified existing Treaty provisions (see section 3.8). It was followed by the adoption of the Fiscal Compact as an intergovernmental treaty outside EU law ('CON*'). The intergovernmental treaties establishing the EFSF and the ESM are similar—and so far the only—acts of intervention into de facto legislative decision-making that under different circumstances could have been dealt with in the form of secondary EU legislation ('LEGS*').

Figure 3.2 also reveals the punctuated and rare occurrences of involvement with legislative decision-making ('LEGS'). For example in 1998 the heads met at a 'Council Meeting of Heads of State and Government' to decide that the final stage of EMU would begin on 1 January 1999. The European Council also intervened with legislative decision-making related to establishing the original Stability and Growth Pact in 1996 and 1997, and the reforms of the Pact in 2005 and during the crisis. Another reoccurring type of intervention into legislative decision-making occurred in relation to the EU budget ('BUD'). The decision about the so-called Agenda 2000 at the end of the 1990s is a case in point. It included decisions about the multi-annual financial framework for the first half of the 2000s, which was particularly relevant in the context of the 2004 enlargement and involved the reform of the highly contested funding policies for the agricultural sector and regional policy.

## 3.5 The Core Working Method: Participation, Secrecy, and Access to Dialogue

The original idea of the European Council setting was that of an informal and confidential fireside chat between the community's top decision-makers (Bulmer and Wessels 1987). Also in the post-Maastricht context the European Council is considered to have 'many club-like attributes' (Hayes-Renshaw and Wallace 2006: 167). The fact that the EU has grown to include 28 member states—all of which need to be represented at the European Council table—undoubtedly makes it more difficult to conceive of European Council gatherings in that way. Yet this section demonstrates that the organization of

European Council meetings is still geared towards stressing the club-like and secretive character of the forum wherever possible. All European Council meetings are closed-door gatherings. They are not open to the public.[43] There is no visitors' gallery, and the video cameras in the room aid communication only among the heads themselves—they do not address transparency. The European Council is not required to televise any of its debates, as is the case with Council meetings dealing with legislative issues. This secrecy element of the European Council's working method applies both to formal and informal sessions. Moreover, many of the more recent modifications of the European Council's core working method can be considered as attempts to restore or preserve the club-like atmosphere of the early days as much as possible—even if this requires the use of high-tech audio-video equipment.

Seated around an oval table with a large empty space in the middle, the heads are equipped with computer screens, microphones, and headphones for accessing the interpretation services. In the middle of the meeting table and at the fringes of it, robot cameras are positioned and zoom in on the current speaker.[44] Instead of a real fireplace, only the flickering of the large flat screen monitors placed in the middle of the oval meeting table may lighten the dark colours of the meeting room in the Justus Lipsius building. The scenery undoubtedly has its bizarre elements. Yet it reveals how much effort is made to adjust the European Council's core working method to a whole range of challenges. The TV robots, the dark brown standard EU conference room furniture, and the booths of the interpreters, who form, by keeping some distance, the outer circle of the meeting room, remind one that the European Council is a grown-up EU institution with many of the routine and bureaucratic features that come with such a status. A new building is being erected next to the Justus Lipsius compound to function as the permanent home of the European Council.

A look around the meeting table also reveals that despite its size and the video screens, the inner circle is kept as small as it can be in a Union of 28. Only the heads are seated around the conference table. The inner table includes individuals—not delegations.[45] Other than in the regular Council session format, the European Council working method does not allow the

---

[43] See European Council Decision 2009/882/EU adopting its Rules of Procedure, published in OJ L315/51, Annex, Article 4.3.

[44] The large photo-gallery on the European Council homepage not only features hundreds of photos of smiling or grim-looking heads who turn up repeatedly at the numerous European Council meetings but also reveals astonishing technical details about the set-up of the meeting table and the atmosphere of the meeting room. See <http://www.european-council.europa.eu/home-page.aspx?lang=en> [accessed 28 April 2014].

[45] The word 'delegation' is still used by the European Council rules of procedure, but it refers to the support staff of the members of the European Council who are granted access to the Justus Lipsius building in which the European Council convenes.

presence of senior officials in the room. Advisors cannot whisper speaking instructions to their superiors, and must wait in a separate room. European Council meetings typically take place at two venues within the Justus Lipsius in Brussels—namely on the so-called '50th floor' and '80th floor'. The meetings normally start with an exchange of views with the EP president and a discussion about a selected topic on the 50th floor in the afternoon. European Council practice ensures that for this particular part of the meeting the Antici Group[46] representative of each member state and of the Commission is allowed to follow the debate among the heads via headphones in a separate room. For the evening, the meeting is moved to the 80th floor as the heads convene for 'dinner'. Technically, this change of location means a tightening of the confidentiality regime, as now no official outside the room can follow the debate. The COREPER ambassadors and the Antici Group representatives are only allowed to wait in the corridors, not knowing what is being discussed inside the room. Individual members of the European Council may leave the room during the discussion to consult with the diplomats. It is possible for a diplomat to enter the room briefly in order to hand over a note to his or her member. Some heads also exchange text messages with their delegations. Yet the emphasis on confidentiality is high. Also the number of members of national delegations who 'are authorized to have access to the building'[47] is limited to 20, and their names and functions need to be pre-registered.

Typically most of the substantial European Council discussions are held on the 80th floor. As one official put it:

You want to be on the 80$^{th}$ floor if you work on decisions.[48]

Moreover, the same official believed that because of the complicated schedules of many heads, European Council discussions are most effective at nighttime. During this time heads are less distracted from other communication, which they have to engage with during the day. This makes them able to concentrate on the discussion. Night-time hours also imply that there are no other scheduling commitments, as the same official explained:

The best is that you can go on as long as it takes. This is not a negotiation tactic. It is simply a practical requirement.

The Lisbon Treaty codified a key element of the core European Council working method outlined above by limiting membership to the heads of state and government, the European Council president, the president of the

---

[46] The Antici Group is a preparatory group of COREPER. Members of this group are traditionally in charge of note-taking during European Council meetings.
[47] European Council Decision 2009/882/EU adopting its Rules of Procedure, published in OJ L315/51, Annex, Article 4.4.
[48] Interviewee EU-25/GEN, 4 March 2013.

Commission, and the HR (Article 15.2, TEU). The two presidents and the HR are non-voting members.[49] The foreign ministers no longer participate in meetings (cf. on the previous arrangement Article 4, TEU, Treaty of Nice). Moreover, the Lisbon Treaty stipulates that the EP president 'may be invited to be heard by the European Council' (Article 15.2, TFEU). In practice the EP president is always invited to address the European Council at the beginning of each meeting. Yet the EP president does not typically attend the full meeting. A change to this arrangement requires unanimous agreement among the heads.[50] The only other person who is allowed to take a seat at the core meeting table, though he or she is not formally a member of the European Council, is the Secretary-General of the Council Secretariat, who is the only civil servant in the room.[51]

The new participation rule reflects the refocusing of European Council activity on face-to-face discussion among the heads—a process that had begun long before the Lisbon Treaty entered into force, as shown below. Officials dealing with European Council meetings do not doubt the effect the changed participation regime has had on the discussions among the heads. As one of them put it:

The foreign ministers left and it became more collegial.[52]

The new working method also reflects the fact that the European Council has developed into a forum that regularly instructs the Council and the Commission on how to proceed with work on specific policy issues. Originally, foreign ministers had enjoyed a crucial role in the preparation of European Council meetings and, as members of the General Affairs Council (GAC), were in charge of institutional issues and horizontal coordination. This role became gradually obsolete in the post-Maastricht period. With the growing diversification of the European Council portfolio and the focus on policy coordination, other Council formations became as important to the work of the European Council as the old General Affairs and External Relations Council had once been.

Moreover, the gradual build-up of the CFSP framework implied that foreign ministers were needed increasingly as foreign affairs decision-makers and not as EU generalists (see chapter 4.3). By making the HR the chair of the Foreign

---

[49] In the sense of Article 235.1, TFEU.

[50] European Council Decision 2009/882/EU adopting its Rules of Procedure, published in OJ L315/51, Annex, Article 4.2.

[51] The position is currently held by Uwe Corsepius—a former senior advisor on EU affairs in the German Federal Chancellery. The Council Secretariat is the administration in charge of European Council meetings. In addition, and depending on the subject, the Directors-General of the relevant directorates inside the Council Secretariat and representatives from the Council Secretariat's legal service are in the meeting room—seated in the outer circle.

[52] Interviewee EU-02/GEN, 4 July 2011.

Affairs Council (FAC) and a permanent member of the European Council, the Lisbon Treaty removed any rationale for involving foreign ministers directly in the proceedings of the European Council. On paper this possibility still exists (Article 15.3, TEU). Between 2005 and the beginning of 2013, largely unnoticed by the scholarly literature, a similar arrangement structured the relationship between the European Council and euro-area finance ministers. Though European Council membership of the Eurogroup president is not foreseen by the Treaty, the prime minister of Luxembourg, Jean-Claude Juncker, assumed the dual role of Eurogroup president and member of the European Council. Juncker's reports on the work of the ministers had a routine character and he functioned as the main interlocutor between the two bodies. As a member of the European Council, Juncker was bound to the prevailing consensus among the heads. Chapter 4.2 discusses these aspects further.

Several of the changes introduced to the European Council's working method by the Lisbon Treaty were in fact prepared much earlier. In view of the historic 2004 enlargement, the European Council adopted a set of quasi-rules of procedure in 2002. In an annex to the presidency conclusions of the Seville European Council of June 2002 a set of 'rules for the organization of the proceedings of the European Council' (European Council 2002) was adopted. It stipulated that 'in principle' the European Council meets four times a year and can convene for extraordinary meetings (European Council 2002, para. 1). Moreover, the Seville rules established that European Council meetings are divided into a small group meeting involving only the heads and the Commission president, and a full-scale group meeting that involves 'delegations' (European Council 2002, paras 6 and 10). This clause codified a routine that already existed. The Seville conclusions also acknowledged the new baseline number of four meetings per year, and emphasized the need for so-called 'restricted' meetings (European Council 2002, para. 6).

The Seville conclusions also regulated more clearly the internal functioning of the European Council. They flagged the need to provide internal 'summary briefings on the outcome and substance of the discussions' while stressing that 'briefings shall be organized in such a way as to safeguard confidentiality of discussions' (European Council 2002, para. 10).[53] Finally, the Seville rules pointed to the importance of the European Council conclusions as the forum's core instrument for exercising leadership. The rules stipulated that an 'outline of the conclusions' must become available shortly before the start of each meeting and that such a document must distinguish between aspects

---

[53] A similar procedure was used to structure the confidential discussions within the Eurogroup. Since July 1999 it has been obligatory for the Eurogroup president to send a follow-up letter on each meeting to the other members of the group summarizing the main results (Puetter 2006: 77).

that do not require further discussion and those that are subject to negotiation at the meeting (European Council 2002, paras 12 and 13).

After the Seville meeting in June 2002 the European Council gatherings were gradually moved to Brussels. The Spanish 2002 Council presidency was the last to convene all semester meetings at home. From the October 2003 European Council meeting onwards all meetings took place in Brussels.[54] Effectively, this step brought the European Council on a par with the Council as a regular EU institution based in Brussels. The change of meeting place, therefore, can be seen as a certain formalization of European Council activity. Equally, and perhaps paradoxically, the move has strengthened the European Council's ability to foster informal and frank exchanges among the heads. Hiding in the grey Justus Lipsius building in Brussels also means that distractions from core European Council proceedings are reduced in comparison to the previous practice of holding meetings at different locations. Moreover, European Council meetings can be called at short notice, as the logistic and bureaucratic infrastructure is concentrated at a single location.

The above review of the European Council's core working method reveals how institutional engineering has led to increasing the consensus generating capacity of the top-level intergovernmental forum. The review also shows the difficulties in fostering policy deliberation in such a highly politicized setting. Yet there is ample evidence of a continuous search for improvement. The comparison between European Council debates and discussions within the context of the informal Eurogroup by a senior EU official illustrates this point further:

> The European Council meetings are more formal and heavy [than those of the Eurogroup]. There is a lot of communication pressure. The heads want to know what to tell the press. But there are real discussions, in particular on the euro area. The ESM, the EFSF, interest rates are debated.[55]

And the same official continues by adding the example of European Council debates on introducing a successor for the Lisbon agenda:

> The EU semester also triggered good debates. The heads are more willing to engage [than in the past] but with 27 it is difficult. But Van Rompuy is really determined to make it happen.

Another senior official offered a similar comparison between policy debates in different intergovernmental forums:

---

[54] Declaration 22 of the Treaty of Nice stipulates that European Council meetings must be held in Brussels when the EU is comprises 18 or more member states.
[55] Interviewee EU-09/ECON, 4 July 2011.

As regards the intensity of debates it is still the strongest in the Eurogroup; then come ECOFIN and the European Council.[56]

## 3.6 The Introduction of New Working Methods: Extraordinary, Informal, and Single-issue Meetings

The quickly expanding decision-making agenda and the fact that heads of state and government have to deal with detailed aspects of policy decisions pose enormous challenges to the European Council's role as an intergovernmental forum for policy coordination and its internal functioning. The review of the dominant agenda items in section 3.4 showed the intensification of the European Council's work around the new areas of EU activity. The modifications to the European Council's core working method reviewed above represent just one set of examples of the way the European Council's internal functioning has been adjusted over time. There are a number of further modifications to the European Council's working method that deserve attention here. This section looks at institutional engineering, which was aimed at making the European Council more reactive to suddenly arising policy issues, crisis situations and increasing workloads. For example, Youri Devuyst (2012: 341–7) quotes the inflexibility in scheduling European Council meetings and the lack of a more sophisticated preparation regime as obstacles to consensus formation and the emergence of a more strategic approach towards CFSP decision-making among the heads. The most obvious example of institutional engineering in response to the increasing demand for European Council decision-making has been to increase the frequency of meetings. As highlighted at the beginning of this chapter, a schedule of monthly meetings is no longer a remote scenario. For those dealing with the European Council agenda the demand for more meetings is out of the question:

There is a push to have more and more European Council sessions.[57]

The schedule of European Council meetings for the last two decades shows an increase in the number of meetings per year (Figure 3.3).

With the intensification of policy coordination in the new areas of EU activity in the second half of the 1990s the number of meetings per year was increased from three to four. At that time the European Council was chaired by the country holding the rotating Council presidency. This meant that each presidency convened two meetings—typically towards the end of the first half of the semester and again at the end of the respective presidency period. This

---

[56] Interviewee EU-07/ECON, 30 March 2010.
[57] Interviewee EU-07/ECON, 30 March 2010.

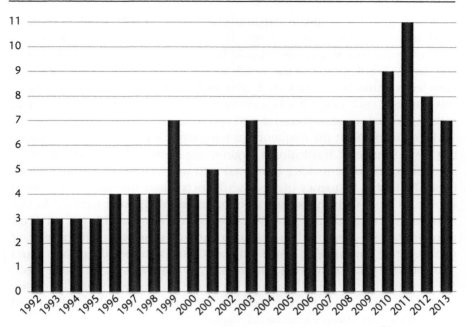

**Figure 3.3.** Number of European Council meetings per year[58]

approach already reflected the routinization of European Council activity in specific policy areas. In 1999, for the first time, the forum met on seven occasions. The schedule for that particular year reveals how much the base workload of the European Council had already increased in previous years. Extra workloads, caused for example by the negotiations of Agenda 2000 and the Intergovernmental Conference, which was preparing the Nice Treaty, could not be accommodated within the regular meeting schedule. Crucially, 1999 was also a year of foreign policy crisis in the Balkans. The North Atlantic Treaty Organization (NATO) intervened in the Kosovo War, and Kosovo was put under United Nations administration. This item dominated the European Council agenda and triggered additional meetings. As the base workload was already at a high level, the foreign policy crisis and irregular items on the EU's decision-making calendar immediately caused a surge in the total number of meetings. In the following years such sporadic increases in European Council activity could be observed several times. Since 2008—the beginning of intensified EU action in relation to the economic and financial crisis—there has not been a single year with less than seven meetings. In fact, the total number of gatherings—including both full European Council and Euro Summit

---

[58] Figures include the aggregate number of all European Council meetings for each year. This includes extraordinary, informal, and euro-area meetings.

meetings—jumped to nine in 2010 and eleven in 2011. This was the period of most intensive crisis management. This immediate crisis management—decisions over bailout packages should be mentioned here—was of less concern in 2012 and 2013, and this is reflected in the falling number of separate Euro Summit meetings (see section 3.8). In 2012 and 2013 respectively there was only one such meeting whereas the base figure of full European Council meetings remained almost unchanged compared to 2011.

The adjustment in the frequency of European Council meetings is indeed the first example of institutional engineering identified here. The growing demand for decision-making translated into more European Council meetings. The higher frequency of meetings, which brings the European Council almost on a par with the regular meeting schedule of senior Council formations, is a systemic feature of the EU's new intergovernmentalism. It is a direct response to the growing demand for consensus generation on the part of member state governments. The European Council's responsiveness to issues of day-to-day decision-making is reflected in an emphasis on particular meeting formats. Extraordinary meetings are the most frequently used working method in this regard. For the reviewed time period, a total number of 29 extraordinary meetings are recorded (Figure 3.4).

There are some inconsistencies as regards the use of the label 'extraordinary meeting'. Some meetings that were convened at short notice (shown in

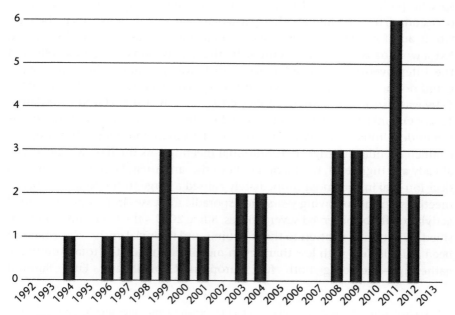

**Figure 3.4.** Number of extraordinary European Council meetings per year

Figure 3.4) are referred to in EU jargon as 'special summits' or 'informal meetings'. The Lisbon Treaty explicitly acknowledges the growing importance of non-regular European Council meetings. Yet it does not entirely abolish earlier differences in terminology. Article 15.3, TEU—the core article on the European Council—stipulates that the European Council meets 'twice every six months'.[59] In addition the president can convene a 'special meeting' whenever 'the situation so requires'. This provision thus suggests that apart from four regular meetings each year, all other additional meetings are referred to as special meetings. The TEU's Title V on external action and CFSP instead mentions that an 'extraordinary meeting of the European Council' (Article 26.1, TEU) can be convened in response to an international foreign policy crisis situation, so as to 'define the strategic lines of the Union's policy'. In the past, the use of the term 'extraordinary meeting' was not completely restricted to foreign policy crisis meetings.[60] In order to overcome these terminological difficulties, all non-regular meetings of the European Council were coded as 'extraordinary' if they were convened less than three months in advance. In fact, the majority of these meetings were convened less than one month in advance.[61] This definition largely captures EU practice in using the terms 'special' or 'extraordinary' in European Council-related communications. There are only four cases in the second half of the 1990s when this terminology was used in relation to events that had been prepared much further in advance.

Looking at the occurrence of extraordinary European Council meetings helps to understand more clearly the changed approach to European Council agenda setting. The assumption on which the analysis is based here is that a meeting announced less than three months in advance is convened because of unforeseen events or workload. More occurrences of this meeting format are interpreted as indicating greater flexibility in European Council agenda setting, and that deliberations are issue-driven. Moreover, meetings convened at short notice also indicate that the European Council often has to take decisions under uncertainty, i.e. the heads are required to agree on a policy response to developments that are unfolding and of which the consequences are only partially understood. Such meetings therefore can be particularly

---

[59] The European Council's rules of procedure stipulate that the European Council should coordinate the timing of the two regular European Council meetings scheduled during each semester with the relevant Council presidency '[a]t the latest one year before' the beginning of the presidency period. See European Council Decision 2009/882/EU adopting its Rules of Procedure, published in OJ L315/51, Annex, Article 1.1.

[60] The Seville European Council conclusions, which contain a set of quasi-rules of procedure for the European Council, reserve the term 'extraordinary' for all meetings of the European Council that take place in addition to four ordinary meetings during a calendar year. See European Council (2002), Annex I, para. 1.

[61] This information has been drawn from the relevant EU websites, the websites of the rotating presidencies, Agence Europe, and media reports. No announcement date could be established for four of the meetings.

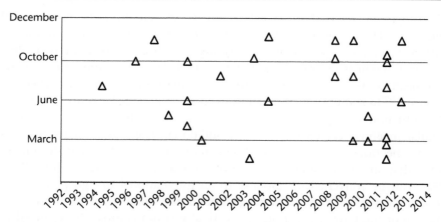

**Figure 3.5.** Distribution of extraordinary European Council meetings over time

important for preference formation. Figure 3.5 shows the distribution of extra-ordinary meetings over time. Foreign policy crises were a major trigger of these extraordinary meetings with the Kosovo crisis in 1999, the terrorist attacks on the United States in 2001, the 2003 military intervention in Iraq, the 2008 Georgia crisis and the military intervention in Libya in 2011 being prominent examples. Between 2008 and 2011, efforts to deal with the consequences of the economic and financial crisis triggered a number of extraordinary meetings—some of them in very quick succession.

Increased flexibility in agenda planning also occurs because of the increased number of regular European Council meetings. There are ample examples of European Council meetings where the agenda was revised shortly before the meeting, individual agenda items were rearranged, or the 'time budget'[62] attributed to these items was changed. With the EU's intensified coordination agendas in economic governance, foreign affairs, and social and employment policy, reaction to extraordinary events has become a regular responsibility of the European Council.

Another important meeting format used by the European Council is the so-called informal meeting. Though there is some overlap with the category of extraordinary meetings, the two are not identical. Of the 29 extraordinary meetings, which were reviewed above, 14 were officially labelled as informal meetings.[63] European Council president Herman Van Rompuy repeatedly used the 'informal' meeting format to make the European Council focus on

---

[62] When preparing a draft agenda, senior officials in the Council Secretariat and the cabinet of the European Council president always note down estimates of how much time to allow for each agenda item.

[63] They were referred to either as 'extraordinary informal' meetings or as 'informal' meetings (the latter however was convened within a period of less than three months).

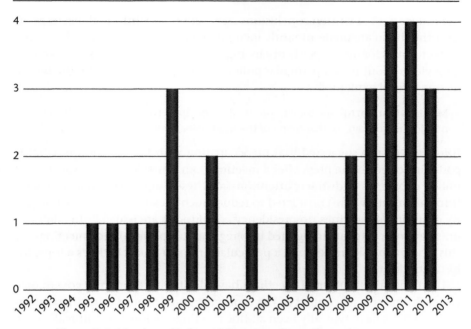

**Figure 3.6.** Number of informal European Council meetings per year

pertinent policy issues and to provide more room for orientation debates. In February 2010 he even sought to emphasize the informal atmosphere by convening an informal European Council in the historical Bibliothèque Solvay in Brussels. There has been an increase in the number of informal meetings over time, as shown in Figure 3.6. European Council president Herman Van Rompuy declared the further development of the European Council's informal working method a priority of his first term in office (see also section 3.7).[64]

The analytical framework of deliberative intergovernmentalism attaches particular relevance to the use of informal working methods, as they are considered to be an indicator of the consensus building capacity of a particular negotiation setting. The European Council originally emerged as a forum for informal policy dialogue among the heads of state and government and the attributes 'fireside chat' and 'club-like atmosphere' were given to early European Council meetings (Bulmer and Wessels 1987; Hayes-Renshaw and Wallace 2006). Yet there is little doubt that the European Council has increasingly taken final decisions on policy in the new areas of EU activity and has resolved major institutional questions on EU governance. Though such decisions do not constitute legislative acts, they imply a certain formalization of European Council decision-making. A European Council meeting is expected

---

[64] As reported by Agence Europe and *Financial Times*, 5 January 2010.

to produce a set of written conclusions (see section 3.9). Informal meetings on the other hand are predominantly focused on orientation debates. This opens opportunities for more openly discussing different policy options and exchanging views about how a particular policy challenge is perceived by the heads. As one official explained:

> Meetings that aim to issue conclusions tend to end up in a drafting session. If you do not do this you can see that many of the heads debate more openly and freely.[65]

Interviewees also suggested that preoccupation with the question of what is communicated to the press after a meeting is an obstacle to more substantial policy debate, as it distracts attention from resolving a particular problem. Informal meetings are considered to reduce such pressure. For the vast majority of informal meetings no presidency conclusions are issued.[66] In addition, orientation debates are integrated into regular European Council meetings. In this case the president reserves a particular time slot and schedules a topic for in-depth debate.

The majority of informal meetings have dealt with economic governance issues. In the special context of the economic and financial crisis these informal meetings have typically been ad-hoc meetings. Before the outbreak of the crisis economic governance issues also featured several times on the agenda of non-ad-hoc informal meetings. Foreign affairs issues on the other hand have so far rarely been discussed at non-ad-hoc informal meetings. In relation to this policy area informal European Council debates have primarily occurred when the EU is faced with a crisis situation, as the presentation on data on extraordinary European Council meetings above reveals. These findings support Devuyst's (2012) observation that in the past there was a lack of strategic focus in European Council debates related to foreign affairs issues. The first full-time European Council president Herman Van Rompuy was aware of this deficiency and championed more informal meetings on CFSP and CSDP matters. As one EU official explained:

> In September 2010 there was a full meeting on foreign policy. The focus was very much on the internal functioning of our institutional set-up after Lisbon.[67]

Another feature of many informal meetings is the focus on a single issue or a small set of issues—as in the case of the September 2010 meeting. Yet the

---

[65] Interviewee EU-25/GEN, 4 March 2013.

[66] The presidency may however release a short press statement or a 'declaration', as often happens in response to a foreign policy crisis. Some informal meetings dealing with EU and euro-area responses to the economic and financial crisis have led to the publication of comprehensive conclusions. This occurred for example in connection with the constitution of the Euro Summit meeting format. However, this practice remains an exception. See section 3.8 for a further discussion of the Euro Summit format.

[67] Interviewee EU-10/EXT, 8 July 2011.

single-issue meeting or thematic European Council, as it is also referred to more recently in European Council jargon, can be considered to constitute a working method in its own right. It is used to refocus attention. This method can be applied to formal and informal European Council meetings alike. The majority of single-issue meetings overlap with either the informal or the ad-hoc extraordinary meeting format. Meetings may be designed to provide room for orientation debates, or may even mark the launch of major policy initiatives. Among the historic examples for single-issue meetings that laid the foundations for new policy initiatives are the 1997 Luxembourg European Council (also referred to as the 'Luxembourg Employment Summit'), which established the EES, the 1999 special Tampere European Council meeting on the creation of an area of freedom, security, and justice, and the 2000 special Lisbon European Council, which adopted the Lisbon agenda. These meetings were planned with a view to allowing focus on an issue of major strategic importance. More recently, single-issue meetings have gained growing importance, as the crowded European Council agenda has required additional efforts to refocus discussion on strategic issues. As one senior official explained:

> We also see single-issue European Councils, for example on research and development, energy security, climate change, or EU2020.[68]

Herman Van Rompuy was a key advocate of this working method and made it a regular feature of European Council gatherings. How much this working method was pushed by the first full-time president was documented by the fact that within his cabinet there was a designated member with responsibility for the coordination of such meetings. For example, the May 2013 European Council was convened as a thematic meeting to deal with energy.[69]

## 3.7 A Full-time President

The creation of the position of an elected president is probably the most intensely debated feature of the reforms in European Council organization introduced by the Lisbon Treaty. Moreover, this arrangement attracted substantial political attention before and during the European Convention. Devuyst (2008: 290–2) highlights the role British prime minister Tony Blair, French president Jacques Chirac, and German chancellor Gerhard Schröder played in demanding reform of the European Council presidency. The three were impatient with the previous regime of the rotating presidency. Devuyst also highlights that the new office was not well received by 'the defenders of

---

[68] Interviewee EU-07/ECON, 30 March 2010.     [69] Interviewee EU-25/GEN, 4 March 2013.

the Community method' (Devuyst 2008: 292). In particular, many of the small and medium-sized member states and the Commission were against the change (Tallberg 2006: 225). The idea was debated controversially in the context of the European Convention in 2002. Ben Crum (2009: 686) notes that 'this proposal [was] met with considerable scepticism, especially from the smaller EU member states'. Fear of having the permanent president acting as an agent on behalf of larger member states relates to the principle of equal access to dialogue. The creation of a permanent presidency is an important case of institutional engineering.

Rational choice institutionalists especially have focused on explaining the delegation of the chair function in EU intergovernmental decision-making (cf. especially Tallberg 2006). An increased demand for formal leadership is considered the key factor in explaining the transition from what hitherto seemed to constitute a pragmatic compromise in dealing with the institutional dilemma of the presidency. This dilemma can be described as follows: on the one hand, there is the quest for formal leadership so as to enable collective decision-making to move forward. On the other hand, there are doubts that the chair will refrain from exploiting this privileged position for his or her own national interests. The rotating presidency regime addresses this dilemma by sharing the chair function between the member states. Enlargement is widely perceived as further exacerbating the inevitable flaws of the rotating presidency system, rendering collective decision-making ineffective and without continuity, and thus causing new demands for formal leadership (Blavoukos et al. 2007; Kollman 2003; Tallberg 2006). With the appointment of a full-time European Council president, however, a new principal-agent dilemma emerges (Wessels and Traguth 2010). Consequently, rational choice institutionalists expect member states to concentrate on controlling the powers of the office holder in post-Lisbon European Council politics (Blavoukos et al. 2007; Tallberg 2006).

Deliberative intergovernmentalism as an analytical framework adopts an alternative perspective on the European Council's new presidency regime. It holds that the changing political role of the European Council in EU policy-making is the main driver of institutional adjustment. The changing decision-making agenda of the European Council and increased demand for generating consensus over policy at the highest political level can best explain the evolution of the office of the permanent president. Factors such as the unprecedented increase in the number of EU member states following the 2004 and 2007 enlargements clearly played a role in creating demand for new leadership. Yet reference to enlargement alone does not explain that demand, or, more precisely, it does not explain demand for a particular kind of leadership. Though member states undoubtedly find it difficult to resist the temptation to clip the powers of the chair, the new position has so far received remarkable support. The argument in this section is that member states agree in principle that the European Council's capacity to forge consensus requires improvement. The following remarks by an official working in the personal administration office of a head of state or government, which were made a few months before the appointment of Herman Van Rompuy, reveal that members of the European Council at the time were ready to concede quite an important role to the future president:

> The future role of the European Council probably evolves in connection with the person of the [permanent] president. The relevant person would need to lead the European Council in an appropriate way. [ . . . ] Many of the heads are hoping that a strong president relieves them a bit from the domestic pressure to permanently demonstrate leadership on Europe with regard to all conceivable issues. If someone could do this, people are ready to transfer authority to this person.[70]

Yet the quote also shows ambiguity about the desired qualities of the office holder—a key feature of the debate at the time. The person was expected to be 'a strong president', while also leading the forum 'in an appropriate way'. The remarks reflect the distinction between the external representation function of the president and his or her internal role. There were indeed various considerations informing the original decision to create the office of an elected European Council president. This was not least illustrated by the debate about who was the right person for this job in the run-up to the Lisbon Treaty coming into force. One group of political commentators lamented that the EU was unable to bring a real political leader to the top. Tony Blair's name was circulated again and again as an appropriate choice. The selection of a renowned political figure of international standing was considered pivotal so as to give the EU a greater role in global politics. Others rather emphasized the need to appoint someone who would be able to act as an honest broker, and who could mediate between smaller and bigger member states. When the former Belgium prime minister Herman Van Rompuy was eventually appointed, he was clearly placed in the latter category. Those who were not disappointed with the decision emphasized Van Rompuy's experience with Belgium's complex domestic politics and the country's fragile federal system.

In order to solve the puzzle of the presidency it is therefore important to identify more clearly how the European Council presidency was exercised during Herman Van Rompuy's first two terms. The Lisbon Treaty includes a heavy hint that consensus generation is one of the core functions of the new European Council president. The Treaty stipulates that the president 'shall endeavour to facilitate cohesion and consensus within the European Council' (Article 15.6, TEU). In addition, other key functions usually associated with

---

[70] Interviewee MS-06/GEN, 3 July 2009.

the assignation of formal leadership competences are highlighted, such as external representation of the EU in CFSP matters, and the preparation and continuity of decision-making and representation of the European Council in relation to the Commission and the EP (Article 15.6, TEU). The Treaty also specifies that the president is elected by a qualified majority for a two-and-a-half year term of office and cannot be active in domestic politics while serving as president. Still, the Treaty provisions leave much room for interpretation. They remain 'rather vague' as one interviewee put it.[71] Not only can an individual office holder place different emphasis on the various aspects of the president's role, but there are also no formal regulations on how to fulfil the role of a consensus facilitator, for example. Van Rompuy himself has developed over time a particular understanding of what the role of the European Council president should be about. As one senior official explained a year before the end of the president's first term:

Van Rompuy still defines the job but he knows what he wants.[72]

Though the Lisbon Treaty also emphasizes the external representation function of the president, his actual powers are directed at the internal process of European Council decision-making. As opposed to the Commission president or a national head of state or government, the European Council president does not command any significant political authority other than the one that is expressed through engineering collective decisions by the heads. As one official pointed out:

The president does not have executive powers. His only advantage is that he is there permanently.[73]

Thus, the focus on facilitating internal decision-making is not just a question of personality—though this undoubtedly matters—but a structural feature of the position. Moreover, the notion of leadership associated with the office of European Council president is more likely to relate to the ability to engineer collective action and facilitate decision-making rather than to pompous gestures and insidious political moves otherwise associated with presidential authority.

The European Council's first elected president Herman Van Rompuy was appointed at an informal European Council meeting in November 2009. His first two-and-a-half year term of office started when the Lisbon Treaty came into force on 1 December 2009. Unlike the newly appointed HR Catherine Ashton, who has continued to attract criticism from the press and parts of the Brussels apparatus for not being a more decisive and visible leader of the

[71] Interviewee EU-10/EXT, 8 July 2011.     [72] Interviewee EU-09/ECON, 4 July 2011.
[73] Interviewee EU-10/EXT, 8 July 2011.

foreign affairs portfolio (see chapter 4.3), Van Rompuy did not become the subject of major criticism after the initial debates about the presidency had resided. Van Rompuy stayed clear of major confrontations and disputes with individual members of the European Council—at least as far as his public image was concerned. In 2012 the European Council prolonged his mandate by a second term until the end of November 2014. It is noteworthy that Van Rompuy's first years in office were not associated with a major role in external representation—a function that was much highlighted in debates surrounding the initial appointment of a permanent European Council president. Instead the internal role of the chair was highlighted. The former Belgium prime minister is generally referred to by fellow leaders and officials familiar with the European Council environment as being an effective chair with the skill to facilitate agreement and a good sense of what issues drive the European Council agenda. The focus on the internal dimension of the presidency and the appraisal Van Rompuy received for it is illustrated by the following quote:

> The president is very good at building up compromises. He is very good and knowledgeable on economic governance.[74]

The same interviewee also believed that Van Rompuy's personal approach towards fulfilling the role of the president matters in this regard:

> Van Rompuy is not the type of politician who always wants to be in the limelight and grabs every opportunity of a TV camera being present. That also means that he hasn't made himself so many enemies yet. Merkel and Sarkozy don't see him as someone who contends their leadership roles.

Another official wanted to replace the attribute 'moderator', which is sometimes given to Van Rompuy, with 'facilitator':

> Facilitator and moderator is a big difference. He [Van Rompuy] is interested in a deal not in a good discussion.[75]

The president maintains close contact with the heads between European Council meetings through frequent telephone conversations, visits to member state capitals, and meetings with heads who have travelled to Brussels. The small presidential cabinet also devotes much of its time to communicating with the capitals, the Commission, the ECB, and increasingly the EP. The head of cabinet calls all capitals ahead of European Council meetings.[76] Several members of the cabinet bring their experiences and networks from previous positions. For example, Odile Renaud-Basso, the Deputy Head of Cabinet in

---

[74] Interviewee EU-02/GEN, 4 July 2011.    [75] Interviewee EU-10/EXT, 8 July 2011.
[76] Interviewee EU-09/ECON, 4 July 2011.

the first years of Van Rompuy's presidency, who had responsibility for the euro area and economic governance issues, was a long-term member of the influential Economic and Financial Committee (EFC) and then director of the EFC secretariat. Richard Corbett, a former British Labour Party MEP, was put in charge of relations with the EP.

How Van Rompuy has interpreted and sought to define the role of the president is illustrated by a programmatic speech he gave at the College of Europe in Bruges very soon after his first appointment. According to Van Rompuy, the main role of the European Council was to mobilize political consensus around collective action in two areas, which he considered vital for the future of the Union and its role in the world—economic governance and foreign affairs:

> This brings me to Europe and to the European Council.
>
> In order to confront such changes [in a globalized context], the members of the Union need to be strong and need to be united. Therefore I believe that the two most important domains of the European Council are economic policy and foreign policy. Simply put: economic policy to be strong, foreign policy to be united.
>
> First on economic policy.
>
> Since my election, I have put economic growth at the top of the EU's agenda. Three European Council meetings are dedicated to the issue this semester. The informal meeting two weeks ago in the Bibliothèque Solvay and the regular Councils of March and June. The Heads of State or Government will address how to enhance growth, how to create jobs, how to be more competitive. [ . . . ]
>
> All the members of the European Council were willing to take more responsibility for these economic issues. Such personal involvement is indispensable. I was glad to find a high level of ambition around the table.[77]

Personal commitment, frequent meetings, and gatherings within a more informal context are seen as vital for constituting European Council leadership. For example, Van Rompuy is said to have pushed hard for the finalization of the EU2020 coordination framework—the successor of the much-criticized Lisbon agenda. He prioritized the issue, as he believed that the model of policy coordination under European Council leadership was pivotal to the EU's ability to deal with contemporary policy challenges. Van Rompuy was even seen as being more active in bringing about the finalization of the EU2020 package than Commission president Barroso[78]—a circumstance that illustrates the growing importance of the European Council and its permanent president in phases of policy initiation and consensus formation around a particular coordination approach.

[77] Van Rompuy (2010b). Also quoted in Puetter (2012b).
[78] Interviewee EU-06/GEN, 3 June 2010.

Van Rompuy's first term of office coincided with the unfolding of the global economic and financial crisis. Generally, interviewees thought that Van Rompuy was well positioned to deal with the economic governance portfolio, and believed that he was respected among the members of the European Council for his role in crisis management:

> Due to the crisis he [Van Rompuy] is perceived as Mr Euro. Internally, everybody refers to him on matters related to saving the euro.[79]

Another senior official thought that:

> Van Rompuy's focus on economic governance reflects his own interests. He can grasp the issues.[80]

A number of routines and working methods through which the European Council president could exercise leadership and help the preparation of policy dialogue within the European Council have emerged during the process of crisis management. Some of these practices deserve further attention as they may well be used beyond the crisis period and also in other policy-making domains.

Four examples are provided here. The first example refers to establishing the routine of regular informal coordination meetings between the European Council president, the president of the Eurogroup, the commissioner for economic and financial affairs, and the ECB president ahead of Eurogroup meetings.[81] During the crisis such meetings were sometimes convened on a weekly basis. In 2013 this practice found acknowledgment in the first set of rules of procedure for Euro Summit meetings.[82] The European Council president thus plays a decisive part in inter-institutional coordination. In this process he assumes the role of a convenor. This role reflects the hierarchy that has emerged between the different bodies. The Eurogroup and the Commission increasingly prepare decisions and policy proposals on the explicit request of the European Council. Ministers seek final approval from the heads, as they do not feel that they are in a position to finalize certain decisions.

The second example of a working method that emphasized the leadership role of the president and was employed for the first time during the period of crisis management was the so-called Van Rompuy task force. The task force approach gave the European Council president direct oversight over EU finance ministers, the Commission, and ECB representatives—the group of decision-makers who normally populate the ECOFIN Council. The task force was charged by the March 2010 European Council to work on a set of

---

[79] Interviewee EU-10/EXT, 8 July 2011.      [80] Interviewee EU-09/ECON, 4 July 2011.
[81] Interviewee EU-09/ECON, 4 July 2011.      [82] Council of the European Union (2013: 3).

proposals for reforming the EMU's institutional architecture.[83] There was no prior example for establishing such a close link between the Council and the European Council.[84] From May until October 2010 Van Rompuy chaired a series of six meetings of the task force. Alongside each finance minister a so-called Sherpa was appointed to take part in the work of the task force. The Sherpas were high-ranking civil servants equipped with a mandate to prepare and pre-negotiate the sessions. They were led by the Austrian senior civil servant Thomas Wieser, who also chaired the work of one of the EU's most senior policy committees: the EFC and its Eurogroup Working Group (see chapter 4.5). Wieser did not only chair discussions among his peers, but was also charged with providing direct support to the European Council president.

The task force approach was noteworthy as it embedded the process of policy evolution and initiation within a densely integrated intergovernmental bureaucratic network rather than giving it to an independent supranational administration. The Commission was an important member of that network, but so were the member state administrations. Besides providing technocratic advice, the role of leading civil servants within this network was to generate consensus among bureaucrats and pave the way for political agreement. By directly overseeing the work of ministers and top-level civil servants the European Council president obtained control of a key resource for EU-level consensus building. The task force delivered a report on 'Strengthening economic governance in the EU'—also referred to as the Van Rompuy report—to the European Council meeting of 28–9 October 2010.[85] The work of the task force resulted in a broad set of revisions to the existing coordination framework (see chapter 1.3). The task force was instrumental in preparing one of the key steps in institutional reform during the crisis period, including a revision of the legislative provisions relating to the multilateral surveillance mechanism.

The third example discussed here was the four-presidents approach,[86] which was first applied in 2012. After Van Rompuy had submitted a report to the European Council meeting on 28–9 June 2012 on the three-step development of a banking union, a budget union, and an enhanced economic union as measures of reinforcing EMU, the European Council mandated Van Rompuy to pursue these ideas further and to develop 'a specific and time-bound road map for the achievement of a genuine Economic and

---

[83] European Council (2010a).

[84] The old working method of the European Council, which included the foreign ministers sitting beside heads of state or government as members, could be considered to represent a similar model. Yet the prime role of foreign ministers at the time was not to function as representatives of a particular policy domain but to assist the European Council in its work on horizontal and institutional issues.

[85] See European Council (2010b).     [86] This term is not used in official EU language.

Monetary Union'.[87] The president was asked to pursue this task 'in close collaboration'[88] with the presidents of the Eurogroup, the Commission, and the ECB. In addition to the above-mentioned informal routine meetings of the Eurogroup president the commissioner for economic and financial affairs and the ECB president with Van Rompuy ahead of Eurogroup meetings, this time Commission president Barroso himself was included in the group. The group was supposed to deal with issues of major institutional reform, including revisions to the policy coordination framework, legislative changes, particularly with regard to the creation of a banking union, and a potential strategy for addressing burden-sharing issues that would emerge in relation to a European-wide banking resolution regime and new collective fiscal policy instruments such as eurobonds. On all these issues the Commission, the Eurogroup, and the ECB commanded the necessary technical and political expertise. Again, as in the case of the other two examples discussed above, the European Council president acted as a convenor of the process and submitted the final reports to the European Council for discussion—an interim report for the October 2012 European Council meeting and a final set of proposals for discussion at the December 2012 European Council.[89] A key role of the European Council president was to test and pre-discuss reform proposals at an early stage with member states on a bilateral basis. Again this showed a changed approach to policy development.

Though Van Rompuy used his role as president to suggest a wide range of institutional options to member states, he also made sure that the actual documents for discussion at the relevant European Council meetings did not contain proposals that he considered unlikely to receive backing from all or at least the vast majority of member states. Even the so-called Van Rompuy Report to the June 2012 European Council meeting,[90] which had triggered the initial mandate for the work of the four presidents on a set of medium- and longer-term reform proposals, omitted several ideas circulated in earlier discussion papers.[91] Collaboration with the presidents of the Commission, the Eurogroup, and the ECB therefore also implied that the final report submitted to the December 2012 European Council would deviate in several ways from the positions taken by the three other bodies. This was most obvious in relation to the Commission.[92] A week ahead of the publication of the final version of Van Rompuy's report to the December 2012 European Council, Commission president Barroso presented the key points of a Commission

---

[87] European Council (2012c).      [88] European Council (2012c).
[89] Cf. European Council (2012a, 2012b) and Van Rompuy (2012b, 2012c).
[90] Van Rompuy (2012a).
[91] Cf. *Financial Times*, 'Van Rompuy scales back eurozone plan', 26 June 2012.
[92] European Commission (2012).

communication on institutional reform.[93] The document contained several reform options that were not proposed by the final report. For example, the Commission communication proposed the creation of a so-called redemption fund to reduce public debt in member states that had debt levels beyond the 60 per cent deficit ceiling stipulated by the Treaty, and flagged the transitory character of intergovernmental arrangements such as the Fiscal Treaty. The Commission document featured a number of analytical statements on the failure of existing policy instruments during the crisis while the Van Rompuy report was a much less eloquently written document that had been prepared mainly with the intention of enabling agreement on a set of conclusions at the December 2012 European Council meeting. The Commission communication criticized the lack of supranational authority, whereas Van Rompuy focused on the decentralized nature of euro-area economic governance.

The episode illustrated the central role of the European Council president in major processes of institutional reform. The final report indeed initiated unprecedented reform steps such as the completion of a banking union, including the creation of a bank resolution fund, and the future creation of so-called fiscal capacity within the euro area. The episode also showed that Van Rompuy did not attempt to play a role similar to the one traditionally assigned to the Commission. Though he voiced his own reform ideas, he did so essentially behind the scenes in bilateral communication and through informal working documents. Similarly, the European Council president effectively acted as a gatekeeper in relation to the other three bodies involved in the discussion of the reform proposals. In a speech at the beginning of the 2013 Irish Council presidency, Van Rompuy once more asserted his leading role as the main coordinator of discussions on further euro-area reform, and defined his relation to the Commission president and the member states therein:

> Yet to secure the eurozone's stability in the long run, there is more that can be done. So whilst we progress on the banking union in the coming semester, as President of the European Council I will lead a process, in cooperation with Commission President Barroso, of thorough consultations with the Member States on how to further improve the integration of our economic and fiscal frameworks.[94]

The fourth and final example of the establishment of a new institutional practice reflecting the key role of the European Council president in maintaining inter-institutional relations was the direct participation of the

---

[93] For a summary of the statements of the three Commission members see Agence Europe, 28 November 2012.
[94] Van Rompuy (2013: 3).

European Council president in the deliberations of particular Council formations. Van Rompuy introduced this novel practice by taking part in two gatherings of the Employment, Social Policy, Health and Consumer Affairs Council (EPSCO), which dealt with the interrelatedness of the economic governance and social and employment policy coordination portfolios in the context of the EU2020 strategy, and the future role of social and employment policy in a reformed EMU. In both cases Van Rompuy declared his ambition to improve horizontal coordination between the two dossiers and the two responsible Council formations—EPSCO and ECOFIN (see chapter 4.4). Van Rompuy's first visit to EPSCO ministers occurred at an informal EPSCO meeting under the Belgium Council presidency on 8 July 2010.[95] The next time Van Rompuy joined EPSCO ministers for a debate was at a regular EPSCO meeting in Brussels on 28 February 2013. At the meeting Van Rompuy, who had requested the debate, asked ministers to provide him with input for the discussion of EMU reform proposals planned for the June 2013 European Council meeting.[96] Van Rompuy's decision to talk directly to EPSCO ministers was unprecedented, and reflected the fundamentally changed relationship between the European Council and the Council in the new areas of EU activity. Van Rompuy himself reportedly referred to his February 2013 visit at the EPSCO Council as 'historic',[97] because of the fact that there now existed the possibility of direct discussion between the European Council president and ministers. On the occasion of both visits the discussions between Van Rompuy and the ministers were held during an informal lunch and breakfast.

Though economic governance clearly dominated the first years of Van Rompuy's presidency, it is possible to draw more general conclusions about the role of the permanent president and the way he exercised and exercises leadership within the forum. Maintaining inter-institutional relations is a key aspect of the work of the European Council president. Besides the arrangements for dealing with the particular challenges discussed above, a number of practices and routines have been established to allow day-to-day inter-institutional cooperation and communication.

Contacts with the Commission play a very important role—notably with its president. Barroso and Van Rompuy established the routine of weekly meetings, which typically take place on Mondays.[98] Before the Lisbon Treaty came into force the creation of the office of a full-time European Council president was frequently criticized for causing friction with the office of Commission

---

[95] Press release, Belgian Presidency of the Council, 8 July 2010, <http://www.employment.eutrio.be/eutrio/defaultNews.aspx?id=31196> [accessed 24 April 2014].

[96] Press release, Irish Presidency of the Council, 28 February 2013, <http://eu2013.ie/news/news-items/20130228post-epscodjei/> [accessed 12 March 2013].

[97] Agence Europe, 28 February 2013.      [98] Interviewee EU-09/ECON, 4 July 2011.

president. However, the actual experience of collaboration between the two presidents during Van Rompuy's first and second terms did not seem to confirm such concerns. Several interviewees described the working relationship between the two presidents as pragmatic, each of them knowing that the other is an important player in EU policy-making. Some officials even thought that a sense of rivalry between the two sometimes made it easier for the European Council president to remind heads of their commitment towards previously established EU policy objectives and to discipline discussion within the European Council. As one interviewee explained:

> He [Van Rompuy] gets along with Barroso. Barroso has passed his honeymoon period, as have many politicians who are in their second term. This means, for example, that there are people who don't want to be lectured about economic governance issues by him. But then Van Rompuy can say: Yes, I understand that you don't want to be lectured by the Commission but it is really important that you do this or that. It is a bit like good cop and bad cop.[99]

As no clear rules were established by the Lisbon Treaty on how to structure the relationship between the two presidents in areas of overlapping competence, the first years were crucial in establishing practices and routines. The sphere of external representation, especially in relation to actors outside the EU, requires constant coordination. Even though arrangements were found for reoccurring international events—such as the agreement that the European Council president speaks for the EU at the UN General Assembly—actors outside Europe tended to attach different expectations to the office of European Council president. Such expectations were not always anticipated in Brussels, and required ad-hoc agreement between the two presidents. As one official described the situation:

> He [Van Rompuy] is perceived by the outside world as the president of the EU—not of the European Council. Therefore close cooperation with the Commission president is important.[100]

Cooperation with the Commission is important not only because of the potential overlap between the responsibilities of the two presidents—the growing significance of the European Council in controlling and guiding processes of policy initiation also requires close coordination. The examples of institutional reform in the context of the economic and financial crisis discussed above show that even in areas where the Commission is mandated by the Treaty to initiate policy, prior agreement within the European Council is essential. For example, the issue of reforming banking supervision within the EU (or at least the euro area) involves changes to core single market

---

[99] Interviewee EU-02/GEN, 4 July 2011.    [100] Interviewee EU-10/EXT, 8 July 2011.

legislation. Moreover, the reform packages showed the inter-relation between areas that are governed through policy coordination and those that are subject to supranational regulation. The European Council president therefore also maintains regular contact with the different members of the Commission—especially with those whose portfolios are central to the European Council's agenda. The practice of regular exchanges between the European Council president and members of the Commission is not without repercussions for other forums and networks in Brussels that are traditionally involved in mediating between member state and Commission interests. This is even felt within the sphere of legislative decision-making, as one senior member state diplomat explained:

> Van Rompuy's and the European Council's top-down approach really clashes with the practice of a bottom-up—Council working groups, COREPER, Council—approach.[101]

Also of particular importance for inter-institutional relations and the work of the European Council is the division of labour between the European Council president and the HR. According to the Lisbon Treaty, they have overlapping roles in representing the EU to the outside world in the field of foreign and security policy, and there was no clear guidance on how the two representatives should work together. As in the case of the relationship between the Commission president and the European Council president, Van Rompuy's first and second terms did not provide evidence of open conflict between the two office-holders over their respective roles in the external affairs domain. Interviews with senior officials involved in European Council organization suggest that Van Rompuy wanted to avoid friction between the two positions from the beginning. As one official explained:

> There is conscious effort by the president not to duplicate the work of the High Representative.[102]

The European Council president meets with the HR on a bi-weekly and sometimes monthly basis. He also meets other members of the Commission and other top EU foreign policy officials on a regular basis.[103] Though the emphasis on economic affairs in the first years of Van Rompuy's presidency makes it difficult to fully assess the scope and frequency of foreign policy contacts within the field of inter-institutional communication, there is little doubt that the foreign policy portfolio is among the president's main activity areas.

---

[101] Interviewee PR-22/GEN, 1 June 2010.    [102] Interviewee EU-10/EXT, 8 July 2011.
[103] Interviewee EU-10/EXT, 8 July 2011.

Another important aspect in understanding the role of the full-time European Council president is his influence over agenda setting. Technically, the transition from the rotating presidency regime to the position of an elected European Council president implied a slight revision of the Council Secretariat's role in agenda preparation. In the past, the rotating presidency has tended to rely heavily on the recommendations of the Council Secretariat with regard to the finalization of the European Council agenda—now the final decision over the agenda clearly lies with the president. The Council Secretariat still prepares draft agendas and provides support, but Van Rompuy consciously uses his prerogative to decide about the agenda.[104] Most importantly, it has become clear that a full-time president is in a much better position to establish strategic priorities and use specific meeting formats to engineer a particular environment for the discussion of selected topics.[105] This is, however, not to say that ex ante coordination with the member states and other EU institutions ahead of European Council meetings is in any way less important today than it was previously. As before, current affairs and crisis situations lead to unforeseen changes to the European Council agenda that are beyond the control of the presidency, or now, the president. However, while in the past the presidency's influence over the agenda became manifest mainly in its ability to schedule some debates of particular interest to the relevant member state in addition to the already-defined agenda items, there is clear evidence that Herman Van Rompuy has managed to influence the European Council agenda to follow far more strategic considerations concerning the evolution of the wider role of the forum in specific areas of EU policy-making. Van Rompuy has arranged for specific policy issues to get attention within the European Council, and consciously developed the different priority areas of the top-level decision-making forum by structuring the deliberations and reserving time for more strategic and forward-looking debates. As one official explained by reference to an example:

It is his [Van Rompuy's] discretion to set the agenda. Innovation and energy for example were put on the agenda by him.[106]

Though the period of intensive European Council activity around the economic and financial crisis has left many EU foreign and security policy observers disappointed with the role of the European Council in fostering strategic orientation and further developing the CFSP portfolio, there is evidence that Van Rompuy has used his agenda-setting prerogatives to establish such a focus

---

[104] Interviewee EU-09/ECON, 4 July 2011.
[105] Examples of decisions by Van Rompuy on the use of particular working methods for discussion of certain agenda items are provided in the earlier sections of this chapter.
[106] Interviewee EU-02/GEN, 4 July 2011.

on foreign policy issues. Van Rompuy has been eager to move foreign policy into the centre of policy deliberations within the forum, as one official explained:

> Van Rompuy wants to establish regularity for foreign affairs in the European Council because you don't handle relations with China through foreign ministries. He wants to create a sense of ownership in relation to external affairs.[107]

The same official also believed that foreign policy issues were mainly held back or did not get the necessary attention from the heads during the relevant meetings on the economic crisis. He did not see a lack of interest or competence on the part of Van Rompuy but rather suggested that from the beginning of his first term as European Council president he was very well aware of all major foreign policy issues, such as the political changes in North Africa.[108] The ambition to develop the foreign policy portfolio is also apparent from Van Rompuy's own bold statements that he sees foreign policy as the second most important area of European Council activity next to economic governance. Van Rompuy's attempts to turn this ambition into practice became manifest for the first time in September 2010 when he flanked the organization of a European Council meeting especially devoted to foreign policy with public statements. During a speech in Paris he admitted that EU foreign policy coordination was a cumbersome process because of decentralized responsibilities but that because of this difficulty, the active engagement of the European Council was essential:

> I should like however to come on to the area of external policy. There our tortoise has more difficulty winning, the challenge is greater. The transfer principle [transfer of decision-making competence to the EU] comes up against obstacles, sensitivities: we cannot issue directives on our relations with the United States or Russia as we do on the quality of chocolate.
>
> The principle of participation, which is certainly necessary in this area, sometimes takes too long. When you have to react to a humanitarian crisis somewhere in the world, you cannot always wait until the 27 have negotiated a response. The challenge in this sphere is a major one.
>
> I have therefore decided, as the first President of the European Council, to tackle it anyway.[109]

During the same speech, which Van Rompuy gave only a few days after the European Council meeting on foreign policy, he emphasized that the meeting had been deliberately designed to begin a new phase of more intensive policy dialogue:

---

[107] Interviewee EU-10/EXT, 8 July 2011.    [108] Interviewee EU-10/EXT, 8 July 2011.
[109] Van Rompuy (2010a: 8).

For the first time, the Heads of State and Government devoted a meeting to the subject of Europe's place in the new world. We concentrated on our relations with the Union's strategic partners, such as the United States, Russia and China.

The episode at the September 2010 meeting on foreign policy provides a good example of the president's role in agenda setting and, at the same time, demonstrates the difficulties in developing the foreign policy portfolio at times of a major EU economic crisis. Van Rompuy was eager to reserve a full meeting to discuss the strategic orientation of EU foreign policy. He deliberately did not introduce more specific policy issues for decision-making to the agenda so as to enable open debate.[110] The meeting was planned to take up only one day unlike a regular meeting[111] over two days with a full agenda. Ahead of the gathering, Van Rompuy reminded the members of the European Council of the aim of creating, through this meeting, a permanent process of policy dialogue over external relations so as to regularly agree 'key messages'[112]—a term also used in other areas of European Council activity—that guide EU institutions and member states in their relations with third countries. After that, Van Rompuy scheduled a number of foreign and security affairs-related debates of which several focused on the strategic orientation of EU foreign policy. Often these debates were organized as informal exchanges so as to allow open and forward-looking dialogue (see section 3.6) and, thus, have not necessarily featured prominently in the European Council conclusions. For example, at its October 2012 meeting the European Council saw an informal debate about the EU's relations with China. The conclusions just noted that an 'exchange of views on the EU's relations with strategic partners' was held.[113] Similarly, Van Rompuy scheduled an open debate about relations with Russia to take place within the context of the Spring European Council in March 2013.

## 3.8 The Euro Summits

The practice of holding additional meetings of euro-area heads of state and government under the chairmanship of the European Council president and the institutionalization of this meeting format as the 'Euro Summit' in

---

[110] Cf. also Agence Europe, 'A look behind the news', 16 September 2010. The column discusses if and why it makes sense to convene a meeting without aiming to decide specific issues.

[111] Officially the gathering had the status of a formal European Council meeting. Yet Van Rompuy also used elements of informal European Council meetings, i.e. concentration on one major subject, opportunities for engaging in orientation debates, and the focus on broader issues.

[112] The formulation is used in Van Rompuy's invitation letter to the heads ahead of the meeting, as quoted in Agence Europe, 15 September 2010.

[113] See European Council (2012b), p. 10.

October 2011 came in response to the steep surge in demand for high-level intergovernmental policy deliberations during the economic crisis.[114] Euro Summits are meetings of the heads of the euro-area member states that are convened in addition to meetings of the full European Council. The working method of Euro Summits can be described as a blend of the informal and single-issue meeting formats of the full European Council outlined earlier in this chapter. The Euro Summit mirrors the Eurogroup of euro-area finance ministers (see chapter 4.2). This section reviews how and why the meeting format was introduced, and how it is related to the general activities of the European Council. Deliberative intergovernmentalism expects greater involvement from the heads as the coordination agenda becomes more elaborate and thus politically more sensitive in the domestic arena. The crisis required decision-making that had immediate consequences for the budgetary positions of individual member states and the stability of the monetary union. This applied to institutional as much as to managerial decisions. The emergence of the Euro Summit format followed that logic.

The idea of additional European Council meetings devoted only to euro-area governance is not entirely new and was floated well before the EU was hit by the economic and financial crisis in 2008. The former French president Nikolas Sarkozy in particular publicly propagated a greater involvement of the heads in important euro-area decisions. The review of the evolution of the European Council agenda over time showed the predominant role that the issue of economic governance had assumed since the introduction of the single currency. As the consequences of EMU's policy coordination framework for domestic policy-making became increasingly apparent, closer involvement of the heads in specific policy decisions was inevitable in order to reach political backing for EU-level decisions. Finance ministers—who traditionally enjoyed a powerful role in EU economic governance—were increasingly scrutinized and sometimes openly challenged by their superiors. Hodson (2011) argues that it was precisely the early success of the Eurogroup in establishing itself as the central euro-area decision-making forum that triggered growing intervention by the European Council. At least part of this activity was aimed at limiting the autonomy finance ministers had enjoyed in euro-area governance so far. European Council and later Euro Summit intervention thus occurred not because of the absence of policy coordination but because of its increasing importance for domestic politics.

[114] Though the term 'Euro Summit' was coined by the euro heads in October 2011 (see section 3.8), European Council terminology still refers to the meetings that often take place on the first day of a full European Council meeting as either 'Euro Summits' or 'meetings of the heads of the euro area'. The European Council website also uses both terms when it comes to the publication of the occasional statements issued after some of these meetings. Both terms are used interchangeably here.

A rather bizarre attempt to gain greater control over Eurogroup decision-making illustrated the changing dynamics particularly well. In July 2007 French president Sarkozy invited himself to a Eurogroup meeting to tell the surprised finance ministers that it was—in contrast to the prevailing opinion inside the Eurogroup—right for France to delay the deadline for achieving the country's so-called medium-term budgetary objective by two years until 2012. Sarkozy had flanked his visit at the Eurogroup with a newspaper interview in which he argued that major decisions affecting growth and jobs should be made by the heads themselves rather than the ministers (Hodson 2011: 46–7). At the time, Sarkozy's brisk proposition that the heads should pursue a more interventionist role in relation to the work of finance ministers was met with scepticism. Member state governments in favour of a more rigid stance on euro-area fiscal targets feared particularly that the further politicization of euro-area decision-making through greater involvement of the heads could lead to an erosion of previously agreed policy objectives. The German government was reluctant to respond to initial French requests to split the discussion within the European Council into an EU-wide process and a euro-area process, as it feared disintegration tendencies in relation to the rest of the EU. Even in the light of the unfolding economic and financial crisis in the second half of 2008, German chancellor Merkel was still said to favour additional bilateral meetings and increased telephone contact between euro-area leaders over the introduction of routine euro-area meetings of the European Council.[115]

Coincidentally, France was the holder of the rotating European Council presidency in the second semester of 2008. Sarkozy first convened an emergency summit of the heads of the four EU members of the G8—France, Germany, Italy, and the United Kingdom—as well as the presidents of the Commission, the Eurogroup, and the ECB in Paris on 4 October 2008 with the aim of preparing an EU position for the November 2008 G8 summit.[116] By 12 October 2008 Sarkozy had opened the first-ever informal meeting of the euro-area heads of state or government. There was no formal mandate from the full European Council for this. Sarkozy effectively created a new practice and set a precedent. The crisis situation lent legitimacy to this move. The following reaction by a euro-area member state finance ministry official revealed the thinking at the time—and the emerging shift in opinion:

---

[115] Interviewee MS-06/GEN, 3 July 2009.—The practice of maintaining intensive informal contacts between members of the European Council or entire networks of members of the European Council on specific issues between European Council meetings is as old as the institution. Already Bulmer and Wessels (1987: 54) had identified 'multiple bilateralism' as a key mechanism that was used to prepare the work of the European Council.

[116] See <http://www.ue2008.fr/PFUE/lang/en/accueil/PFUE-10_2008/PFUE-04.10.2008/sommet_crise_financiere_internationale.html> [accessed 11 January 2013].

Sarkozy got a bloody nose with his appearance in the Eurogroup [in July 2007]. How do you imagine the heads agree on rules for the nationalization of banks or new surveillance mechanisms at the EU level in the current crisis? They lack the technical knowledge. The finance ministers should stay in control of these processes. Of course, there is pressure from Sarkozy to activate more often [the discussion among] the heads. He doesn't like the finance ministers. But you don't always have to bow to such pressure. Sometimes that is ok. In fall 2008 it was good that they [the heads] met in Paris and issued a common statement. This was good because the citizens realized it.[117]

Representatives of non-euro-area member states criticized the move. For them the meeting came at a time when it had just become apparent that the crisis functioned to some extent as a trigger for the revival of EU-27 economic governance. Problems such as the instability of the banking sector and the issue of finding a common EU position for the G8 and G20 were not limited to the euro area.[118] The first group of countries to receive financial assistance included only non-euro-area member states. Moreover, the looming issue of institutional reform called for agreements among all EU member states. As one official explained at the time:

We are now learning very fast that we bring together all EU-27. Any balancing of interests must include the EU-27 alltogether.[119]

The Czech presidency in the first semester of 2009 demonstrated this dilemma. A second informal meeting of the euro-area heads following the début in Paris was seen as too controversial during the presidency of a non-euro-area member state. Instead German chancellor Merkel acted as the host of a mini-summit of the EU's G8 members plus the presidents of the Commission, the Eurogroup, and the ECB in Berlin in February 2009. The chancellor and the Czech presidency reportedly thought that using this meeting format—which was also referred to as a G4 summit (the three G8 members plus the EU institutions)—would put off the question of further euro-area meetings for some time.[120]

It was European Council president Herman Van Rompuy who eventually introduced the routine practice of informal meetings of euro-area members of the European Council. As the sovereign debt situation in Greece rapidly deteriorated in the first half of 2010, a more explicit commitment by the euro-area heads to support Greece was needed. Moreover, agreement on an

---

[117] Interviewee MS-10/ECON, 18 February 2009.

[118] For a discussion of EU coordination activity in relation to the G20 summits of the relevant period see Hodson (2011: 95–113).

[119] Interviewee, PR-19/ECON, 10 March 2009.

[120] Interviewee MS-10/ECON, 18 February 2009. The Berlin meeting was coordinated with the Czech presidency, which could portray it as a preparatory meeting ahead of a full European Council meeting shortly afterwards.

arrangement for a likely bailout had to be reached. Uncertainty prevailed among European Council members, as it was still unclear what financial resources were needed and how grave the situation was.[121] A declaration of support for Greece following an informal European Council meeting in February 2010 did not succeed in calming the situation. As it was apparent that only euro-area member states were ready to make financial commitments, Van Rompuy convened a separate meeting of the euro-area faction within the European Council at the fringes of the regular Spring European Council meeting on 25–6 March 2010. This gathering was not confirmed officially until the very last minute.[122] It took place on the first day of the two-day European Council meeting under Van Rompuy's chairmanship. The meeting resulted in a press statement by the euro-area heads announcing that they would provide financial assistance to Greece. The statement also mandated Van Rompuy to convene a task force on institutional reform (see section 3.7). This mandate was also endorsed by the full European Council. Moreover, the euro-area statement explicitly called for an increased role for the European Council in institutional reform and economic policy coordination.[123]

As early as 7 May 2010 Van Rompuy chaired the next euro-area meeting, which gave final approval to the financial aid package that had been pre-negotiated by the Eurogroup in the meantime. The discussions at the meeting also turned to the issue of institutional reform.[124] As at the previous informal euro-area meeting in March, a press statement resembling an extract from the usual European Council conclusions was issued—bearing no letterhead or official reference number.[125] On the fringes of the regular December 2010 European Council, Van Rompuy again convened a separate informal meeting of the heads of the euro area, thus turning this meeting format into a routine arrangement. This time the euro-area heads, prior to the full European Council meeting, pre-negotiated the text for a limited amendment of the Treaty under the simplified revision procedure (Article 48.6, TEU), allowing the implementation of a permanent financial assistance mechanism—the ESM. The heads of the euro area also issued a statement saying that they were committed 'to do whatever is required to ensure the stability of the

---

[121] The press briefings in connection with the European Council meeting of the heads on 25–6 March 2010 reveal this. Merkel, Sarkozy, and Juncker were careful to use language suggesting that the discussion was ongoing and requesting flexibility over anticipated institutional adjustments.— Cf. Agence Europe, 26 March 2010.

[122] Cf. Agence Europe, 24 and 25 March 2010.

[123] Statement by the Heads of State and Government of the Euro Area, 25 March 2010, <http://www.consilium.europa.eu/uedocs/cmsdata/docs/pressdata/en/ec/113563.pdf> [accessed 16 January 2013].

[124] Agence Europe, 8 May 2010.

[125] 'Statement of the Heads of State or Government of the Euro Area', 7 May 2010, <http://ec.europa.eu/commission_2010-2014/president/news/speeches-statements/pdf/114295.pdf> [accessed 16 January 2013].

euro area as a whole'.[126] This time the statement was acknowledged in the main European Council conclusions.[127]

The practice of holding euro-area meetings as a supplement to full European Council meetings—held either ahead of a regular European Council meeting or between European Council meetings—was continued throughout 2011. The euro-area meetings emerged as the key venue for deciding on the various financial assistance packages. They focused on discussing institutional reform and policy coordination matters before they were discussed by the full European Council, and became an important venue for consensus formation within the euro area. Finally, on Sunday, 23 October 2011, the informal euro-area forum assigned itself the status of a permanent meeting format under the name 'Euro Summit'—the first time this name was used in official EU language. Within hours the euro-area heads had their decision rubber-stamped by the full European Council. Reference to the relation between the two meeting formats in the European Council conclusions was kept short:

> The European Council agreed on the need for coherence of the activities of the euro area and the European Union, with due respect for the integrity of the European Union as a whole and its operation at 27. [ ... ] The President of the Euro Summit will keep the non-euro-area Member States fully informed of the preparation and outcome of the Summits.[128]

The conclusions also stipulated that members of the Euro Summit were free to select their own president. This meant that the European Council president and the president of the Euro Summit could be two different individuals. However, Van Rompuy was immediately assigned this role until the next election of a European Council president. He then was formally confirmed in this double role as European Council and Euro Summit president in March 2012 for another two-and-a-half years. Further steps to complete the institutionalization of the Euro Summit format were taken only a few days later on 26 October 2011, when the euro-area heads adopted a catalogue of provisions regulating the role of Euro Summits in economic governance and also the work of the Eurogroup and its relationship with the European Council and the Euro Summit. These provisions were communicated through a 'Euro Summit Statement'. The document stated that Euro Summits would be convened 'at least twice a year', and would be devoted to providing 'strategic orientations on the economic and fiscal policies in the euro area'.[129] The statement also established a clear hierarchy between the euro-area heads and the ministerial meetings of the Eurogroup (see chapter 4.2). The Eurogroup prepares the Euro

---

[126] 'Statement of the Heads of State or Government of the Euro Area', 7 May 2010.
[127] European Council (2010c), Annex III.     [128] European Council (2011), para. 7.
[129] Euro Summit Statement, 26 October 2011, para. 31, <http://www.consilium.europa.eu/uedocs/cms_data/docs/pressdata/en/ec/125644.pdf> [accessed 16 January 2013].

Summit. Another step towards the further institutionalization of Euro Summits was taken with the adoption of the Fiscal Treaty (see chapter 1.3), which largely reiterated the 26 October 2011 conclusions on the introduction of Euro Summit meetings. The Fiscal Treaty referred to the heads of the euro-area member states and the president of the Commission as the members of the Euro Summit, and stipulated that the ECB president is 'invited to take part in such meetings'[130]—a formula also used in relation to the Eurogroup. Relations with the EP were organized in the same way as in the case of full European Council meetings.[131] Again following the example of the full European Council, the Euro Summit adopted its own rules of procedure (Council of the European Union 2013).

So soon after the Lisbon Treaty came into force, the creation of the Euro Summit format constitutes a somewhat puzzling adjustment. Why change an institutional setting that had just undergone substantial review? The preference for euro-area countries to make decisions among themselves was not new, and the Eurogroup (see chapter 4.2) provides for that possibility. This section indeed cautions against putting too much emphasis on the institutional rivalries between euro-area and non-euro-area countries when it comes to explaining the emergence of the Euro Summit format. The emergence of the Euro Summit format rather confirms one of the key claims of the analytical framework of deliberative intergovernmentalism: processes of intensive intergovernmental policy deliberation develop and become more sophisticated initially at a lower level, and then spread to the highest level as the repercussions on domestic politics are felt more strongly. The Euro Summit follows several years of Eurogroup coordination at ministerial level. The creation of financial assistance mechanisms and the tightening of budgetary policy coordination in the context of the crisis required a constant generation of political consensus on particular policy measures among the heads. Several of these decisions touched on the very existence of the euro area and, indeed, the fate of individual national governments. The above review of the trajectory of the top-level meeting format shows that the idea of introducing exclusive meetings of euro-area heads was not new. Yet earlier attempts to form such a meeting format were resisted even by euro-area member states. Unlike the Eurogroup, which concentrates on the day-to-day political management of euro-area affairs, the European Council must generate wider political consensus among all EU member states. Precisely because euro-area decision-making increasingly dominates the EU's economic governance agenda as a whole, the involvement of the European Council is indispensable to avoid disintegration. Yet the euro-area bailout decisions especially went beyond anything that had

---

[130] TSCG, Article 12.1.    [131] TSCG, Article 12.5.

hitherto been decided collectively so far, and posed a particular challenge to the euro area.

The bailouts and the establishment of the ESM as a permanent rescue mechanism for the euro area have in fact provided a departure from the previous no-bailout doctrine. This has required close agreement among euro-area countries. The institutionalization of top-level euro-area meetings however, may not constitute an insurmountable challenge to the unity of the European Council, at least for the foreseeable future. The changing frequency of euro-area meetings speaks to this point. While there were four meetings in 2010 and 2011 respectively, only one Euro Summit per year could be recorded for 2012 and 2013. At the same time, euro-area policy coordination remained a dominant issue on the agenda of the full European Council. So far, the Euro Summit has more of the character of a euro-area working group of the European Council than of a competing institution. The provision of the Fiscal Treaty that at least one of the two envisaged Euro Summit meetings per year are held with the participation of non-euro-area members also speaks to this point, and effectively amounts to obliging the European Council to have more meetings that are fully dedicated to economic governance. Finally, Van Rompuy's dual role as chair of both configurations helped to mitigate differences and tensions.

## 3.9 The European Council Conclusions as an Instrument for Exercising Leadership

The previous sections of this chapter showed how much European Council deliberations in the post-Maastricht era have focused on governing the fragile coordination processes in the new areas of EU activity. The constant generation of commitment among the EU's top-level decision-makers to pursue commonly agreed policy objectives at the national level and by coordinated action in global politics is at the heart of European Council action. The heads intervene regularly in Council and Eurogroup decision-making—also in relation to short- and medium-term policy issues. Moreover, the European Council effectively frames and structures the various coordination processes by defining the responsibilities and relationships of the various other EU institutions and member state administrations. These roles require the European Council to communicate its consensus on a regular basis and make clear the implications of its decisions, even though these decisions do not constitute legal acts. The more the European Council gets involved in complex decision-making, the greater is the need to follow a more structured approach in communicating European Council decisions to EU-level institutions, member state administrations, and increasingly the outside world. This section reviews the main instrument through which the European Council traditionally communicates its position in this regard. The role of the so-called European Council conclusions as an instrument for exercising leadership is discussed with reference to key examples of European Council intervention in the post-Maastricht era.

At the time of the rotating presidency the European Council's concluding statement was referred to as the presidency conclusions. Since the Lisbon Treaty came into force just the word 'conclusions' is used. The formal status of the conclusions matters. Their adoption by the European Council does not constitute an official act of the EU. The conclusions are also not to be confused with the adoption of formal decisions by the European Council. There are a number of so-called European Council decisions identified by the Treaty (see Tables 3.2 and 3.3 in section 3.3). Such decisions involve, for example, the appointment of the Commission, the number of Council configurations, the limited amendment of Part III of the TFEU, or the adoption of the European Council's own rules of procedure. Formal European Council decisions in this sense are official acts of the EU and are published in the so-call L-series of the *Official Journal of the EU*—in which all legal acts of the Union are published.[132]

However, the bulk of European Council activity does not concern the adoption of such formal decision-making acts but revolves around what is communicated in the conclusions. Through this document the European Council can exercise political control in various ways. The spectrum includes such diverse matters as executive decision-making, strategic guidance, specific policy decisions, statements on the EU's stance towards international developments, or instructions directed at other EU institutions. The European Council conclusions are a key reference document in the various policy coordination processes. They state common objectives and establish procedures for policy review. They have also been used to deal with important institutional issues below the level of treaty changes. Thus, the conclusions are much more than a public statement or a collection of messages to the outside world. With the rise of new intergovernmentalism in the post-Maastricht era the conclusions have developed into an increasingly complex collection of guidelines and instructions that direct policy and institutional activity at various levels of decision-making.

Since the mid-1990s the document is being read increasingly carefully by a quickly growing number of EU officials and civil servants dealing with EU affairs in the different branches of member state administrations. Anecdotal evidence from officials working on EU policy coordination topics

---

[132] The European Council may also adopt formal decisions that are directed at a particular institution or actor and do not need to be published in the *Official Journal*. See Article 12, European Council Decision 2009/882/EU adopting its Rules of Procedure, published in OJ L315/51.

in the three new areas of EU activity suggests that many of them know the relevant passages of the conclusions that are related to their respective field of expertise word for word, and refer to them as documents defining the overall direction of policy. In the mid-1990s John Peterson (1995: 72) hinted at this phenomenon for the first time, and quoted an EU official saying: 'If you can cite a European Council conclusion in a debate, you're away.'

The European Council conclusions are used to establish the basic calendar of administrative activities. The importance of the document in the daily life of ministerial bureaucracies at the member state level and, within the Commission's Directorates-General (DGs), signals the growing influence of the European Council on Council and Commission activity.

The focus on the conclusions as a key instrument for exercising leadership also implies a certain formalization of European Council decision-making.

The importance of the documents is rated so highly by European Council members that considerable time is devoted at European Council meetings to editing passages and to inserting or deleting items. The heads confer with their advisors about the wording of individual paragraphs or even sentences. Briefings prior to the meetings point to the potential pitfalls if certain language is agreed. A key aspect of the preparation of each European Council meeting is the preparation of different sets of draft conclusions by the General Secretariat of the Council and, more recently, the cabinet of the European Council president. As the meeting draws closer the individual sections are reworked and rearranged, taking into account initial reactions to the draft conclusions. The growing importance of the conclusions as an instrument for exercising leadership also became apparent when the Helsinki European Council of December 1999 focused on the reform of Council decision-making in the advent of EU enlargement. The conclusions of the Helsinki meeting demanded that future presidency conclusions should be 'more concise (maximum 15 pages) thereby focusing them on the political decisions taken on the items actually discussed at the meeting'.[133] The wording reveals that the authority of the conclusions rests primarily on the fact that they reflect the prevailing political consensus within the European Council. They do not constitute a contract between European Council members that has relevance beyond the actual debates within the forum. As the European Council started to take an increasingly proactive role in specific policy-making processes in the late 1990s the previous practice of using the conclusions also for broad political statements was rejected by the Helsinki conclusions.

The centrality of the conclusions for European Council activity is formally acknowledged by the European Council's first set of rules of procedure, which

[133] European Council (1999a), Annex III.

was adopted under the provisions of the Lisbon Treaty.[134] The rules of procedure assign to the European Council president the task of preparing draft conclusions or guidelines for establishing such conclusions. The provisions also acknowledge the role of the rotating Council presidency and the Commission in this process, and stipulate that the GAC discuss draft conclusions before each meeting of the European Council.

The Treaty does not include a general provision that the European Council works through the adoption of conclusions. Reference to the word 'conclusion' in relation to the European Council occurs only in the context of the provisions on the adoption of the broad economic policy guidelines (Article 121.2, TFEU) and on the review of the EU's employment situation in preparation for the employment guidelines (Article 148.1, TFEU). It is stipulated that the European Council should 'discuss a conclusion on the broad guidelines' (Article 121.2, TFEU) or 'adopt conclusions' on the employment situation (Article 148.1 TFEU). In both cases the Treaty obliges the Council to take into account the European Council conclusions when taking the final decision on the relevant set of policy guidelines.

Though reference to the word 'conclusion' does not occur in the relevant paragraphs, similar provisions, which suggest an act of documenting the result of European Council deliberations, can be found in key articles relating to the European Council's role in governing the CFSP and other EU external action. Article 22, TEU stipulates that the European Council 'shall *identify* the strategic interests and objectives of the Union'[135] (Article 22.1, TEU; see also Article 26.1, TEU) and speak of 'decisions of the European Council' when referring to the act of determining strategic interests and objectives and the time horizon of the relevant policy decision and the means provided by the member states and the EU. The 'decision' by the heads is published in the European Council conclusions, and the Council is obliged to follow it (Article 26.2, TEU). Again, such a 'decision' does not constitute a legal act.

In the case of all three policy areas referred to above, the European Council's actual policy-making role goes well beyond adopting guidelines under the procedures specified by the Treaty. In fact, these guidelines account for only a relatively small portion of the total number of conclusions adopted by the European Council on economic governance, foreign affairs, and employment policy. The political relevance of the European Council conclusions cannot thus be derived solely from the Treaty provisions. This also becomes clear from the way in which the focus and content of the conclusions have changed over time. The conclusions have become more specific and started to identify

---

[134] See European Council Decision 2009/882/EU adopting its Rules of Procedure, published in OJ L315/51.
[135] Emphasis added by the author.

concrete tasks and deadlines for the Council, the Commission, and member state governments. Officials now refer to this practice as 'tasking'. Tasking occurs regularly, and typically includes a request to prepare a report or to pre-negotiate a particular decision. In some cases the European Council simply asks the Commission and the Council to implement a particular decision immediately—even if that decision involves legislative action. This practice challenges the previously prevailing view among ministers and within the Commission that final policy decisions are not taken at the level of the European Council. One official put it quite bluntly:

The European Council tasks the Council. It doesn't always proceed smoothly.[136]

Another official explained:

The heads want to take the lead. They are ready to overrule ECOFIN as they did in June 2009 on financial supervision and also the Eurogroup as they did in March 2010 on International Monetary Fund involvement [in connection with financial support for Greece].[137]

The conclusions are also used to communicate decisions relating to the structure of important decision-making routines and the functioning of core EU institutions. Some of these decisions even have a constitutional dimension, despite the fact that they are not formal amendments of the EU treaties. This practice has been included as a particular activity and referred to as informal constitutional decision-making ('INF-CON') in the matrix of European Council decision-making (see section 3.2).[138] There are several examples of European Council conclusions that constitute de facto modifications of decision-making routines and institutional competences, and are related to collective decision-making within one of the new areas of EU activity. The creation of the Eurogroup in 1997 constituted such a de facto amendment of treaty provisions, and was communicated in the form of a European Council conclusion.[139] The Lisbon Treaty only codified this decision more than a decade later. The launch of the EES was communicated via the conclusions, and the coordination process was launched with immediate effect.[140] The new coordination routine was then incorporated into the Amsterdam Treaty, which came into force only in May 1999. Similarly the European Council gave the green light for establishing an enhanced bureaucratic infrastructure

---

[136] Interviewee EU-02/GEN, 4 July 2011.     [137] Interviewee EU-07/ECON, 30 March 2010.

[138] The modification of institutional arrangements through informal acts is by no means restricted to the sphere of European Council decision-making. For example, Jeffrey Stacey's (2010) study of inter-institutional informal accords concludes that institutional change in the EU can hardly be identified through the study of treaty changes but requires the analysis of informal dynamics.

[139] See European Council (1997b), para. 44.

[140] See European Council (1997a), para. 13–30.

for CFSP coordination. The Helsinki European Council in December 1999 authorized the Council to put the necessary committee infrastructure in place.[141] In February 2000 a formal Council decision on the establishment of an interim Political and Security Committee (PSC) followed.[142] A year later the Council followed up with a decision on transforming the PSC into a permanent committee. As stated in the decision, the Council acted on the grounds of the Helsinki European Council conclusions and the Nice European Council conclusions of December 2000, which acknowledged the progress made so far and authorized the creation of a permanent committee structure.[143] The relevant provisions were incorporated in the Treaty of Nice, which, however, did not come into force until February 2003. Again, the European Council conclusions served as the main reference document authorizing the implementing decisions taken by the Council. More recent examples include the adoption of financial assistance packages for struggling euro-area countries following the decision of the informal European Council in February 2010, and the creation of Euro Summits discussed above. Even the Fiscal Treaty, formally signed as an intergovernmental agreement between 25 EU member states outside EU law, received indirect endorsement from the March 2012 European Council conclusions, which stated that '[i]n the *margins* of the European Council the participating Member States signed the Treaty on Stability, Coordination and Governance in the EMU'.[144] The 2012 annual report of the European Council featured a photograph of the ceremony, and described the agreement on the Fiscal Treaty as one of the key achievements of the year.[145] The signing ceremony with the 25 heads and Commission president Barroso had indeed been presided over by European Council president Herman Van Rompuy.

Finally, the role of European Council conclusions as an instrument for exercising leadership is illustrated with regard to European Council deliberations located at the intersection of non-legislative and legislative decision-making. The European Council may initiate legislative activity or flank legislative decisions by reaching non-legislative consensus. Without such consensus, the implementation of specific policies may otherwise be deemed ineffective or impossible. Contrary to the European Council's pre-Maastricht role as a final arbitrator in relation to failed legislative negotiations in core areas of community decision-making, contemporary European Council involvement in the legislative process occurs most often in relation to policies that are located at the intersection of community method decision-making and policy

---

[141] See European Council (1996), annex I.
[142] See Council Decision 2000/143/CFSP on setting up the Interim Political and Security Committee, 14 February 2000.
[143] See Council Decision 2001/78/CFSP on setting up the PSC, 22 January 2001.
[144] European Council (2012c); emphasis added.   [145] See European Council (2013).

coordination. An early example of such dynamics was studied more systematically by Andrea Lenschow (2002) in relation to the field of environmental policy-making. Though environmental policy belongs to the core areas of community method decision-making, policy coordination also matters as a governance method in this area (cf. also Sabel and Zeitlin 2008). Lenschow argues that European Council intervention played a crucial role in bringing about recognition and legitimacy for the procedural framework of environmental policy integration. This framework requires actors from different fields of EU policy-making to coordinate horizontally whenever policy decisions have environmental repercussions. It can relate to law-making initiatives but is not restricted to them. Initially, this procedural principle was introduced at an administrative level within the Commission in the early 1990s through an initiative by DG Environment. However, according to Lenschow (2002: 26–7) it was only after the Cardiff European Council in June 1998 that the principle was used more effectively. The Cardiff European Council conclusions contained a set of instructions to member state authorities and the Council in accordance with the envisaged procedural framework.[146]

Another case in point is the link between core single market legislation and the wider economic governance agenda. The European Council directly oversaw the reform of the EU's legislative *acquis* in the field of financial sector supervision and regulation. In the context of the efforts to fight the consequences of the economic and financial crisis, the issue of EU financial market regulation gained sudden prominence, and the heads wanted to control the process. Though the Commission tabled the concrete proposals for new legislation, the European Council effectively controlled the timing, scope, and implementation of the reform process, and asked the Commission and the Council at various stages to act in a particular manner. European Council intervention occurred first in September 2009 following the so-called Larosière report, and later in June and September 2012.[147] The issue of financial sector regulation featured prominently in the various reform proposals developed under the leadership of Van Rompuy within the European Council on reforming EMU's institutional architecture. Decision-making on banking union followed a similar pattern to the earlier case of the Larosière report.[148] An official familiar with the dossier thought that the European Council's activism in the wake of the Commission-sponsored Larosière report was a

---

[146] See European Council (1998).

[147] See e.g. European Council (2009, 2012c) and the Commission's communication on European financial supervision, COM(2009) 252, 27 May 2009, in which the Commission formally asks the European Council to endorse the proposed legislative package.

[148] For a more detailed account on the link between new intergovernmentalism and legislative decision-making in the field of financial sector regulation and banking union see the contribution by David Howarth and Lucia Quaglia in Bickerton et al. (2015).

good example of when and why the European Council intervenes in Commission and Council decision-making:

> Larosière is a good example. This involves a delegation of competences by the member states. At the same time, there are also always cases where the European Council instructs the Council to work on topics nobody [in the Council] had expected to get. The VAT debate is the best example. I guess it was Chirac who once put this on the [Council] agenda.[149]

Another official assessed the situation similarly, and thought that the European Council closely monitored all crucial legislative activity with a view to whether individual dossiers touched on contentious political issues. The official also observed that the transition from the rotating presidency model to the elected chair model was crucial in constituting the leading role of the European Council in relation to important legislative initiatives:

> There is a difference in approach and philosophy. Van Rompuy is an advocate of a top-down approach. In this regard there is a huge change but the European Council will still leave it to the Commission to develop legislative proposals.[150]

Throughout this section it has been demonstrated how the European Council exercises leadership through its conclusions. The authoritative character of the conclusions is demonstrated by the way the Commission and the Council follow this document. In many ways the conclusions have become the central reference document for areas of EU decision-making that are governed outside the community method and policy issues that are located at the intersection of policy coordination and community method decision-making. Philipp de Schoutheete (2011) argues that the conclusions are a powerful instrument in the field of intergovernmental and community method decision-making because all EU heads and the Commission president are represented at European Council meetings. In his view this makes it very difficult for any member of the relevant administrations to ignore the conclusions. It also binds the Commission. Moreover, this section has demonstrated that the conclusions may contain quite far-reaching modifications to the EU's institutional framework.

What is then the status of the conclusions? Philipp de Schoutheete (2011: 2) aligns himself with Jacques Delors by calling the European Council conclusions an instrument of soft law. Yet this concept may not fully reveal what the conclusions are. This is not only because the concept of soft law is inherently problematic, as it seeks to tackle the question of what normative authority the conclusions have by ranking them below the level of hard law (cf. Armstrong 2011b). Seen from the perspective of deliberative intergovernmentalism, the

---

[149] Interviewee EU-07/ECON, 7 April 2009.     [150] Interviewee PR-16/GEN, 3 June 2010.

conclusions have evolved as an instrument of leadership because they reflect the active political consensus within the European Council. The above quote from the 1999 Helsinki European Council conclusions reveals this very well. As long as this is the case, the impact of the conclusions will be anything but 'soft'. This is especially true for the increasingly important practice of tasking the Council and the Commission, but it also applies to the regulation of procedural routines outside the framework of the Treaty.

Moreover, the process of adopting the conclusions should not be conflated with the dynamics of decision-making under the community method. The conclusions are based on unanimous agreement. There is no authority higher than the European Council that could enforce the conclusions against the prevailing consensus within it. This also implies that there are very few limitations to what the European Council may deal with in its conclusions. As examples of modifications to the EU's institutional framework show, there is little that can prevent the European Council from deviating from Treaty provisions as long as there is strong enough agreement among the heads.

As an instrument for exercising leadership within the EU's multi-level system, the conclusions have formalized the way the European Council relates to other institutional actors, and communicates its consensus. There is little doubt that the focus on communicating political consensus through the conclusions also implies a certain formalization of decision-making within the European Council. Finding agreement on the conclusions often determines the choreography of meetings. This may at times hamper informal debate. The diversification of the European Council's working methods, as advocated by Van Rompuy, have responded to this problem by helping to disentangle informal debate and decision-making on the conclusions. Though the conclusions may have a disciplinary effect even inside the European Council they are first and foremost an instrument for exercising leadership in respect of other EU institutions and member state administrations.

## 3.10 Conclusions

This chapter has demonstrated that the European Council is assuming a new role in EU policy-making in the post-Maastricht era. Policy-making in the new areas of EU activity relies heavily on the leadership of the European Council. Leadership is constituted by the European Council's potential to generate consensus among the EU's most senior decision-makers. This places the forum at the centre of the EU's new intergovernmentalism. Adding to earlier analysis of the occurrence of policy deliberation processes in EU governance this chapter has provided evidence that within the context of the EU's new intergovernmentalism there is 'deliberation all the way up'.[151] The salience of economic governance, foreign and security affairs and employment and social policy coordination implies that the centre of gravity in contemporary EU politics has shifted to the European Council. This new political role of the European Council goes hand-in-hand with a complex process of institutional engineering aimed at making the high-level forum adapt to new demands for consensus seeking among member states and the involved EU institutions—notably the Commission. Most importantly, this chapter has shown that reforms of the European Council's working methods have focused on improving the consensus generation capacity of the forum. Institutional change within the European Council setting is driven by the key institutional logic identified by the analytical framework of deliberative intergovernmentalism. The political ambition to govern the new areas of EU activity through coordinated action rather than autonomous supranational resources have translated into a particular institutional design. European Council activity in the post-Maastricht era have also confirmed the argument that the more elaborate the coordination framework becomes, the more high-level intervention is needed in order to ensure policy implementation within domestic arenas of governance. There is clear evidence that increasing numbers of issues are referred to the European Council for final decision-making. The European Council president and the personal offices and administrations of the heads of state or government actively draw issues into European Council decision-making and divert them away from Council formations and line ministries. Interviews with national and EU officials have shown that this trend is attributed to the salience of policy issues in domestic politics and concerns over national sovereignty. The findings in this chapter thus support interpretations of the Lisbon Treaty as not leading to a process of 'creeping intergovernmentalization' (Wessels and Traguth 2010: 311). The Lisbon Treaty as such is indeed not seen as the only major factor triggering institutional change within the European Council environment. This powerful dynamic was set in motion long before the Lisbon Treaty, in the late 1990s. Yet given this underlying dynamic the Lisbon Treaty provisions have paved the way for it to play out even more strongly, thus further emphasizing the leading role of member state governments.

The matrix of European Council decision-making drawn up at the beginning of this chapter provides the basis for understanding the relative importance of individual areas of European Council activity and allows for better distinguishing between coexisting institutional logics. Depending on whether the European Council deals with the new areas of EU activity, takes major

---

[151] The formula is owed to a comment by Kenneth Armstrong, <http://uacesoneurope. ideasoneurope.eu/2011/01/28/deliberation-all-the-way-up/> [accessed 28 April 2014].

institutional decisions, or acts as a formal decision-making forum, there are differences in what is expected from the European Council in terms of how it operates internally and what results deliberations among the heads need to produce. The matrix of European Council decision-making also allows us to distinguish more systematically between traditional spheres of European Council decision-making and those activities that have been added to the agenda only during the post-Maastricht era.[152]

The European Council undoubtedly continues to be the central forum for preparing all major institutional decisions within the EU. The Lisbon Treaty has codified this role and empowered the European Council to take some of these decisions even outside the framework of formal Treaty revisions. Moreover, the European Council selects senior EU personnel and negotiates the EU budget. This chapter, however, has demonstrated that the most substantial additions to European Council competences since the SEA have occurred in the form of additional policy-making responsibilities in the new areas of EU activity. In each field the European Council has been placed at the centre of the relevant coordination process. Though scattered across the TEU and TEC/TFEU, these provisions have defined a distinct method of decision-making outside the classic community method.

The Lisbon Treaty is widely seen as a treaty that has empowered the European Council because of the revisions it introduced to the European Council's working method. These changes are often related to enlargement and the growing complexity of EU decision-making, which in turn are believed to trigger new demands for formal leadership, as rational choice institutionalists argue. Yet this chapter has demonstrated that the Lisbon Treaty is only the latest in a series of attempts at institutional engineering. The main reason for the growing interest in the efficient functioning of the European Council is found to be the forum's changing mandate. Never before has the European Council had such wide-ranging policy-making responsibilities. The Lisbon Treaty reacted to this new reality by formally strengthening the role of the European Council and reforming central aspects of its working method. There is little doubt that a larger Union implies greater pressure on European Council logistics. However, without understanding the new political role of the European Council, the argument that a larger Union triggered more centralized decision-making routines remains superficial. Not least the fact that many Council formations—and especially those dealing primarily with legislative portfolios—escaped more radical changes to their working methods illustrates that enlargement alone cannot explain institutional change.

---

[152] Philipp de Schoutheete's 2002 review of the European Council provides a concise and pointed overview of the European Council's traditional role in European integration and governance. Cf. de Schoutheete (2002).

The changing political role of the European Council in EU policy-making can also be documented by analysing the forum's agenda. Economic governance and foreign affairs far outweigh all other European Council activities. At the time immediately prior to and during the first half of the ten-year Lisbon agenda period, employment and social affairs coordination also assumed a very prominent role. Moreover, the total time spent on fostering agreement among the heads on coordinated policy action has dramatically increased since the late 1990s. This is reflected not least in an increase in the frequency of European Council meetings over the last two decades. Though the European Council continues to fulfil its traditional function as a forum for concluding 'history-making' and 'super-systemic' decisions (Peterson 1995), dynamism in European Council activity is triggered predominantly by the constantly increasing demand for collective policy responses within the new areas of EU activity. Thus, this study shares common ground with earlier accounts of the European Council's role in EU policy-making, which emphasized that consensus-oriented decision-making within the European Council is a precondition for the integration process moving forward (Bulmer and Wessels 1987; Bulmer 1996). However, deliberative intergovernmentalism emphasizes the European Council's role in the new areas of EU decision-making in the post-Maastricht era, and stresses the link between new policy-making responsibilities and institutional change. During the time of revived single market integration in the 1980s, European Council agreement was required primarily for dealing with major institutional decisions and unlocking disagreement about pivotal legislative initiatives. Policy development and implementation, however, were left to the community method procedures and were dealt with by the Commission, the Council, and the EP (Armstrong and Bulmer 1998). Reviewing European Council agenda data from the second half of the 1990s onwards has shown that intervention to resolve legislative conflict within the Council occurs very rarely and is not a dominant activity of the forum. Moreover, when the heads do focus on legislative activity, this activity often concerns policy issues located at the intersection of coordination and community method decision-making. Deliberative intergovernmentalism thus holds that there is substantial change in European Council activity, and points to the fact that these changes can only be fully understood by juxtaposing the post-Maastricht European Council agenda with the time when European-level politics were dominated overwhelmingly by the process of single market integration under the community method.[153]

---

[153] Wessels (2008) refers to research on the headline statistics of the European Council presidency conclusions covering the period 2000–7 to demonstrate that the overall agenda composition has remained essentially stable over time. The analysis presented in this chapter suggests that the post-Maastricht agenda of the European Council was established in the second half of the 1990s, when policy coordination in the new areas of EU activity got underway in earnest.

This chapter has provided key insights into the process of constant institutional engineering and adaptation within the European Council setting, which can be traced to the late 1990s. The study of the European Council's working methods has demonstrated how much the internal organization of the forum is geared towards increasing its capacity to generate consensus over policy among the EU's top decision-makers. The review of the European Council's core working method has demonstrated that the Lisbon Treaty marks only the latest in a series of attempts at institutional engineering. Throughout the first decade of the new millennium the European Council's internal organization has become increasingly focused on face-to-face debates among the heads.

The growing importance of the European Council in policy-making has also triggered a gradual formalization of the work. These changes have included the introduction of confidential debriefing notes and more careful preparation of European Council conclusions. At the same time, the informal dimension of European Council deliberations has also been emphasized. Such a focus on informality underlines how much institutional engineering is aimed at strengthening the consensus generation potential of the forum. The exclusion of foreign ministers and delegations from the meetings, and insistence on the confidentiality principle, are the most important elements mentioned here.

It would be wrong to apply to the European Council the notion of an epistemic community because of the highly political character of the discussions among the heads. However, the interviews with senior officials familiar with European Council proceedings confirm that substantial debates over policy occur increasingly regularly within this forum and that such debates are considered vital for finding common policy responses and achieving a sustainable working consensus. The attempt to focus debates on substantial policy issues is also clear from the action taken by the European Council president Herman Van Rompuy to adjust European Council proceedings with a view to engineering policy debates. Informal European Council meetings are scheduled to provide more room for orientation debates and allow greater concentration on one or a small number of issues. Moreover, the president regularly schedules informal orientation debates during full European Council meetings, so as to allow frank discussion without the pressure to adopt conclusions.

Since the second half of the 1990s a clear trend is observable to complement regular meetings of the European Council with an increasingly large number of extraordinary and special meetings. Single-issue meeting or so-called thematic European Councils refocus attention on key policy issues. The use of such working formats is a response to demands for coordinated EU responses to unforeseen policy challenges. This practice documents greater flexibility in agenda setting. Moreover, meetings are issue-driven and the heads must often make decisions under uncertainty. These are further clear indications for the deliberative potential of European Council meetings and their role in preference formation among the EU's top decision-makers. The decision to hold all meetings at one location has allowed for further flexibility in agenda setting and made it possible to convene the forum at short notice.

With the discussion of the role of the new full-time European Council president, this chapter has added to the debate about how the Lisbon Treaty has affected the work of the European Council. The experience of the first two terms of European Council president Herman Van Rompuy shows that the main political role of the president has been to guide and organize the work of the European Council internally. The president embodies the new role of the European Council in the post-Maastricht era. Van Rompuy actively works towards engineering political agreement and improving the consensus building capacity of the European Council through a strategic development of the forum's working methods. Moreover, a key part of the president's work is focused on maintaining inter-institutional relations between the European Council and the other core EU decision-making bodies. The president has thus become a crucial actor in organizing the interplay between EU-level and member state resources, which is vital to the functioning of the decentralized governance framework. The president is also pivotal in underpinning the European Council's new role in developing and initiating policy. By coordinating member state and EU-level bureaucratic resources and decision-making processes the president enables the European Council to exercise political leadership. Finally, the position of the European Council president has so far triggered relatively little contestation on the part of member state governments. This chapter has thus challenged accounts that have expected the European Council president to focus primarily on representing the EU in the global arena or in relation to its citizens. Moreover, it has questioned rational choice institutionalist arguments that the quest for formal leadership implicit in the creation of the office of a full-time president was primarily linked to enlargement. Rather, it has emerged that the changing European Council agenda and the focus on policy-making within the new areas of EU activity have been triggered mainly by the quest for full-time leadership.

The new practice of meetings of euro-area heads within the context of the Euro Summit has again confirmed the base institutional logic identified by deliberative intergovernmentalism. The sustained intensification of economic policy coordination within the Eurogroup and the introduction of financial assistance schemes and tighter budgetary coordination in the wake of the crisis have triggered an even stronger demand for consensus generation among the euro area's most senior decision-makers. Ministers could no longer organize the necessary political support alone. The creation of the Euro Summit format has not constituted a break in the trajectory of European Council development, but rather follows from the enormous growth in European Council activity related to the economic governance portfolio. Understood as a particular European Council working method, the euro-area meetings have added to the time the heads devote to this portfolio and further pushed up the frequency of European Council meetings. So far, an open conflict between the two meeting formats has been avoided due to the fact that the same individual chairs both forums. Moreover, the Euro Summit closely mirrors European Council practice and routines.

Finally, analysis of the new role of the European Council in EU policy-making is underpinned by a discussion of the European Council conclusions as an instrument for exercising leadership. The conclusions derive their political authority from the active political consensus among Europe's most senior decision-makers. The documents do not represent enforceable contracts. Though the conclusions may also have a disciplining effect also on discussions within the European Council, they are primarily instruments for communicating the European Council's position to other actors. The transformation of the conclusions into an increasingly detailed policy document again illustrates the European Council's new role in policy-making. The European Council conclusions are also an important instrument used to stipulate informal constitutional decisions and major institutional modifications outside the context of formal treaty changes. The examples reviewed in this chapter suggest that the European Council conclusions are one of the major sources of informal institutional change in contemporary EU decision-making, next to those that are identified as being at play in the field of legislative decision-making (Farrell and Héritier 2003, 2007; Stacey 2010).

# 4

# The Council: from Law-making
# to Policy Coordination

The previous chapter demonstrated how the European Council developed into the new centre of political gravity in the context of post-Maastricht European Union (EU) politics. This assessment is somewhat at odds with established conceptualizations of the Council of the European Union ('the Council') as being the 'heart of EU decision-making' (Lewis 2013: 143). Indeed, no matter what is decided in EU politics and no matter how it is decided—whether under the community method or in the context of inter-governmental policy coordination—the issue is likely to go through the Council. This chapter does not reject the notion of the Council as the heart of EU decision-making, but argues that the traditional understanding of the centrality of Council decision-making requires qualification on several fronts. First, following the argument of the previous chapter, the functional central-ity of the Council in EU politics can no longer be understood without closely considering the relationship between the European Council's oversight role in the new areas of EU activity and Council decision-making. Second, the trad-itional role of the Council as the prime legislative institution of the Union is challenged by the fact that the European Parliament (EP) became an effective co-legislator, and that the relative importance of legislative decision-making declined in the post-Maastricht era with the rise of new intergovernmentalism. This chapter thus aims to recast the role of the Council in contemporary EU policy-making by reviewing its role in governing the new areas of EU activity. The main argument is that the organization and internal functioning of the Council are being radically transformed as the focus shifts from law-making to intergovernmental policy coordination. As outlined in chapter 2, the analytical framework of deliberative intergovernmentalism starts from the assumption that the EU's new intergovernmentalism evolves in the context of an institutional infrastructure that was previously oriented primarily towards community method decision-making. In this sense, well-known textbook descriptions of the Council as a legislative institution continue to be largely valid (e.g. Hix and Høyland 2011: 49–74). Yet the functional differentiation of different aspects of Council decision-making is increasing substantially with the rise of new intergovernmentalism. The shift in emphasis from law-making to policy coordination is not trivial. It has repercussions on how the Council operates and on which decision-making routines and practices prevail. This chapter traces the changing character of Council decision-making and the introduction of new working methods that are tailored towards consensus generation in the new areas of EU activity. The case of the Council as an institution that was shaped initially through the classic community method is particularly well suited to substantiating the argument that the new intergovernmentalism characterizes contemporary EU decision-making. This new intergovernmentalism has distinctive features and emphasizes particular decision-making practices that were not associated with earlier forms of intergovernmental decision-making under the community method or within the context of more loosely integrated settings of international cooperation. Reviewing Council activity in the context of the analytical framework of deliberative intergovernmentalism particularly challenges the rationalist literature on Council decision-making, which identifies the evolution of formal decision-making procedures as its central question (see chapter 2). This chapter argues that in the post-Maastricht era the main dynamic of institutional change is located elsewhere. During this period, legislative decision-making practices in the Council have by and large been relatively stable, even despite the adjustment of voting rules in relation to EU enlargement.

As with the European Council, the rise of new intergovernmentalism implies not only qualitative changes in Council activity but also quantitative ones. Meetings last longer and pivotal groupings of ministers meet more frequently. There is a rapid expansion of activities at the level of senior expert committees that prepare the work of the Council. The growing importance of the European Council does not actually lead to a reduction in Council activity, but rather to an overall increase in intergovernmental exchanges. Yet with the rise of new intergovernmentalism, the relationship between the two institutions has become rebalanced, in the sense that some dossiers that were previously dealt with mainly at the Council level have been increasingly influenced by European Council input. A senior official described the changing relationship between the Council and the European Council as follows:

> Thus, the process changes from bottom-up—with the Council formations coming up with proposals to the European Council—to top-down.[1]

This institutional trend is also felt within the domestic arena. Nederlof et al. (2012: 167) observe, with reference to the Netherlands, that even in political

---

[1] Interviewee EU-07/ECON, 30 March 2010.

systems that consider the prime minister as a first among equals rather than as overly powerful, 'regular cabinet ministers increasingly lose out' when it comes to European Council-related decision-making.

This chapter reviews the EU's most senior forums for policy deliberation among ministers: the Economic and Financial Affairs Council (ECOFIN), the Eurogroup, and the Foreign Affairs Council (FAC). Legally speaking the Eurogroup is not a Council formation. Yet it de facto acts as the euro-area division of the ECOFIN Council. The Employment, Social Policy, Health, and Consumer Affairs Council (EPSCO) is another important case that is analysed here. It does not meet as frequently as the three other forums but it plays a central role in the governance of the social and employment coordination portfolio. The EPSCO Council is different from the other groupings, in the sense that it is a so-called hybrid Council, populated by ministers from different government portfolios who rotate depending on the issues under discussion. Because of the existing legislative EU social policy *acquis* the EPSCO Council agenda is still dominated by legislative decision-making. The EPSCO Council therefore represents an important test case for the coexistence of policy coordination processes and legislative decision-making.

Another characteristic feature of post-Maastricht institutional change within the Council is the proliferation of dedicated expert committees, which were created specifically to support policy coordination rather than legislative decision-making. The most senior of this new group of committees are reviewed here. These committees fulfil a dual function. They prepare decision-making and policy dialogue within the relevant Council formations, and provide the institutional infrastructure for coordinating the work of member state administrations at all stages of the policy process. The sharing of decentralized administrative resources located at the level of member states and the EU is a key feature of the new intergovernmentalism. Also the European External Action Service (EEAS) is considered in this regard. Finally, this chapter turns to the changes within the general operation of the Council that were triggered by new intergovernmentalism. Here, the examples of the General Affairs Council (GAC), the rotating presidency, and the Committee of Permanent Representatives (COREPER) are discussed.

## 4.1 Reforming the Council

> First pillar issues are relatively straightforward—procedurally. Soft coordination is more complicated.[2]

The functional differentiation of Council work requires the adjustment of a range of decision-making routines. Therefore it would be wrong to analyse

---

[2] Interviewee PR-01/ECON, 4 November 2009.

the political decisions on Council reform that were taken by the end of the 1990s and in the early 2000s by focusing mainly on changes to voting procedures. Rather, these decisions addressed multiple aspects of Council decision-making. Some of these decisions require further attention as their implications cannot be fully understood without considering them more explicitly in relation to specific Council activities—notably in relation to the question of whether the Council legislates or engages in intergovernmental policy coordination.

The issue of Council reform was addressed systematically by the European Council and the GAC in a series of meetings. Background reports from the Council's Secretary General provided the basis for these discussions (cf. especially Council of the European Union 1999; Council of the European Union 2001, 2002a, 2002b). The most important steps on general Council reform were taken at the 1999 Helsinki and 2002 Seville European Councils. Moreover, the October 2002 European Council approved the much-debated list of weighted votes for Council decision-making in the enlarged Union.[3] Finally, the Lisbon Treaty incorporated and developed further some of the previous decisions on Council reform. The Council's rules of procedure were revised in 2002 and again in 2009 so as to reflect European Council guidelines and the Lisbon Treaty.[4] What is clear from the relevant European Council conclusions and the background reports is that enlargement is seen to exacerbate existing problems in the functioning of the Council. Enlargement is not considered to be the sole source of these problems. This was clearly expressed by the Helsinki European Council guidelines on Council reform:

> Reforming the functioning of the Council is an important component of the broader institutional reform process to prepare the Union for enlargement. The scale of the coming enlargements coupled with the wider scope of the Union's action could well slow the Council down, and ultimately even paralyse it. That risk is already perceptible now and represents a threat to the smooth operation of the Union, given the Council's central role in Union decision-making. Hence the need for a comprehensive review of the Council's working methods [.][5]

Next to enlargement, 'the wider scope of the Union's action' is considered to be the main reason that reform is needed. Moreover, the mobilization of consensus over policy among the EU's most senior decision-makers was conceived as the key issue for contemporary Council decision-making, as the Helsinki guidelines continued to stress in the subsequent paragraph:

---

[3] See European Council (2002), Annex I.
[4] Reference to these documents is made at various points throughout this chapter.
[5] European Council (1999a), Annex III, p. 6.

The Council must have an overview of all Union policies. For it to do so, there has to be at the heart of the system a single chain of coordination capable of ensuring that Union action is consistent with the will of its political leaders.[6]

The main issues that were identified by the Helsinki and Seville European Councils as requiring reform were the role and functioning of the GAC (see section 4.6.1) and the Council presidency (see section 4.6.2), the number and portfolios of individual Council formations, the speedy functioning of the Council as a legislator, and the transparency of Council proceedings. Moreover, both the Helsinki and Seville European Councils included a number of hands-on recommendations on conducting Council meetings more efficiently.[7]

The first case of institutional engineering considered here concerns the role of informal working formats within the Council environment. The creation of the Eurogroup as a separate forum for informal discussion, apart from the regular ECOFIN Council formation, constitutes the most radical case of institutional engineering in this regard, but also the other Council formations studied here have witnessed a sustained trend towards holding important policy debates during informal parts of the sessions, and also in the context of informal Council meetings where no formal decision-making is foreseen. It is important to notice that not all informal working formats imply that there are no decisions. In many ways the situation mirrors the one in the European Council. In areas of non-legislative decision-making the Council governs by adopting conclusions and decisions that are based in most cases on unanimous agreement. This practice requires more emphasis on substantial policy debate and consensus generation. In addition, some Council debates are deliberately designed not to encourage final agreement in order to allow orientation debates, which help participants to a better understanding of how individual ministers and their respective governments are likely to approach certain policy issues.

The Helsinki European Council conclusions of December 1999 explicitly acknowledged the growing importance of informal working formats in Council decision-making. The guidelines featured a separate paragraph on the practice of 'informal ministerial meetings'.[8] It was stipulated that informal meetings 'are designed to permit as free as possible an exchange of views on topics of general scope'. The text also stressed that these meetings 'are not Council sessions and cannot replace the Council's normal activities'. The maximum number of informal meetings per semester was restricted to five, the issuing of an 'official agenda' was explicitly forbidden, and so was preparation

---

[6] European Council (1999a), Annex III, p. 6.

[7] See European Council (1999a), Annex III and European Council (European Council 2002), Annex II.

[8] European Council (1999a), Annex III, para. 20.

for such meetings with the help of 'Council documents'. It was highlighted that no 'formal conclusions or decisions' could be finalized at such meetings. Moreover, the Helsinki conclusions restricted to two the number of 'assistants' who could accompany a minister. Though the Helsinki definition of informal meetings hardly covered the full range of informal working methods that were and are used by ministers at meetings, the very fact that the Helsinki conclusions tried to regulate this aspect of Council activity showed the increased relevance of informal working methods.

The following sections on individual Council formations show that so-called informal Council meetings, as referred to in the Helsinki conclusions, represent only one among many informal formats used within the Council environment. Also regular Council meetings feature informal gatherings such as breakfasts and lunches. Though informal meeting formats are often associated with backroom negotiations on difficult legislative issues, this chapter shows that since the end of the 1990s informal working methods have proliferated, owing especially to non-legislative decision-making. A key function of informal working methods is to allow for excluding not only the wider public but also officials, who would otherwise assist ministers during Council sessions. Informal formats instead emphasize face-to-face exchange between ministers. They typically involve the minister plus one senior advisor, or just the minister. Officials are not allowed to follow the conversations in a separate room and no minutes are circulated among member state officials or the diplomats of the Permanent Representations. Informal meeting formats limit the risks of leaks, and ministers are encouraged to conceive of discussions as an occasion for reaching direct agreement among them or for having a more open debate about alternative policy options. This is a precondition for consensus generation within the context of intergovernmental policy coordination.

Council decision-making on legislative issues under the community method requires a higher degree of formality. Decisions are final and need to be recorded. The relevant COREPER comprising ambassadors, deputy ministers, and civil servants from the capitals, who assist their superiors, attend Council meetings too. Meetings are minuted and officials follow the proceedings in the meeting room or on video screens in dedicated rooms in the Council building. Already prior to the 2004 enlargement, when the EU comprised only 15 members, over 100 people could be found in the meeting room. Enlargement exacerbated this problem dramatically.

Another key aspect of the decisions on Council reform since the late 1990s requires consideration here: the new regulations on transparency. These regulations concern also the distinction between legislative and non-legislative Council activity. Though the transparency rules were intended primarily to make Council decision-making more accessible to outside observers, they have ramifications and side effects beyond this. Most importantly, they have led to the most radical procedural distinction between legislative and non-legislative Council decision-making to date. First the Seville European Council[9] and then the Lisbon Treaty introduced new standards on transparency of legislative decision-making in the Council:

> The Council shall meet in public when it deliberates and votes on a draft legislative act. To this end, each Council meeting shall be divided into two parts, dealing respectively with deliberations on Union legislative acts and non-legislative activities.[10]

This provision effectively exempted the entire sphere of intergovernmental policy coordination from the requirement to televise debates. The 2009 version of the Council's rules of procedure explicitly exempted 'acts concerning inter-institutional or international relations or non-binding acts (such as conclusions, recommendations or resolutions)'[11] from the requirement to be debated in public. Indirectly, and perhaps unintentionally, the new rules on transparency have revealed that some of the most important Council formations spend most of the time debating non-legislative issues. Anyone who expects to be able to follow lengthy debates among finance ministers or foreign affairs chiefs on the Internet will be disappointed. The public is excluded from all substantive policy debates that take place in the Eurogroup and in the FAC and ECOFIN Council.[12]

Another aspect of reform is the decision by the 2002 Seville European Council to restrict the number of Council formations. This is generally seen as a response to growing 'inefficiency and a certain lack of coherence' (Hayes-Renshaw and Wallace 2006: 35) of the previous functional division of labour within the Council. The Lisbon Treaty itself mentions two specific configurations: the FAC and the GAC. All other Council configurations have been established by a European Council decision. The current list is based on the 2002 Seville European Council decision. It identifies a total number of ten configurations including the FAC and the GAC.[13] The discussion about the

---

[9] In 2002 the Seville European Council had already decided that some stages of the Council debates on legislative proposals, which required co-decision with the EP, would be open to the public. See European Council (2002), Annex II, section E.

[10] Article 16.8, TEU.

[11] Article 8.1, Council Decision 2009/937/EU adopting the Council's Rules of Procedure, published in OJ L325/35.

[12] The Council's rules of procedure encourage public policy debates only on the general work programme of each Council formation, regardless of whether it deals with legislative or non-legislative issues. See Article 8.3, Council Decision 2009/937/EU adopting the Council's Rules of Procedure, published in OJ L325/35.

[13] See Council decision (2009/878/EU), establishing the list of Council configurations in addition to those referred to in the second and third subparagraphs of Article 16(6) of the Treaty on European Union, 1 December 2009.

number of Council formations bears particular importance for governing the new areas of EU activity. Though a smaller number of Council configurations may suggest better horizontal coordination of neighbouring policy portfolios the example of the EPSCO Council also shows the difficulties in merging policy portfolios that are represented by different line ministries at the national level into one Council formation (see section 4.4).

## 4.2 The Eurogroup and the ECOFIN Council

The Eurogroup and the ECOFIN Council, together with the FAC, are the most senior groupings of ministers within the EU setting. Not only do they meet most frequently, they also include many of the most high-ranking members of national governments next to the heads of state or government. Political agreement among Europe's finance ministers is often a precondition for making headway in pursuing major coordination initiatives, even well beyond the sphere of fiscal policy coordination. The Maastricht Treaty assigned the ECO-FIN Council the lead role in EU economic governance. The 1997 decision of the European Council to allow the formation of a separate informal euro-area forum for policy dialogue among finance ministers—the Eurogroup—provides for a de facto modification of this arrangement. As a result ECOFIN and the Eurogroup effectively share political leadership within the economic governance portfolio with the Eurogroup having the upper hand on all euro-area-related decision-making, and ECOFIN dealing with overarching coordination topics that involve all EU member states. The Lisbon Treaty acknowledged this practice more explicitly for the first time, and made reference to the Eurogroup as a routine informal group of top euro-area decision-makers. This section discusses the ECOFIN Council and the Eurogroup as examples of two major political bodies in the context of the EU's new intergovernmentalism. It is demonstrated how the working methods of the two bodies were constantly reformed and how the idea that informal working formats are pivotal for generating political consensus among finance ministers informed the choice of particular working formats and the evolution of decision-making routines. Moreover, this section explains that similar to the European Council the Eurogroup and ECOFIN witnessed an intensification of policy coordination activity from the end of the 1990s and that these developments triggered demands for changes of the presidency regime. Similarly, the focus on the strengthening of the consensus generation capacity of the forums is considered to have been central to attempts at institutional engineering. Instead, enlargement is considered as an event exacerbating previously existing deficiencies rather than as the major rationale behind change. It is also considered how the multi-speed character of integration in the field of economic governance impacted on a key precondition for success-ful policy deliberation: equal access to policy dialogue for all concerned actors. The differentiation between euro-area and non-euro-area members certainly deserves particular attention in this regard. Finally, this section reviews the relationship between the finance ministers and the European Council from the perspective of the Eurogroup and ECOFIN.

### 4.2.1 *Working Methods: the Emphasis on Informal Policy Dialogue*

Within the Council context, the Eurogroup represents the most developed institutional infrastructure for informal policy dialogue so far. Over time the ECOFIN Council working methods have also undergone important changes. In both cases informal working formats are seen as instruments for generating political consensus among finance ministers, and complement or entirely replace the standard Council working method. Next to the desire to create a separate group of euro-area ministers, a key motivation for founding the Eurogroup was the search for a new format for regular discussions among finance ministers. For the first time the so-called minister-plus-one approach was used as the standard working method. The Eurogroup setting was designed to emphasize face-to-face discussion among finance ministers, the commissioner for economic and financial affairs, and the European Central Bank (ECB) president as the euro-area's most senior political representatives.[14] Right from the start, the Eurogroup model has represented a radical departure from previously established working formats within the Council. Meetings have been organized for ministers and their core advisors—typically deputy finance ministers—rather than delegations. All meetings have been held behind closed doors so as to enable frank exchanges of views. The frequency of Eurogroup meetings has been high from the beginning. Since the end of the 1990s the group has followed a schedule of monthly meetings. It typically meets on the night before the ECOFIN Council. The creation of the Eurogroup has thus effectively doubled the number of meetings for euro-area ministers per year, as the Eurogroup complements and does not replace the ECOFIN Council gatherings. This drastic expansion of the meeting schedule of finance ministers has coincided with the launch of the single currency. Since 2008, when the EU started to take measures against the consequences of the economic and financial crisis, the Eurogroup has often been convened for meetings more than once a month. Additional meetings have often been

---

[14] A detailed analysis of the Eurogroup's role in economic governance and its informal working method is provided by the author elsewhere (Puetter 2006). This section therefore provides only a short summary of the main features of the Eurogroup's core working method and concentrates on discussing more recent changes to the Eurogroup's working method and its role in the economic governance set-up.

called at short notice to finalize bailout decisions or to address other unforeseen crisis situations. Moreover, the Eurogroup has met before and after European Council and Euro Summit meetings to prepare decisions by the heads or to follow up on urgent implementation requests. This practice has been formally acknowledged by the Euro Summit's rules of procedures, which stipulate that the Eurogroup is 'convened within the fifteen days preceding a Euro Summit meeting'.[15] In addition, Eurogroup videoconferences have taken place to finalize agreement in urgent situations.

The intensification of policy dialogue among euro-area finance ministers following the launch of the single currency in the late 1990s has also led to longer sessions. Eurogroup meetings are known to last well into the night. In contrast to many regular Council meetings the Eurogroup takes a more flexible approach to agenda planning and the duration of individual meetings. Urgent policy issues imply that group members often cannot afford to break up meetings before a solution is found. As the Eurogroup decides by consensus, discussions regularly involve interventions from all, or at least a large number of, Eurogroup participants. The Eurogroup's former president Jean-Claude Juncker explicitly defended this approach at his last hearing in front of the EP's Economic and Monetary Committee in January 2013, arguing that it was quite appropriate to hold hour-long debates among ministers. Juncker said it was essential to hear the views of all ministers who wanted to express their opinion, as the euro was a common currency.[16] The statement revealed a particular self-conception of the Eurogroup, which had already matured during the earlier years of Eurogroup activity. Key governance procedures and coordination routines are accepted by individual ministers only insofar as they can claim ownership for them. The Eurogroup's key role in EU crisis management has represented the toughest test so far for the Eurogroup's informal working method, as it has dramatically increased the pressure on finance ministers to find agreement repeatedly within a relatively short period of time. Though Eurogroup consensus is often cumbersome, there is little evidence that during the various stages of crisis management there has ever been a risk of the discussion process being suspended. As one official explained:

> The Eurogroup worked very well in the crisis. Everything was discussed and reviewed by ministers: bailout, banking system; people pre-discussed domestic approaches.[17]

The Eurogroup's distinct institutional setting and working method clearly shows its focus on policy coordination. The group has established itself as

---

[15] See Council of the European Union (2013: 3).
[16] Agence Europe, 10 January 2013.
[17] Interviewee EU-16/ECON, 9 March 2009.

the political centre of fiscal policy coordination under the Stability and Growth Pact (SGP). Despite the fact that the SGP procedures involve formal decision-making whenever stability programmes are reviewed or official reprimands are issued, it has quickly become apparent that SGP coordination has relied essentially on an underlying working consensus established by the Eurogroup (Puetter 2004).

Moreover, Eurogroup ministers have repeatedly resisted calls for a greater formalization of Eurogroup decision-making. It has been believed that the status of the Eurogroup as a forum for informal policy coordination better reflects the decentralized character of economic governance within the context of Economic and Monetary Union (EMU).[18] Instead, modest formalization of the Eurogroup's status, rather than of its decision-making method, has been allowed. The Lisbon Treaty codified the status of the Eurogroup as the key coordination forum of the euro area by acknowledging the right of euro-area member states to establish such an institutional infrastructure (Article 137, TFEU). Yet the Lisbon Treaty avoided putting the Eurogroup on a par with the Council. The provisions concerning the Eurogroup's status and working method were specified in a separate protocol,[19] which acknowledged the need to 'develop ever-closer coordination of economic policies within the euro area', and to regulate the conditions under which 'enhanced dialogue between the member states whose currency is the euro' takes place. The protocol also acknowledged the specific format of Eurogroup meetings by stipulating that '[t]he Ministers of the Member states whose currency is the euro shall meet informally'.

However, like the European Council, the Eurogroup has been unable to avoid further formalization of its decision-making procedures, as it must reach final decisions on a number of issues, and must also communicate these decisions to other institutions, the markets, and the wider public. However, compared with the European Council and the Council formations, which are studied in this chapter, the Eurogroup has remained a highly informal institution. For example, the group has so far carefully avoided publication of a comprehensive set of conclusions or press releases. Instead, Eurogroup discussions are followed by way of a letter from the Eurogroup president, which is sent only to the ministers and provides a summary of the main points of the debate. The Eurogroup occasionally issues statements on specific issues whenever it is believed essential that financial markets or other institutional actors need to be aware of the Eurogroup consensus. The

---

[18] Cf. Puetter 2007a.

[19] Protocol No. 14 on the Euro Group, as attached to the Lisbon Treaty. The group is commonly known as the 'Eurogroup': also in EU jargon and many official communications. However, the Lisbon Treaty, the TSCG, and some of the rare Euro Summit and Eurogroup statements refer to the name Euro Group.

Eurogroup's role as the central forum for dealing with the development and implementation of crisis response measures has led to an increase in the number of statements it releases each year. This may be interpreted as a sign of a greater formalization of the Eurogroup: for example, the Eurogroup issued short statements on the conditions for financial assistance packages that were adopted during the crisis. These statements provided the basis for the release of credit tranches by the European Financial Stability Facility (EFSF) and the European Stability Mechanism (ESM).

The introduction of the office of an elected president (see section 4.5) can be seen as another step towards greater formalization, as can the upgrading of the Eurogroup's administrative infrastructure (see section 4.5.1). Also the increasingly hierarchical relationship with the European Council may not be without consequences. Commenting on Sarkozy's visit to the Eurogroup in 2007 Begg (2008: 12) warns that a more hierarchical relationship between the heads and the Eurogroup, and the prospect of further direct intervention, could prove dangerous for the working consensus established within the intimate Eurogroup setting. Hodson (2011: 38–53) argues that the formalization of the Eurogroup has impacted negatively on some of its informal qualities. Hodson investigates the trade-off between the original informal working method, which provided the biggest potential for consensus generation among Eurogroup members, and the increasing formalization of the Eurogroup's status and decision-making in relation to episodes of SGP-related decision-making between around 2005 and 2010.

The conclusions of the Euro Summit of 26 October 2011 state that the Eurogroup is responsible for the 'daily management of the euro area',[20] thus assuming that the Eurogroup executes decisions and works under the guidance of the heads of state and government. The conclusions also stressed that the Eurogroup has 'a central role in the *implementation* by the euro area Member States of the European Semester'.[21] Finally, the Eurogroup was assigned responsibility for the preparation of Euro Summits (TSCG, Article 12, para. 4), including preparation of the agenda and drafting Euro Summit statements.[22] In practice, the Eurogroup assumes a similar role in relation to meetings of the full European Council as far as the euro-area economic governance portfolio is concerned.

It remains to be seen what implications the new relationship with the European Council and the Euro Summit has for Eurogroup decision-making in the long run. The Sarkozy episode and the instances of European Council intervention in SGP-related decision-making studied by Hodson reveal the growing politicization of Eurogroup decision-making. Yet the fact that the

---

[20] Statement, Euro Summit, 26 October 2011, para. 32.     [21] Emphasis added.
[22] Euro Summit, rules of procedure, Council of the European Union (2013).

European Council and the Euro Summit enjoy by now a more institutionalized role in resolving highly political issues may also create new room for finance ministers, especially with regard to policy implementation, as they have an explicit mandate to act in a specific field. Experiences with finalizing and monitoring bailout decisions during the crisis may support such an assessment. Seen from within the Eurogroup the changing relationship with the heads does not provoke only negative reactions, as one official tried to explain:

> The Eurogroup had always good discussions but the results often did not go to the higher levels in domestic politics. The heads could make a difference on the OMC[23] issues.[24]

In 2010 Eurogroup president Jean-Claude Juncker addressed the relationship with the European Council in a letter to fellow group members. By making reference to the EU's Growth Strategy for the Decade 2011–2020 (EU2020) process, Juncker struck a more combative tone:

> Of course, the European Council will determine the overall scope and features of the EU2020 package, but I see a very strong case for the Eurogroup making its views clear, even presenting them to the President of the European Council in the same way that we have previously exchanged views with the President of the Commission on similar topics.[25]

Yet later in the letter Juncker acknowledged that the changed inter-institutional dynamics required the Eurogroup to reconsider the kind of output it produces:

> But we will need to be more aware of the onward transmission of our work and prepare ourselves accordingly. Where we are preparing positions on issues that will be discussed by the European Council, we need to ensure that we provide our contribution in a way that will best serve the discussions of the European Council.[26]

For a long time the Eurogroup had concentrated informal discussion among finance ministers. As a consequence there was an emptying out of the ECOFIN agenda as regards discussion on substantial policy issues. Interviews with senior officials reveal that ECOFIN meetings were no longer attended in full by all ministers. Many tended to leave after the morning sessions. The Euro-group was seen to be more relevant and to feature more interesting discussions, especially by those finance ministers who participated in both forums. This may not be surprising, as structurally the EU's economic governance architecture is clearly centred on euro-area decision-making. However, it would be wrong to ignore the relevance of the ECOFIN Council as a key player

---

[23] Open method of coordination.     [24] Interviewee EU-09/ECON, 4 July 2011.
[25] Juncker 2010: 4.     [26] Juncker 2010: 7.

within the EU's new intergovernmentalism. Despite the fact that the Eurogroup took charge of major parts of the fiscal policy coordination agenda under the SGP, the proliferation of coordination processes in the field of socio-economic governance in the late 1990s and the eventual launch of the Lisbon agenda gave ECOFIN a prominent role in relation to all overarching coordination topics, which were meant to involve all EU member states and not just the euro area. More recently, the EU2020 framework confirmed this role of the ECOFIN Council. This means that despite the emergence of the Eurogroup, ECOFIN Council engagement in intergovernmental policy coordination procedures has expanded ever since the late 1990s. Indeed, other key actors within the socio-economic governance portfolio conceive of ECOFIN as the dominant political institution in this area (see section 4.4.2). A decline in focus on ECOFIN debates among finance ministers thus threatens the viability of an overarching EU coordination agenda that goes beyond macroeconomic stabilization within the euro area.

The ECOFIN Council has indeed become subject to institutional engineering, so as to make it a more attractive forum for substantial policy deliberation among all EU finance ministers. The 2004 enlargement again increased pressure for reform dramatically. Yet the discussion of the Eurogroup above shows that problems with the original ECOFIN working method were revealed at a much earlier stage. At an informal ECOFIN meeting in Vienna in April 2006 ministers concluded that an improvement of ECOFIN working methods would be necessary in order to make policy coordination more effective and efficient. These improvements were targeted at facilitating debate on 'strategic issues, promoting exchange of views on best practices and benchmarks, and ensuring better guidance for Member States' reform priorities'.[27] An official was quoted saying that the 'main reason for considering reform is to try to make the ECOFIN Council meetings more attractive; if nothing is done ministers will stop attending and start just sending top officials'.[28] Officials also reported the use of unconventional measures, such as changing the locks of the meeting room and issuing passes to participants so as to avoid unauthorized access to the meetings. The measures were said to have lowered the number of officials attending the meeting to close to 150, down from 200.[29]

The reform of working methods was discussed again at an informal ECOFIN in Helsinki in September 2006 and new guidelines were adopted at the next regular ECOFIN meeting in October the same year. The ECOFIN conclusions stated that ministers would be 'accompanied by a delegation of 3 persons in

---

[27] Press release published by the Austrian Council Presidency on the results of the informal ECOFIN meeting, Vienna, 7–8 April 2006, <http://www.eu2006.at/en/News/information/0804InformalECOFIN.html> [accessed 23 August 2011].

[28] As quoted in *European Voice*, 'Ministers bid to spice up rigid Ecofin meetings', 16 March 2006.

[29] *European Voice*, 'Ministers bid to spice up rigid Ecofin meetings', 16 March 2006.

the meeting room'. Moreover, it was said 'that the Presidency may reflect on possibilities to ensure confidential deliberation in the context of the Ecofin Council'.[30] This made it possible for the presidency to move items to the informal parts of the meeting—typically the breakfasts and lunches—more easily. Informal parts of ECOFIN meetings are usually restricted to ministers and deputy ministers and thus resemble the minister-plus approach of the Eurogroup. Usually, no notes are circulated on the informal parts of the meetings, and internal debriefings are rare. As seen in the case of the Eurogroup, ministers tend to prefer this environment, as they are less afraid of leaks. This is seen as a key precondition for having more open debates in which individual participants are more open to changing their views on particular policy issues.

Another innovation has been the change in the seating order in the ECOFIN meeting room. Ministers sit face-to-face in an inner circle in the centre of the room. The delegations are seated around them. It is reported by interviewees attending the meetings that ministers are quite involved in negotiating detail directly among themselves, often one word at a time, in both the formal and informal parts of ECOFIN meetings. It is, however, clear that ministers would not engage in such exchanges in the public parts of the meetings, which are televised.[31] Another important change concerns ECOFIN's language regime. Though there is no formal requirement to speak only one language, and interpretation services are provided during ECOFIN meetings, there is evidence that the use of English as the main working language has become common practice. This experience is also shared with the Eurogroup, which witnessed a similar development earlier. The use of a single working language is a key factor enabling face-to-face debate.—As one participant in the meetings explained:

> English is becoming more and more the only language. Whenever you want to say something serious you better do this in English. [...] The breakthrough came with Lagarde, who was a very eloquent president. She stopped using French and this was important and underlined the changed approach.[32]

The same official believed that ECOFIN is increasingly witnessing substantial debates over policy, which requires ministers to adjust their behaviour.[33] The official also thought that other Council formations have a weaker stand in many political debates because their members cannot base their arguments on economic grounds:

---

[30] Council of the European Union, press release 2,753rd Council meeting, Economic and Financial Affairs, Luxembourg, 10 October 2006, p. 13.

[31] Interviewee MS-05/ECON, 9 December 2009.

[32] Interviewee MS-05/ECON, 9 December 2009. The then French finance minister Christine Lagarde chaired the ECOFIN Council during the 2008 French Council presidency.

[33] This view is echoed by others; Interviewee MS-10/ECON.

I always tell my ministers you can win an argument in ECOFIN based on economic arguments but don't just present figures; it is a much more political process.[34]

The first two years of EU reactions to the global economic and financial crisis in particular provide an example of how the intensification of EU-wide economic policy coordination have translated into specific ECOFIN working practices. Crisis coordination gave a boost to the informal ECOFIN breakfast as the key venue for EU-27 policy coordination.

Since the beginning of the crisis [ECOFIN] ministers have become much more active. The interest in joint discussions has dramatically increased. This in particular concerns debates which focus on an exchange of views and the discussion of options—rather than on arriving at formal conclusions. People talk about banks, the implications of the crisis, Larosière and so on.[35]

A year further into the crisis the same official still believed that he 'never saw such interactive debates in ECOFIN as during the crisis'.[36] Another official commented on the informal ECOFIN discussions by highlighting that just before the EU started to respond to the crisis ministers became increasingly eager to engage with colleagues so as to find answers to the new situation, as they were unclear about appropriate policy responses: '[i]n autumn 2008 there was so much uncertainty'.[37] Yet another official thought that ECOFIN discussions went so well during the early stages of the crisis that the forum managed to reclaim ground somewhat in relation to the Eurogroup, which later became the centre of crisis management again:

The crisis changed the importance of ECOFIN compared to the Eurogroup. It changed from one day to the next.[38]

The expansion of the informal ECOFIN breakfast agenda and the allocation of more time to this particular meeting format started with the Czech presidency of the Council in the first half of 2009. The informal meetings were also used by the president of the Eurogroup to brief all EU finance ministers of euro-area discussions. In addition, the commissioner for economic and financial affairs and the ECB president provided ministers with comprehensive briefs.[39] During the crisis the informal meetings developed into the main forum of G20 coordination and became an important location for discussing crisis response options and country-specific information.

---

[34] Interviewee MS-05/ECON, 9 December 2009.
[35] Interviewee EU-07/ECON, 7 April 2009.
[36] Interviewee EU-07/ECON, 30 March 2010.
[37] Interviewee PR-11/ECON, 5 November 2009.
[38] Interviewee EU-04/ECON, 12 November 2009.
[39] Interviewee EU-17/ECON, 12 March 2009.

Particularly during the first years of the crisis, the informal breakfasts proved to be a format for involving all EU member states in policy dialogue on economic governance issues. The early cases of banking resolution, which affected countries both inside and outside the euro area, as well as the fact that the United Kingdom, as a non-euro-area member state, held the G20 presidency in 2009, facilitated a constructive attitude towards the discussion process:[40]

> Sometimes the breakfast lasted for three hours while the normal ECOFIN was only one hour. What was also new was that they were really negotiating about language [for common positions].[41]

Another diplomat thought that the move to vitalize the ECOFIN breakfast was crucial in coordinating all EU member states, rather than just those in the euro area, back onto the economic governance agenda:

> ECOFIN wasn't engaging in any meaningful surveillance anymore. But the Eurogroup is doing this very intensively and we need this for the whole EU. In particular, in times of crisis people need to understand the economic situation in the entire EU—not only in the euro area. People were not happy with this. Again Sweden was leading the way. In 2007, therefore, the ECOFIN breakfast was created in response to a growing demand for an open and frank exchange about the economic situation. Then a lot of other sensitive issues were put on the breakfast agenda.[42]

### 4.2.2 The Presidency Regime

The Eurogroup was the first group of EU ministers to be chaired by an elected president. The Eurogroup moved unilaterally to create the position of an elected president in September 2004.[43] The position was filled for the first time in January 2005 by Luxembourg's prime minister and finance minister Jean-Claude Juncker, who remained in office until January 2013. Like the European Council president, the Eurogroup chair is elected for a period of two-and-a-half years.[44] Another parallel with the European Council setting is that the office of Eurogroup president was initially associated mainly with its external representation function. Such a view was fuelled by the infamous spat between the Belgian Eurogroup president Didier Reynders, who held the rotating Eurogroup presidency throughout one full year in 2001 and the ECB president Wim Duisenberg—each of them claiming the title of 'Mr Euro'. In fact, the Eurogroup president plays a very important role in the internal functioning of the group. As one official explained:

---

[40] For a review of the results of EU-level G20 coordination see Hodson (2011).
[41] Interviewee EU-04/ECON, 12 November 2009.
[42] Interviewee PR-02/ECON, 3 November 2009.   [43] Cf. Puetter (2006: 82).
[44] Protocol No. 14 on the Euro Group, Article 2, as attached to the Lisbon Treaty.

The presidency question is less important to how we are perceived outside Europe but it has an effect on internal processes. [...] As we are into the crisis we don't have a problem with the spokesperson. Almunia [then commissioner for economic and financial affairs] does his job very well. That helps a lot. The presidency of ECOFIN and the Eurogroup does matter so much for the internal processes. The Eurogroup [example] shows that a longer mandate can calm the process and increase the consistency of the work.[45]

The job of the Eurogroup president shares many features with that of the European Council president. Because of the Eurogroup's informal working method the role of the president as someone who summarizes the group consensus and can remind group members of the results of previous discussions is particularly important. Moreover, acceptance of the person chairing the Eurogroup by its members is considered an important factor. As another official explained:

Since Juncker took over the Eurogroup [presidency] it has really improved a lot. It is just much, much better, you can see it in the summaries and conclusions. He is just very effective in pulling people together. He can pull consensus together and ensure consistency.[46]

The same official also detected that the permanent presidency arrangement had led to an improvement in the preparation of Eurogroup meetings and also helped to maintain the group spirit among the ministers during crisis situations. Juncker himself described the role of the Eurogroup president as someone who reminds members to commit themselves to acting in the interest of the euro area. In a letter to his colleagues in 2010 he stated:

I will be asking of each of you a clear indication of that commitment, to work together in the Eurogroup to support the interests of the eurozone, and to carry that eurozone interest into discussions with our global partners. I will also be asking you to consider the impact of your domestic policies on all of us within the eurozone. I will be asking you to provide support to each other through our peer review processes and, where necessary, to help each other to take the hard political decisions required in the difficult economic circumstances that we face.[47]

Unlike the European Council president and the High Representative (HR) as chair of the FAC, the Eurogroup president is not a full-time president but selected from within the current Eurogroup membership. The transition in the Eurogroup presidency in 2013 from Juncker to the Dutch finance minister Jeroen Dijseelbloem revealed how difficult it has become to uphold this model given the drastically increased workload of the Eurogroup. Speaking at a press conference following the 14 December 2012 European Council meeting,

[45] Interviewee EU-07/ECON, 7 April 2009.
[46] Interviewee EU-16/ECON, 9 March 2009.
[47] Juncker 2010: 2.

Juncker himself pointed to this problem as an important issue behind the discussion about the future Eurogroup president. Juncker doubted that prime ministers or finance ministers of larger member states would be able to reconcile their commitment as chair of the Eurogroup with their domestic engagements. At the same time, Juncker argued, larger member states command more powerful administrations, which can give support to the office-holder more effectively than was possible for his home administration in Luxembourg.[48] In a similar vein, another member of the European Council who was tipped to be the next Eurogroup president, the Finish prime minister Jyrki Katainen, rejected the idea of holding the office of Eurogroup president as being unrealistic.[49] Despite the fact that the Eurogroup's second president was not appointed as a full-time president, this option was at no point off the table. Following a Euro Summit statement in October 2011 the creation of the position of a full-time president was possible in principle. Moreover, the Eurogroup president no longer needs to be selected from the group of current euro-area finance ministers but can be also picked from outside this group.[50] For example, less than half a year after Dijseelbloem's appointment, French president Hollande and German chancellor Merkel proposed the transition to a full-time presidency for the Eurogroup.[51]

The mention of Katainen's name during the search for a suitable successor for Juncker illustrates another critical feature of the Eurogroup presidency. The Eurogroup president needs to have close ties with the European Council. As prime minister of Luxembourg, Juncker was automatically a member of the European Council. Though no rule existed that the Eurogroup president would attend European Council meetings, Juncker de facto played a similar role in the European Council as the HR plays as chair of the FAC. The leading role of the European Council in key policy coordination portfolios and the importance of the FAC and the Eurogroup for European Council preparation suggested that in the future the Eurogroup president would at least be invited to attend parts of European Council meetings. The provisions on Euro Summit meetings explicitly foresee the participation of the Eurogroup president.[52]

In contrast to the Eurogroup and the FAC, the ECOFIN Council is still chaired by a rotating Council presidency. An initiative of France and Germany during the Convention process to include ECOFIN in the group of bodies

---

[48] Agence Europe, 14 December 2012.    [49] Agence Europe, 13 December 2012.

[50] Statement, Euro Summit, 26 October 2011, Annex I, para. 5.

[51] The idea was first floated by Hollande as part of a statement on France's vision for EU development in mid-May 2013 (Agence Europe, 17 May 2013). It was then endorsed by the French president and the German chancellor in a joint press statement, which was issued at a meeting between the two heads in Paris at the end of May 2013. See Bundesregierung (2013: 9).

[52] See TSCG, Article 12, para. 4. The 2013 Euro Summit rules of procedures stipulate that the Eurogroup president 'may be invited to attend' (Council of the European Union (2013: 4)). In practice the Eurogroup president always attends Euro Summit meetings.

chaired by an elected president failed to find sufficient support (Bunse et al. 2005). The idea of a more stable presidency regime for ECOFIN, however, still circulates among practitioners involved with ECOFIN affairs. The arguments levelled in favour of such an arrangement converge with statements made in relation to the Eurogroup presidency. One official, for example, thought that the position of the ECOFIN president was becoming increasingly complex and required great familiarity with the dossier, which was very difficult to achieve in the context of the rotating presidency regime:

> For ECOFIN a longer presidency would be a good thing. [ . . . ] The chair needs to become familiar with an enormous amount of legal and procedural issues. At the same time he or she gets a huge amount of requests from the member states and the ECB onto the table. That you have to digest, while at the same dealing with your own domestic politics issues, which are actually far more important to you.[53]

The official estimated that a period of two months is usually required before the minister in the chair feels fully comfortable with the process. Several interviewees believed that the presidency was a crucial factor influencing the quality and conduct of ECOFIN debates, and thought that the right president could make a difference. For example, reference to the personal leadership style and the expertise of the Swedish finance minister Andras Borg was made to illustrate this point.[54] However, the issue of a permanent ECOFIN president is also seen as a potential source of conflict between euro-area and non-euro-area countries. Whereas for euro-area members it is difficult to imagine a permanent ECOFIN president coming from a non-euro-area country, there is suspicion among those from the latter group of countries that a permanent ECOFIN presidency would be just another attempt to reinforce the prerogatives of euro-area members.[55]

### 4.2.3 *Enlargement and Multi-speed Integration*

The analysis has so far demonstrated the link between a changing decision-making environment within the Council and the rise of new working methods that put greater emphasis on consensus generation processes and routinized informal policy dialogue rather than formal procedures designed to structure and regulate legislative decision-making. The main rationale for Eurogroup and ECOFIN Council reform is a changing decision-making agenda. Enlargement has exacerbated previously existing deficiencies within the economic policy coordination set-up, but did not cause them in the first

---

[53] Interviewee EU-07/ECON, 7 April 2009.
[54] Interviewee EU-04/ECON, 12 November 2009.
[55] Interviewee MS-05/ECON, 9 December 2009.

place. However, the question of how the increase in EU membership impacts on core decision-making routines, which are identified by deliberative inter-governmentalism as central elements of the EU's post-Maastricht institutional infrastructure, deserves particular attention, as does the multi-speed character of EMU integration. There are indeed a number of issues that can be linked specifically to enlargement, though the changes in voting rights and the threat of deadlock in Council decision-making are not among them. The impact of enlargement has been most strongly felt in ECOFIN. Even informal debates, in which the most restrictive participation regime applies, may cause simple logistical problems. As one official explained with regard to the informal ECOFIN breakfast discussions:

> We plan a table round to take 2½ hours. This defines certain limits. The patience of ministers then is the problem. Everyone likes to speak, in particular if they know the topic well, but often they lack the patience to follow what the other 26 have to say.[56]

Another official elaborated on the impact of enlargement on the ECOFIN Council by saying:

> It depends on whether we vote or decide with consensus. For voting not much has changed but for consensus [decisions] it is more difficult because of the group size. Before enlargement you had ministers who were used to speaking up. Now, many new colleagues keep silent.[57]

A slightly different perspective is adopted by a diplomat from one of the new EU member states who believed with reference to the ECOFIN breakfasts that participation levels were improving but highlighted that friction between the EU-wide and exclusive euro-area coordination agendas gave rise to new frustrations among ECOFIN participants, especially from the new member states:

> There is currently a lot of frustration in ECOFIN with the coordination during the crisis. For example, we had clear agreement that we collectively coordinate the position for the G20 meeting in London, all 27 member states, but this is not really happening. There is then a special summit in Berlin with only the big three and some other EU member states present. There is not enough discussion in ECOFIN about this and we are presented there with what others have already concluded.[58]

The same official echoed other interviewees by praising the Swedish finance minister Andras Borg as one of the key figures within ECOFIN who could integrate the group and advocate a credible EU-wide coordination agenda:

---

[56] Interviewee EU-07/ECON, 7 April 2009.
[57] Interviewee EU-04/ECON, 12 November 2009.
[58] Interviewee PR-02/ECON, 3 November 2009.

The Swedish minister has become one of the most important advocates in ECOFIN for better EU-27 discussion and reminds colleagues regularly that there needs to be more open and transparent coordination within the Council.

During the 2010 Swedish Council presidency Borg, as president of ECOFIN, even tried to accommodate growing concerns within the euro area that the crisis would require the creation of a financial assistance mechanism within the EU-wide coordination agenda.[59] Borg was well aware that the growing focus on bailout scenarios had the potential to deepen the rift further between euro-area and non-euro member states.[60] Even before EU crisis management started to focus on financial assistance measures, officials familiar with the ECOFIN dossier were concerned about the prospect of expanding EU-wide coordination. One official expressed his/her main concern quite bluntly:

The British are just completely anti-euro area! They don't care at all. [...] The British opposition is also leading to a complete blockage of meaningful EU-27 cooperation. [...] Sweden and Denmark are frustrated. Both countries are doing everything the euro area is doing.[61]

The above comments reveal the obstacles in the way of EU-wide coordination. Denmark and Sweden are generally eager to expand economic policy coordination through the same mechanisms as the euro-area countries, yet the two member states do not aim to become part of the euro area in the foreseeable future. For many new member states that share an interest in intensified coordination the current situation is even more disappointing in the sense that they especially suffer from the attitude of the euro-area countries that consider the Eurogroup as the main venue for substantial policy debate. Ministers feel excluded from key debates despite the positive experiences with the ECOFIN breakfast format. Moreover, institutional decisions on euro-area governance affect new members as soon as they have joined the euro area. The Polish finance minister Jacek Rostowski, whom many interviewees described as a leading contributor to informal ECOFIN debates, became an outspoken critique of the current situation and demanded an opening-up of the Eurogroup. At the beginning of the Polish Council presidency in July 2011 a public controversy erupted about the participation of non-euro-area member states in the Eurogroup. The Polish presidency argued that holding this office required being informed about Eurogroup proceedings. Rostowski and the Polish prime minister Donald Tusk made it clear that they did not share the Eurogroup's approach of excluding others. Neither

---

[59] The financial assistance instruments EFSF and ESM were created as funds for the euro-area countries, and do not provide EU-wide financial support.
[60] Andras Borg, letter published by *Financial Times*, online edition, 16 November 2010.
[61] Interviewee EU-16/ECON, 9 March 2009.

concealed in public that they had clashed on this issue with Eurogroup members.[62] Eurogroup president Juncker allegedly responded to the wave of criticism by sending an invitation to Rostowski to take part—in his function as ECOFIN president—in the first Eurogroup meeting under the Polish Council presidency on 11 July 2011. Speaking in Warsaw on the first day of the Polish presidency prime minister Tusk even made a public statement on the matter:

> I respect that the Eurogroup can hold its own autonomous meetings. However, the Polish minister—as a representative of the presidency—will be present at those meetings, for informational reasons[.] He should be up to date and aware of the discussions in the Eurogroup.[63]

Finally, on the day of the July Eurogroup meeting Rostowski declared that he had decided against taking part in the gathering, as such a step would have been controversial. Nevertheless it is reported that the Polish finance minister was allowed to follow parts of an irregular Eurogroup telephone conference on Saturday, 2 July 2011.[64] The Polish government again raised the issue of getting access to euro-area policy dialogue in connection with negotiations about the Fiscal Treaty. It threatened to block agreement if there was no opening-up of euro-area debates related to the institutional architecture of EMU and general economic reform. A clause included in the Fiscal Treaty required at least one session per year of the Euro Summit to be devoted to discussion among all signatory states, i.e. all EU member states minus the Czech Republic and the United Kingdom. The Fiscal Treaty also stipulated that non-euro-area member states always take part in meetings that focus on the competitiveness of the EU and on the institutional architecture of the euro area (TSCG, Article 12, para. 3). Interestingly, the discussion showed that arguments for separating Euro Summit and European Council discussions, as much as those of Eurogroup and ECOFIN Council, are somewhat limited when it comes to discussing initiatives for wider reform. The drop in the number of Euro Summit meetings in 2012 and 2013 to just one per year may speak to this point. The negotiation of the Fiscal Treaty and coordination experiences in ECOFIN however also showed that the strained relations between the United Kingdom and most of the rest of the EU member states were a key obstacle in defining more agreeable institutional arrangements for policy dialogue between euro-area and non-euro-area countries.

---

[62] Agence Europe, *Bulletin Quotidien Europe*, 4 July 2011.
[63] As quoted by the *European Voice*, 7 July 2011.
[64] As reported by EUobserver.com, 3 July 2011, <http://euobserver.com/19/32581> [accessed on 18 July 2011]. Formally it is within the sole competence of ECOFIN to deal with legislative decisions as required for the six-pack. However, in practice the Eurogroup agrees most of these decisions in advance.

## 4.3 The Foreign Affairs Council

EU foreign ministers traditionally belong to the group of top-level government representatives who meet most frequently for common discussions
within the Council. Moreover, like the finance ministers in the ECOFIN
Council and the Eurogroup who saw EMU-related economic policy coordination as their dominant portfolio, EU foreign ministers dramatically expanded
their policy coordination agenda with the rise of the Common Foreign and
Security Policy (CFSP). Foreign ministers were assigned a central role in CFSP
decision-making at Maastricht, Amsterdam, and again by the Lisbon Treaty.
Despite the EU's earlier attempts to engage in closer coordination under the
European Political Cooperation (EPC) framework, the depth and scope of
CFSP decision-making is without precedent, and this is reflected in the agenda
of ministers' EU-level meetings. Repercussions on the institutional infrastructure, which have been triggered by this enhanced focus on foreign and security policy coordination, are much less trivial than an outside observer might
assume. Though one would generally expect the prime role of foreign affairs
ministers to be dealing with foreign and security policy issues, the process of
EU integration as such has long constituted a major (and for some perhaps *the*
major) activity of EU foreign ministers. The member states' chief diplomats
have traditionally played a crucial role in coordinating and overseeing general
EU activity. They have been involved in negotiating major treaty changes, and
they have taken an active role in paving the way for EU enlargement, in
resolving decision-making deadlock, and in assisting the meetings of the
heads within the European Council. In other words, the explicit focus on
policy coordination within their own core domain of decision-making is a
rather recent activity of EU foreign ministers and this activity has inevitably
implied a reorganization of working procedures and methods.[65]

### 4.3.1 *Refocusing the Agenda*

The pre-Maastricht role of EU foreign ministers as general coordinators of
Council decision-making and integration politics was reflected in the original
name of their Council formation: the GAC. Indeed, with the rise of CFSP as
a new area of EU activity this role changed significantly. Preoccupation with
CFSP issues is said to have impacted negatively on the foreign ministers'
classic role as coordinators of general EU affairs from the mid-1990s (Hayes-

---

[65] Obviously, foreign ministers were pivotal to the functioning of the EPC framework as the
predecessor of the CFSP. Yet both the absolute and relative importance of the foreign and security
policy coordination portfolio has increased considerably with the Maastricht Treaty and the
succeeding treaties.

Renshaw and Wallace 2006: 36–7). These developments coincided with the launch of the Eurogroup and the restructuring of the ECOFIN agenda, which was discussed in the preceding section. As with economic governance the new responsibilities of foreign ministers under the CFSP framework added to the existing workload and overburdened the Council's agenda. Foreign policy coordination consumed most of the time during meetings (Hayes-Renshaw and Wallace 2006: 36–37), rather than the topics falling under the traditional catalogue of GAC responsibilities. The new policy coordination responsibilities required adapting to a new reality. The task of assessing the EU's external relations, the overall foreign policy situation, and the coordination of relevant policy action dominated Council meetings. This difference in thematic focus was addressed with the first major reform of the GAC in 2002.[66] From then on the ministers convened under the new umbrella of the General Affairs and External Relations Council (GAERC). The related 2002 update of the Council's rules of procedure emphasized that GAERC covered 'two main areas of activity, for which it shall hold separate meetings, with separate agendas and possibly on different dates'.[67] EU external action including CFSP and CSDP (Common Security and Defence Policy) coordination was identified as a distinct activity. The first meeting which was organized according to the new GAERC structure took place in July 2002. Starting with the next meeting in September 2002 the practice of splitting the two thematic areas of GAERC activity into two consecutive meetings was established. These meetings in most cases took place on the same day but, in procedural terms, were treated as distinct events with press releases and Council conclusions adopted separately at each meeting—one set under the heading 'External Relations' and the other under 'General Affairs'. The splitting up of GAERC ran somewhat counter to another reform decision included in the Seville package, namely the reduction of the overall number of Council configurations. Though GAERC was formally considered to constitute one Council formation it de facto presented a case of functional differentiation. Moreover, despite the fact that the same minister would in most cases represent her or his country at both meetings, the split of the meeting agendas followed a similar logic as the split of Eurogroup and ECOFIN meetings, which are both attended by the same ministers but follow different agendas.[68]

The Lisbon Treaty codifies this de facto separation of foreign affairs and general affairs portfolios, and constitutes the two meeting formats as two

---

[66] The decision was part of the reform package adopted by the Seville European Council. See section 4.1.

[67] See Article 2.2, Council Decision 2002/682/EC adopting the Council's Rules of Procedure, published in OJ L230/7.

[68] This obviously only applies to finance ministers from the euro-area countries. Finance ministers of non-euro-area countries participate only in the ECOFIN Council meetings.

distinct Council formations. The two formations are also the only two Council configurations that are explicitly referred to in the core text of the Treaty. Moreover, the Lisbon Treaty renames the external affairs meetings and assigns the term 'Foreign Affairs Council' to gatherings of foreign ministers dealing with CFSP and CSDP issues (Article 16, TEU). The decision to constitute the FAC as a distinct decision-making structure for policy coordination again parallels the case of the Eurogroup, which was also recognized as a distinct institutional environment by the Lisbon Treaty.[69]

The CSDP portfolio of the FAC is co-managed by ministers of defence. Defence ministers also meet under the umbrella of the FAC and they normally do so once every semester. There are dedicated sessions for discussions among defence ministers that are not attended by foreign affairs chiefs. The sessions are normally scheduled to take place on the same day. For example, on 19 November 2012 the FAC's 3,199th session took place under the heading 'foreign affairs/defence'. It involved a meeting of defence ministers before lunch and one of foreign affairs chiefs in the afternoon.[70] Both sessions were chaired by the HR Catherine Ashton. Among the instruments to encourage horizontal coordination between the two groups of ministers are joint informal working lunches. For example, at the November 2012 meeting the lunch was used to discuss the case of Mali, including plans for an EU military training mission.[71] Horizontal coordination of policy fields, which are each governed through coordination, is a peculiarity of the CFSP and CSDP portfolios. It bears some resemblance to experiences within the EPSCO Council setting, which also comprises representatives from different line ministries under the umbrella of one Council formation (see section 4.4). Next to the defence portfolio, the FAC also currently comprises two additional portfolios relating to policy areas that deviate from the policy coordination logic of the CFSP and CSDP portfolios and involve ministers from other line ministries. One meeting per semester deals with development cooperation issues. Typically this meeting is organized like the meetings of foreign affairs and defence ministers described above. It features two distinct sessions for each group of ministers. Both sessions are chaired by the HR.

The trade policy portfolio follows a rather different pattern. Though it formally features under the FAC framework it remains functionally separated from the other activities of this Council formation. The semester meetings of

---

[69] The main difference between the FAC and the Eurogroup in this regard is that the FAC is constituted as a separate body in the core Treaty text, while the status of the Eurogroup is detailed by a Treaty protocol.

[70] See Council, press release PRE 059/12, Brussels, 15 November 2012.

[71] See press release by the Cypriot Council presidency, 19 November 2012, <http://www.mfa.gov.cy/mfa/mfa2006.nsf/All/C75B5BF2B8DB67DFC2257ABB00365A4E?OpenDocument> [accessed 6 May 2013].

trade ministers are chaired by the rotating presidency, and not the HR. They do not typically take place on the same day as the meetings of ministers of foreign affairs. Moreover, the trade dossier differs markedly from the other dossiers as it is operated under the community method. It involves legislative decision-making as well as the delegation of negotiation powers to the Commission.

Despite this institutional diversity the new FAC regime implies a clear lead role for foreign ministers. The chief diplomats are those who carry overall political responsibility for major foreign affairs decisions and convene most often—on a monthly basis, on average. This enables them to develop a coordination routine. The evolution of a distinct CFSP-related coordination infrastructure with the FAC at its centre is indeed seen by many interviewees as a crucial step in developing EU foreign and security policy. Yet some interviewees also flagged differences between coordination practices within the Eurogroup and FAC settings. Eurogroup finance ministers were seen as having been more successful in developing common positions on important policy issues. For example, one member state official with longstanding experience in EU foreign policy coordination believed:

> The routinization of the process has not yet led to a working consensus but agreement can be reached much quicker now than in the past. This is the main advantage of permanent forums [for coordination]—there is a much better understanding of differences.[72]

And a diplomat from one of the Permanent Representations explained why in his/her view the FAC did not yet achieve the same standing as the Eurogroup as regards its role as a shaper of the coordination process:

> Foreign ministers tend to be much less EU-centric in their thinking than finance ministers—it is very difficult to predict what they will do.[73]

And yet another official with close familiarity with the FAC dossier explained that generating personal commitment on the part of ministers was the main goal of collective discussions:

> Collective discipline is quite important [in the post-Lisbon foreign policy regime]. Ministers need to feel confident that they can rely on each other.[74]

### 4.3.2 Working Methods: Participation Regime and Gymnich Meetings

The working methods used for meetings of foreign ministers reflect the refocusing of the decision-making agenda. As observed in the case of the

---

[72] Interviewee MS-14/EXT, 30 June 2009.   [73] Interviewee PR-03/EXT, 12 March 2009.
[74] Interviewee, EU-24/EXT, 17 November 2011.

ECOFIN Council, institutional engineering both targeted the core working method applied to formal meetings, and aimed to create more room for informal debate about key issues concerning CFSP and CSDP coordination processes. Yet some of these changes occurred only after some delay. After the transformation of the old GAC into the GAERC format, GAERC external affairs meetings continued to apply the conventional structure of Council meetings with delegations. The inner table was made up of the foreign ministers and their deputies. In addition other delegation members took seats at an outer table. This practice continued after the 2004 enlargement. Not until the introduction of the new FAC format by the Lisbon Treaty at the end of 2009 was the seating order changed to include only the ministers around the inner table. Deputies were placed around the outside. Compared with before, the total number of participants populating the meeting room was brought down by this arrangement. Still the number of people with access to the meeting room is considerably higher than for Eurogroup meetings or the informal ECOFIN breakfasts. The most frequently used format for restricted informal face-to-face discussion among ministers on key foreign affairs developments are the lunches, but these lunches are also used to confer with other ministers, as the above example of the joint lunch with the defence ministers showed. This somewhat limits the potential for more routinization when compared to the Eurogroup context and ECOFIN breakfasts and lunches. Moreover, due to the way FAC meetings are organized there is less room for slippages in the schedule. For example, whenever foreign affairs ministers convene on the same day as development ministers or defence ministers, the proceedings are structured as two predefined meeting blocks that can overlap.

Another important venue for informal discussion among EU foreign ministers are the so-called Gymnich meetings, which were first introduced in 1974, and were named after the location of the first meeting—the Gymnich Castle. The Gymnich format has received increasing attention in connection with the development of the CFSP and CSDP coordination agenda. Gymnich meetings stretch over half a day or a full day, and are reserved for open discussion on important items on the coordination agenda. The Gymnich format explicitly does not aim to reach formal conclusions. A senior foreign ministry official from a member state underlined that ministers were aware of the difference working formats can make in the CFSP context. The official explained that an expansion of the Gymnich format had already been envisaged prior to the Lisbon Treaty coming into force, to improve the quality of debates among ministers.[75] As with the European Council, which revealed the

---

[75] Interviewee MS-08/EXT, 11 December 2009.

role of the European Council president in promoting informal debate, the HR, as the permanent chair of the FAC, became an advocate of the Gymnich informal meeting format. This advocacy also involved attention to logistical detail. For example, ahead of a Gymnich meeting in Cyprus on 7–8 September 2012, Agence Europe quoted a source from the Cypriot presidency reporting that the HR Catherine Ashton had insisted on having the informal meeting at a remote location outside the capital, Nicosia, to allow ministers a more open exchange of views, because they would better be able to escape media attention.[76] The HR was also said to use the informal Gymnich meetings to introduce strategic and long-term issues for discussion among ministers. In the case of the Cyprus meeting, for example, the focus was on education and water.[77]

A contested issue is the role of particular groupings of member states within the CFSP setting. Though the foreign affairs portfolio is not a multi-speed integration setting, like the economic governance field, there are also institutionalized forms of closer cooperation that are perceived to challenge the idea that all actors have equal access to policy dialogue. The dominant role of the so-called EU-3—the group of the biggest EU member states France, Germany, and the United Kingdom—is seen as particularly problematic because it pre-empts debate at times within the full FAC. Though closer coordination between the three biggest member states is seen to help the EU to react more swiftly to external policy challenges—the negotiations about Iran's nuclear programme being a case in point—the limited access of other EU member states to EU-3 policy dialogue may impact negatively on the EU's ability to mobilize all its member states to act in a consistent and coherent manner. As one interviewee explained with reference to the Political and Security Committee (PSC) discussions (see section 4.5.2), the EU-3 format had implications for the way meetings were conducted:

> During breaks within PSC meetings you can see the ambassadors of the 'big three' consulting—they are almost like a presidium.[78]

And a diplomat from a non-EU-3 member state was frank in rejecting this format as being incompatible with the idea that CFSP coordination needed to mobilize broad political support for a policy decision among all member states:

> We want to see the EU break free from EU-3 dominance.[79]

---

[76] Agence Europe, 5 September 2012.  [77] Agence Europe, 6 September 2012.
[78] Interviewee EU-01/EXT, 9 March 2009.  [79] Interviewee PR-05/EXT, 24 November 2009.

### 4.3.3 *The Role of the High Representative as Chair*

The post of HR was originally created by the Treaty of Amsterdam.[80] In many ways this position can be seen as a response to the earlier failures of the EU to build a viable policy consensus in the field of foreign and security policy coordination within the original coordination framework defined by the Maastricht Treaty, and as a consequence of the lack of general visibility of this policy field (Cardwell 2009: 20). In its original conception the role of the HR was to act as an external spokesperson for EU foreign policy, and at the same time to have some limited instruments at hand to encourage coordination and policy initiative. The first HR, Javier Solana, could rely on his own small administrative infrastructure—the Policy Unit (section 4.5.3). Yet Solana's role in EU foreign policy was perceived mainly as focused on external representation rather than on organizing internal consensus over policy or even on preserving such consensus.[81] As one member state diplomat explained while looking back at Solana's time in office:

> Solana is essentially a representative to third countries but not someone reminding member states on compliance with common positions.[82]

Most importantly, Solana lacked the powers of the chair. The new provision of the Lisbon Treaty that the HR chairs the FAC thus marked an important change—both for the office of HR as well as for the FAC as an institution. The move constituted another important attempt at institutional engineering that aimed to increase the consensus formation capacity of the external affairs forum. Therefore, it should be of little surprise that the debate about the role the HR should play within CFSP and CSDP decision-making sparked controversy. The external and internal functions associated with the office demand very different qualities and profiles. Other than Van Rompuy and Juncker, who emphasized their internal role as chairs, the HR is committed to a strong external representation role by default, as this was the main rationale for creating the position in the first place. It is estimated that the HR spends

---

[80] Giesela Müller-Brandeck-Bocquet and Carolin Rüger (2011) assemble a broad collection of contributions on the position and role of the HR in EU external action covering both the external and internal dimension of the position.

[81] Solana's role in external representation did mean that he fully replaced the external representation function of the rotating presidency. The position led rather to a modification of the previous regime, and the respective roles of the HR and the rotating presidency in external representation changed from one presidency to the next, depending on the foreign policy situation. For example, Quaglia and Moxon (2006: 351) in their analysis of the consecutive Italian and Irish Council presidencies in 2003 and 2004 conclude that in the field of CFSP 'the establishment of the High Representative has diminished the role of the presidency as external representative of the Union'. Other rotating Council presidencies played a crucial role in external representation with the 2008 French presidency, for example, acting as an important interlocutor for the conflicting parties during the Georgia crisis.

[82] Interviewee PR-07/EXT, 12 November 2009.

more than two-thirds of her time just on travelling.[83] In addition, there are various external representation commitments in Brussels.

An official close to the new HR believed that the responsibility to chair the FAC indeed significantly altered the job of the HR as the new focus on consensus formation has repercussions on how other aspects of the job are emphasized and interpreted. The official rejected the idea that Ashton had no relevant experience in chairing Council meetings, but rather emphasized the particular character of FAC debates:

> She [Ashton] was familiar with chairing [Council sessions] in areas of first pillar decision-making but not in the foreign affairs area. This is quite a different set-up. The Council functions differently in this field. Being in the presidency involves also the responsibility to deliver—not only to comment on [decisions]. Solana had much greater room for manoeuvre because he was not chairman. In the chair you can't pretend that you didn't hear something. You are even responsible for unity. [ . . . ] Every FAC is now a big thing. I think for the High Representative—I think she would agree—it is the biggest event of the month.[84]

Ashton's role as the first permanent chair of the FAC shows characteristics similar to the roles of Van Rompuy and Juncker as chairpersons of the European Council and the Eurogroup respectively. Expectations that the HR would stabilize the processes of internal consensus formation especially in crisis situations were high. Several interviewees referred to the strong leadership of the French 2008 Council presidency in the context of the Georgia crisis as an example illustrating the need of a presidency that was insistent when it came to mobilizing support in the different capitals. One diplomat formulated expectations immediately prior to the transition to the permanent chair regime this way:

> Decisions in the capitals are decisive in crisis situations. If the presidency and the PSC manage to get all member states to agree to the same line at an early stage, the chances [of achieving a stable common position] are much better.[85]

A key instrument for the HR as chair is to supervise the process of agenda setting and meeting preparation. Besides her small cabinet staff the HR can now rely on the EEAS as a bureaucratic resource. Ashton is said to have asserted her competence to fulfil this role from early on as stressed by the official quoted above, who is closely familiar with Ashton's role as chair:

> We [the HR] think we should lead on everything. [ . . . ] We had to make clear that it was for Ashton to do the agenda even of Gymnich meetings and everything.[86]

---

[83] Smith (2013: 12) provides the number of 250 days by referring to interviews with EEAS officials.
[84] Interviewee, EU-24/EXT, 17 November 2011.
[85] Interviewee PR-03/EXT, 12 March 2009.
[86] Interviewee, EU-24/EXT, 17 November 2011.

As illustrated in the section above on working methods, Ashton used the Gymnich meeting format to advance particular topics for discussion. Compared to the example of the long-time Eurogroup president Jean-Claude Juncker, who was assertive about his role of reminding Eurogroup members of previous informal agreements reached within the group, Ashton was more careful not to overemphasize her role as chair. Yet the FAC is considered to have developed self-policing dynamics, implying that ministers check each other for failing to adhere to commitments made within the forum.[87] Much as the domestic political career of the Eurogroup president—who is not a full-time chair—was considered to impose limits on the chair's role, there is little doubt that Ashton's various commitments and especially her time-consuming external representation responsibilities implied restrictions on how much effort she could invest with regard to her role as a chair. Yet there is little doubt that she fully recognized the importance of the chair position to the FAC's role as a forum for policy coordination. In their analysis of Ashton's role in agenda setting, Sophie Vanhoonacker and Karolina Pomorska (2013) offer clear evidence that the establishment of the EEAS helped Ashton to control the agenda of FAC meetings more assertively. They also attest that Ashton's negotiation skills were crucial in overcoming inter-institutional conflicts surrounding the launch of the EEAS, and that the HR deliberately focused on establishing the credibility of the new institutional structures as well as emphasizing key EU foreign policy priorities. Vanhoonacker and Pomorska view the internal quarrels surrounding the installation of the EEAS (see section 4.5.3) and the initial malfunctioning of the new bureaucratic support structures as the most important factors in preventing further evolution of the HR's agenda setting role.

Finally, the HR provides a crucial link between the European Council and FAC activity. As a participant in European Council debate the HR is bound to adhere to agreements reached among the heads. The European Council itself leaves little doubt about its ambition to supervise the work of the FAC and the HR. After a European Council meeting devoted to the discussion of the strategic orientation and internal organization of EU foreign policy coordination in September 2010 (see chapter 3.7), Herman Van Rompuy explained in a press statement his view of how the pattern of coordination with regard to preparing EU positions towards third countries should be:

> Our key messages [to third countries] should be mandated by the European Council, [and] prepared and implemented by the Foreign Affairs Council, the Commission and the high representative.[88]

---

[87] Interviewee, EU-24/EXT, 17 November 2011.
[88] As quoted in Agence Europe, 'A look behind the news', 23 September 2010.

Somewhat ironically, preoccupation with the economic crisis between the years of 2008 and 2013 made it very difficult for the FAC in general and the HR in particular to receive the same degree of attention from the European Council as the euro-area finance ministers and the Eurogroup did. In any case the role of the HR as a chair of the FAC shows clear parallels to the roles of the European Council and Eurogroup presidents. It is also evident that the key aim of giving the HR a privileged role in internal decision-making was to enhance the consensus generation capacity of the FAC.

## 4.4 The EPSCO Council

The EPSCO Council is another important Council formation in the context of the EU's new intergovernmentalism in the post-Maastricht era. EPSCO ministers were placed at the centre of a series of new coordination processes in the field of social and employment policy coordination that were initiated by the European Council in the late 1990s and early 2000s (see chapter 3.3). EPSCO became the Council formation responsible for employment coordination under the so-called Lisbon process and the Amsterdam Treaty's new Title VIII on employment. Later it was also assigned responsibility for the new social inclusion portfolio. EPSCO is also affiliated with EU-level social dialogue and new efforts to stimulate coordination on pension policies and on the implications of ageing populations. It can be said that EPSCO is the central coordination forum for a number of social open methods of coordination (OMCs). The case of EPSCO is of particular relevance to the study of institutional change in the context of the EU's new intergovernmentalism as the Council formation did not manage to obtain a position as prominent as those of the Eurogroup, ECOFIN and the FAC despite the long list of coordination responsibilities added to its agenda. Moreover, many of the social OMCs that are coordinated by the EPSCO Council apparently no longer receive the same level of political attention as they did by the end of the 1990s and early 2000s. Despite the fact that EPSCO, the main political forum for a number of coordination processes, enjoys a similar procedural status to that of the Eurogroup, the ECOFIN Council, and the FAC, its post-Maastricht era institutional trajectory diverges with regard to a number of aspects. Deliberative intergovernmentalism as an analytical framework can help us to better understand why and how these divergences have occurred and what impact EPSCO's particular institutional setting might have had for the wider field of intergovernmental policy coordination under the EU's main social OMCs. The main argument advanced in this section is that EPSCO's current institutional infrastructure is still dominated by legislative decision-making. This feature in particular prevents more radical transformation, as observed in the case of the more senior groupings of ministers that were studied earlier in this chapter. EPSCO working methods have so far failed in providing an institutional environment that is more conducive to successful policy dialogue. Current EPSCO working methods do not level the same potential for consensus generation around key coordination objectives that can be observed elsewhere. This section thus also offers an explanation as to why political leadership has remained considerably weaker in relation to a number of key social OMC mechanisms than in other new areas of post-Maastricht EU activity. Yet the EPSCO context also shows evidence of fresh attempts at institutional engineering, which are targeted at removing existing obstacles to coordination.

### 4.4.1 *The Core Working Method: a Hybrid and a Mega Council*

EPSCO is a so-called mega Council. This is also revealed by its full name: the Employment, Social Policy, Health and Consumer Affairs Council. EPSCO combines several policy portfolios within one Council formation, although these portfolios are represented by two, three, or sometimes even four different line ministries at member state level. This makes the EPSCO Council different from the Eurogroup, the ECOFIN Council and the FAC. All of the three latter groupings are based on the principle that the same minister attends all meetings. In order to ensure consistency the ECOFIN Council and Eurogroup working methods, for example, rule out alternation between ministers of finance and the economy, who in some countries enjoy overlapping competences. The case of the FAC showed that potential alteration of members was deliberately excluded with the decision to create a separate GAC formation (see section 4.6.1). The EPSCO format can be considered a consequence of the decision to limit the overall number of Council formations (see section 4.1). In order to avoid too much confusion and to facilitate the preparatory process, the work of EPSCO is organized within two different 'slots'—health and social. Typically, EPSCO meetings are scheduled in such a way that the two slots are kept apart from each other. Though formally assembled under one roof, 'EPSCO health' and 'EPSCO social' do not overlap much in organizational terms. However, each slot comprises a range of policy issues that may not be dealt with by the same line ministries at member state level. The field of social policy, on which this section concentrates, comprises three 'legs'—employment policy, social policy proper, and equal opportunity policy.[89] Each of the three areas reflects different decision-making mechanisms and policy-making trajectories. Whereas employment policy is a prime example of the EU's new intergovernmentalism and part of the wider OMC

---

[89] Terminology used within EPSCO. Interviewee EU-19, 25 June 2009.

agenda in the broader field of EU socio-economic governance, the social policy portfolio largely stands for EPSCO's role as a legislative decision-making body. Decision-making in social policy legislation has very much determined EPSCO's pre-Maastricht profile. However, more recently the social policy portfolio has also comprised coordination processes, for example the social inclusion portfolio. Finally, the area of equal opportunity policy also combines classic elements of EU social policy-making under the community method and mechanisms of soft coordination, some of which even pre-date the so-called Lisbon social OMCs.

The EPSCO process is thus anything but straightforward. This is reflected in the preparatory structure underpinning the work of the Council formation. Community method decision-making within EPSCO follows the EU's legislative calendar, and is structured largely by the Commission. In this field also the Permanent Representations and the relevant Council working groups in which the social, labour and health affairs counsellors of the Permanent Representations meet play an important role. Instead, work in the field of the social OMCs relies heavily on input from two dedicated expert committees for policy coordination issues—the Employment Committee (EMCO) and the Social Protection Committee (SPC)—see section 4.5.4. Other than the Eurogroup, ECOFIN, and the FAC, which all saw their preparatory structures being streamlined and expanded, EPSCO struggles to combine input from a plethora of preparatory bodies. Coordination with the capitals is considered to be in part complex and cumbersome. As an official from a Permanent Representation with responsibility for EPSCO coordination and experience in national-level decision-making explained, it has often happened that leading officials in a national line ministry were not well acquainted with the relevant EPSCO file. Often instructions have been received from colleagues in the capitals who were not EU social affairs specialists. In some instances, instructions have come from departments with global responsibility for EU decision-making rather than dedicated coordination units within the line ministries.[90] Another official noted that competition between different line ministries involved in EPSCO preparation in the capital has sometimes been particularly damaging to soft coordination procedures. Individual domestic actors, for example, have insisted on specific language being used at the meetings. Though this practice is well known in the sphere of legislative decision-making, the official considered it to run counter to the idea of soft coordination, which requires a greater degree of flexibility on part of representatives, and attributed such behaviour to a lack of awareness about the way decisions should be taken within the EU setting.[91] Other interviewees were

---

[90] Interviewee PR-21/ECON, 12 November 2009.
[91] Interviewee PR-20/ECON, 4 November 2009.

less negative about their respective experiences with the preparatory structures in the domestic arena, but also thought that the process was 'heavy and time-consuming'.[92] However, there was broad agreement among those familiar with EPSCO proceedings that EPSCO's complicated organizational structure has had negative repercussions on how ministers relate to this Council formation. As one official explained:

> The process has become very bureaucratic [...]. For the ministers this is not one of the exciting Council formations.[93]

Another official with long-term experience of the EPSCO portfolio was also under no illusions about how much interest the relevant ministers in his/her country show in attending EPSCO meetings:

> The previous ministers always cancelled last minute.[94]

According to yet another official, ministers usually take quite some interest in EPSCO proceedings when they are new in office but tend to lose this interest after a period of about two years.[95] It is indeed a common practice that member states are represented only at the level of deputy ministers during EPSCO meetings or at least during large parts of these meetings. The complicated structure of EPSCO as a mega Council makes it difficult for individual ministers to relate to each other, and to establish a closer working relationship or even develop a group spirit as in the Eurogroup, ECOFIN, and FAC settings. A key condition of successful policy dialogue and consensus generation identified by deliberative intergovernmentalism is thus lacking with regard to the EPSCO context. One of the officials made explicit reference to the ECOFIN context when explaining EPSCO practice:

> It [EPSCO] is completely different from ECOFIN. There are hardly any close personal relations between ministers. You already see this when people are gathering with their delegations in the meeting room. In ECOFIN this is totally different. There everyone is running throughout the room. People give each other a hug and share a joke. [...] EPSCO is an accumulation forum within which you see little real exchange of views.[96]

EPSCO meetings see ministers rotating depending on the agenda item listed for debate. Individual ministers may thus only attend a short part of the full meeting. In some cases they only enter the room for the discussion of a single agenda item. As is the case with many other Council formations that are

---

[92] Interviewee PR-17/ECON, 5 November 2009.
[93] Interviewee EU-21/ECON, 11 November 2011.
[94] Interviewee PR-15/ECON, 24 November 2009.
[95] Interviewee PR-21/ECON, 12 November 2009.
[96] Interviewee EU-07/ECON, 7 April 2009.

focused on legislative decision-making, EPSCO participants tend to read from prepared speaking notes rather than engaging in open debate. Moreover, given the scope of the EPSCO agenda and the need for stricter time management, individual interventions are limited to no more than two minutes. It is reported that many ministers do not expect such a tight schedule when they first arrive at EPSCO meetings. They are then put off by the lack of opportunity for real exchanges.[97] There are also apparently differences between different constituencies within the EPSCO Council. For example, employment ministers are said to stay in office longer than their colleagues, and are considered to maintain a greater degree of continuity than other ministers.[98]

The lack of close interaction between individual ministers also follows from the fact that the frequency of EPSCO meetings is much lower than is the case for the other groupings of ministers studied in this chapter. Typically the EPSCO Council is convened four times a year, of which three meetings are devoted to social issues and one deals with health policy. In addition, there is normally one informal meeting per semester.[99] One EPSCO meeting is always organized directly before the Spring European Council meeting, which requires EPSCO input. The trend during the 2000s was to have fewer rather than more sessions: for example, at some point the practice of holding an EPSCO meeting in October was questioned.[100]

The relative importance of legislative decision-making within EPSCO's overall agenda represents another major obstacle to the evolution of particular routines for consensus-oriented policy dialogue, as observed with regard to the other formations studied in this chapter. EPSCO's traditional role in developing and administrating the EU's legislative agenda in the field of social policy implies different patterns of interactions than those found within the context of policy coordination processes. The focus on legislative decision-making is considered to foster divisive attitudes rather than a spirit of open discussion:

> The issues [under discussion in EPSCO] partially imply a high degree of awareness of the majority decision-making rule and the existing majorities. The actors always have in mind what the possible coalitions currently are.[101]

Such orientation towards majority decision-making is considered to be different from the area of OMC decision-making, within which 'the mainstream among the representatives is going to be decisive'.[102] According to another

---

[97] Interviewee EU-07/ECON, 7 April 2009.    [98] Interviewee EU-19/ECON, 25 June 2009.
[99] The informal meetings often stretch over two or three days, because they are organized in order to bring the different groups of line ministers in the EPSCO formation together in a series of separate gatherings.
[100] Interviewee EU-19, 25 June 2009.
[101] Interviewee PR-20/ECON, 4 November 2009.
[102] Interviewee PR-20/ECON, 4 November 2009.

interviewee most of the discussions between officials in charge of EPSCO preparation in the capitals, and at the Permanent Representation with their respective ministers, concern legislative issues. The official thought that it was rare for soft coordination issues to be tabled for direct discussion with the minister. Ministers are said to consider soft coordination issues in the social policy field as less relevant to citizens.[103]

The clash between EPSCO practices in the field of legislative decision-making and policy coordination routines is also reflected in the way informal discussions among ministers are organized. Next to the one or two informal EPSCO meetings per year, the main forum for informal discussion is the EPSCO lunch, which is scheduled to take place at every EPSCO meeting. As a rule, lunches are attended by only one minister per country. Occasionally, special lunches with ministers from two different line ministries from the same member state will take place. The EPSCO lunch is a venue for both 'policy debates and very tough negotiations'.[104] The difficulties arising from this combination of very different decision-making modes are recognized by several interviewees. One official argued that EPSCO's ability to deal with soft coordination issues would be strengthened if at least one informal meeting per semester were devoted exclusively to non-legislative issues.[105] The same official also noted that coordination between succeeding presidencies was particularly relevant for non-legislative policy portfolios. EPSCO is chaired by the rotating Council presidency, and there is no prospect of this changing in the foreseeable future.

Since the new rules on transparency entered into force the overburdening of informal EPSCO debates with legislative issues is reported to have increased even further. While soft coordination topics have received less attention, negotiation related to legislative acts is considered to have become even more opaque than was the case before the introduction of the new transparency rules, because they have moved increasingly into the informal parts of the meetings.[106] Unlike during regular non-public Council sessions, no minutes are taken during informal lunches, and access is restricted. As ministers are simply not prepared to discuss sensitive issues in public, formal EPSCO debates have simply become shorter. As one official explained with reference to a pivotal EPSCO meeting during the complicated negotiations concerning the revision of the much contested EU working-time directive:

---

[103] Interviewee PR-21/ECON, 12 November 2009.
[104] Interviewee EU-19, 25 June 2009.
[105] Interviewee EU-21/ECON, 11 November 2009.
[106] Interviewee EU-21/ECON, 11 November 2009.

> [The] negotiations on the working-time directive lasted for 11 hours. We started with it during lunch and finished close to midnight—to reconvene at the public meeting for the decision.[107]

The EPSCO Council can therefore be considered a hybrid Council, comprising both enormous legislative responsibilities and coordination issues. Compared to the Eurogroup, the ECOFIN Council, and the FAC, there is little evidence of further developing the functional differentiation between different working methods since the launch of the series of social OMCs in the late 1990s and early 2000s.

### 4.4.2 Relations with ECOFIN and the European Council

EPSCO's difficulties in playing a stronger role in policy coordination are also revealed by the fact that it sees itself as competing with the ECOFIN Council. For example, the decision to work with so-called integrated policy guidelines after the half-time review of the Lisbon strategy further institutionalized ECOFIN's role as the prime decision-maker in the wider socio-economic governance portfolio. Though there is no evidence that ECOFIN and the Eurogroup interfere directly with EPSCO's internal process as regards the drafting and adopting of employment guidelines, there is a structural asymmetry between the three bodies.[108] For example, it would be inconceivable for finance ministers meeting in the Eurogroup and ECOFIN to make their coordination processes depend on EPSCO conclusions. EPSCO, to some extent, has to accommodate to the macroeconomic guidelines prepared by the finance ministers, and must avoid policy recommendations that might be in contradiction to these guidelines. Moreover, whereas the Eurogroup and ECOFIN interact constantly with the European Council, EPSCO does not. The work of the EPSCO Council is focused primarily on preparing a position on employment policy coordination ahead of the European Council's spring meeting in March each year. Yet there is little interaction between EPSCO and the European Council afterwards. It is largely left to EMCO and SPC as the responsible expert committees to deal with follow-up work.[109] That EPSCO's role in the field of policy coordination is often dependent on Eurogroup and ECOFIN decision-making is seen quite clearly. The following blunt statement by a senior official dealing with the EPSCO portfolio illustrates this sentiment very well:

> There is competition with ECOFIN.[110]

---

[107] Interviewee EU-19/ECON, 25 June 2009.
[108] Interviewee EU-19/ECON, 25 June 2009.
[109] Interviewee EU-19/ECON, 25 June 2009.
[110] Interviewee EU-21/ECON, 11 November 2009.

And a diplomat from one of the Permanent Representations admitted that unlike the Eurogroup and ECOFIN, the EPSCO Council is hardly in a position to push important topics that will find recognition by the European Council:

> We always hope to see our topics in the European Council but this is not always the case.[111]

EPSCO's inability to provide leadership on key policy issues was illustrated during the economic and financial crisis. Despite the fact that during the early stages of the crisis several EPSCO ministers thought that the crisis context would provide a particular opportunity for EPSCO to revive the social policy coordination portfolios,[112] the forum has been unable to position itself more clearly within the wider context of crisis management. This became particularly apparent during the Czech presidency in the first half of 2009. In reaction to growing uncertainty about jobs and the wave of welfare spending cuts in a large number of EU member states the Czech presidency decided to work towards convening a special meeting of the European Council on social issues—a so-called 'social summit'. Yet EPSCO was not involved in the preparations.[113] The initiative eventually failed to result in a fully-fledged European Council meeting as envisaged by the rotating presidency, as key EU leaders such British prime minister Gordon Brown, German chancellor Angela Merkel, and the French president Nicolas Sarkozy expressed their concern that there was no sufficient basis for discussions about concrete policy initiatives among the heads.[114] This view was also echoed by Eurogroup president Jean-Claude Juncker,[115] who, however, lamented the inconsistent communication by the Czech presidency, which had first promised a special European Council meeting and then decided to downgrade the so-called summit to a half-day meeting of the heads of the member states that formed the so-called troika of successive Council presidencies, the Commission president, and the top-level representatives of the EU's social partners.[116]

The episode revealed the differences between the relationship that EPSCO enjoys with the European Council on the one hand, and the links forged between ECOFIN and the Eurogroup with European Council decision-making on the other hand. Whereas crisis-related decision-making in the European Council follows preparation by the Eurogroup and ECOFIN, and triggers follow-up coordination by finance ministers, EPSCO activities have been out of tune with European Council crisis management. One diplomat, with a view

---

[111] Interviewee PR-17/ECON, 5 November 2009.
[112] Interviewee EU-07/ECON, 7 April 2009.
[113] Interviewee EU-19/ECON, 25 June 2009.
[114] Interviewee EU-19/ECON, 25 June 2009.
[115] Agence Europe, 31 March 2009.
[116] Agence Europe, 7 May 2009.

to EPSCO's failure to play a stronger role in crisis management, even sarcastically remarked:

It is ok that ECOFIN takes the lead—for me. Because EPSCO is a waste of time for ministers.[117]

The difficulties of the EPSCO Council in playing a leading role as a forum for policy coordination in a new area of EU activity reveal a number of structural problems with far-reaching repercussions for the socio-economic governance portfolio. Without the political mobilization of relevant line ministers there is hardly any prospect of more vigorous coordination of social and employment policies. Moreover, in the post-Maastricht era the close link between European Council debates and discussions among ministers is pivotal for individual policy initiatives to command the necessary support within the domestic context. Such ties between EPSCO and the European Council remain underdeveloped.

Two unprecedented interventions by European Council president Van Rompuy can be understood as responding to this institutional logic, which is at the core of the analytical framework of deliberative intergovernmentalism. Once again, Van Rompuy's moves can be read as particular attempts at institutional engineering. The European Council president made two personal appearances at EPSCO meetings (see also chapter 3.7). Van Rompuy's first visit to an informal EPSCO meeting under the Belgium Council presidency on 8 July 2010[118] was a reaction to the above-described disastrous failure to convene an EU social summit a year earlier. The visit also coincided with the launch of the EU2020 strategy—the successor of the Lisbon agenda. As with the Lisbon process, EPSCO enjoys a procedural role similar to ECOFIN as a leading Council formation in the EU2020 process. Yet the Lisbon process experience showed that EPSCO found it very difficult to develop an institutional role similar to that of ECOFIN. Van Rompuy's visit therefore can be seen as an attempt to flag up that EPSCO is required to play such a role in order to avoid the EU2020 process suffering from difficulties similar to those faced by the original Lisbon process. Van Rompuy's next debate with EPSCO ministers at an EPSCO meeting in Brussels on 28 February 2013[119] came from a similar motivation. Both the Lisbon process and EU2020 are built on the idea that there is a growing synchronization of all areas of socio-economic governance. Van Rompuy's decision to ask EPSCO ministers directly for input into the discussion about EMU reform—the core domain of Eurogroup and ECOFIN

---

[117] Interviewee PR-21/ECON, 12 November 2009.

[118] Press release, Belgian Presidency of the Council, 8 July 2010, <http://www.employment.eutrio.be/WorkArea/DownloadAsset.aspx?id=31212> [accessed 12 March 2013].

[119] Press release, Irish Presidency of the Council, 28 February 2013, <http://eu2013.ie/news/news-items/20130228post-epscodjei/>[accessed 12 March 2013].

activity—sent a similar message. Van Rompuy implied that EPSCO should play a more proactive role in EU socio-economic governance alongside the Eurogroup and ECOFIN, and under the overall leadership of the European Council. His activism was finally echoed by a joint Franco–German press statement—also referred to as the Merkel–Hollande-paper—at the end of May 2013, in which the two heads demanded that Euro Summits 'task other Euro area Ministers, for example employment and social affairs, research and economics ministers, to take work forward on specific Euro area matters' (Bundesregierung 2013: 9).

It is still difficult to see how EPSCO will reform its core working method to accommodate a greater role in the field of social and employment policy coordination. However, Van Rompuy's initiative and the apparent failure of social and employment affairs ministers to respond to the crisis more vigorously through collective action seem to have created more awareness within EPSCO. At an EPSCO Council meeting in October 2012 several ministers reportedly demanded joint meetings of ECOFIN and EPSCO in the context of a debate about EPSCO's future role in the European Semester. Ministers also demanded clarification of the respective roles of each Council formation in the process.[120] Though the idea of so-called jumbo Council meetings, which bring together ministers from two different Council formations, is considered to be impossible to implement because of the sheer size of such a meeting,[121] the issue of horizontal coordination between the two portfolios certainly remains on the agenda.

## 4.5 The Proliferation of Expert Committees and the New Bureaucratic Intergovernmental Infrastructure

Council decision-making is also a sphere of expert committees and working groups, bringing together officials representing the different member states as well as the Commission. These committees and groups can be considered as forums for intergovernmental decision-making (see chapter 2.1). At first sight the evolution of EU comitology is primarily a function of legislative decision-making, as numerous technical and smaller political obstacles need to be resolved before ministers can engage in meaningful negotiations. This aspect of comitology has been studied extensively. The relevant literature emphasizes the crucial role that committees play in policy evolution and design, but also in finalizing legislative decisions that are not reopened but only rubber-stamped by ministers (cf. Häge 2008). Comitology is seen as an instrument

---

[120] Agence Europe, 4 October 2012.    [121] Interviewee EU-22/ECON, 24 November 2009.

used by member states to gain greater influence over the Commission's role in devising and proposing legislation long before it enters the stage of political debate among ministers. The introduction of comitology into the sphere of legislation can therefore be seen as an important modification of the policy initiation role of the Commission under the classic community method, though it is debatable how much it actually limits the Commission's room for manoeuvre, depending on the relevant comitology process (Majone 2005: 91). Comitology in the sphere of legislative decision-making constitutes the prime example of deliberative supranationalism (Joerges and Neyer 1997; Joerges 2002), as the inclusion of policy experts into the process provides for a rationalizing element in negotiations between member state governments in the field of community method decision-making, or whenever executive powers are exercised at EU level on the basis of an earlier act of competence delegation. There is strong evidence that comitology in the field of legislative decision-making fostered the functional integration of national and Commission-based bureaucratic resources (Bergström 2005). What has received much less attention in the literature so far is the emergence of a parallel comitology infrastructure in Council decision-making, which is focused mostly on policy coordination and executive decision-making outside the core domains of the classic community method. This committee infrastructure is kept functionally separate from other EU comitology. The inherent logic of close intergovernmental policy coordination leads to the evolution of particular features of this type of committee governance. Though there are similarities in institutional design—and of course also committees operating in both spheres of decision-making—there are also notable differences. The establishment of the EMU, CFSP, and CSDP policy domains, as well as the new coordination mechanisms in the area of social and employment policy, has led to the proliferation of new forums for expert-level policy dialogue and decision-making. The work of these committees is closely tied to Eurogroup, ECOFIN, FAC, and EPSCO decision-making. In addition the growing involvement of the European Council in day-to-day decision-making has led to a closer involvement of expert committees in preparatory work for meetings among the heads. The direct link between the work of individual committees and discussions among ministers and the heads is a defining feature of this particular type of comitology, which distinguishes it from more encapsulated expert settings that were observed in the field of legislative decision-making. Moreover, the EU's coordination committees play a crucial role in connecting member state, Commission, EEAS, and ECB bureaucracies. As policy initiation and implementation require permanent and close cooperation below the top level of political decision-making, committee representatives and their relevant unit assume a crucial function within the domestic environment, as they need to channel work from different branches of the administration into the EU-level coordination process and to distribute information and requests from that process back into the home administration. The central role of the coordination committees is reflected in the reorganization of ministerial hierarchies and processes at the domestic level.

The new coordination committees have all been created in the post-Maastricht era. They are populated by senior member state officials, plus their counterparts in the Commission, the ECB, and the EEAS. The PSC and the Economic and Financial Committee (EFC) fall into this category. Also, the EMCO was originally composed of highly senior officials (see section 4.5.4). These senior committees have obtained a central position in the coordination process. They relate to the work of other less senior committees and working groups—often in a hierarchical manner. PSC and EFC members typically enjoy direct access to the top-level decision-makers in the domestic arena. The Commission is represented at director-general level. All substantial policy decisions pass through these committees. Moreover, senior coordination committees have become more and more involved in the process of preparing European Council meetings. The evolution of such permanent top-level committees is a specific feature of deliberative intergovernmentalism. The emphasis on seniority and proximity, especially of PSC and EFC members to the top political appointees within the hierarchies of national administrations, is also not without repercussions for COREPER, which is traditionally considered the most senior EU umbrella committee to have a bird's-eye view of Council decision-making (see section 4.6.3).

The new tier of EU comitology follows its own institutional logic, as it is focused primarily on policy coordination. Coordination committees have also been subject to constant institutional engineering. Their consensus generation function as well as their potential to facilitate the functional integration of decentralized bureaucratic resources, which are located at the national level and within various EU-level bodies, constitutes an important parallel to comitology within the sphere of classic committee method decision-making. As in the case of decision-making among ministers the differences in this regard are due to the different format of decision-making. Consensus generation and the mobilization of bureaucratic resources do not so much revolve around particular acts of legislative decision-making, but rather are continuous features of committee work at all stages of decision-making.

To substantiate understanding of the EU's main coordination committees, this section offers an in-depth review of the role and internal functioning of the EFC and the PSC as prime examples of how key institutional dynamics identified by deliberative intergovernmentalism are at play. It is demonstrated how the central roles of the EFC and PSC are mirrored in the organization of domestic decision-making processes and the parallels in their institutional trajectories are identified. Finally, an overview is provided of the main so-called

OMC committees, which have gained importance ever since the launch of the 2000 Lisbon agenda.

### 4.5.1 *The EFC and the Eurogroup Working Group*

The role of the EFC as the most senior expert committee in the field of euro-area and EU economic governance resembles in many ways the role of the PSC in CFSP and CSDP decision-making. Given the scope and the implications of EU economic governance decisions for domestic and EU-level policy-making, the EFC is probably the most powerful EU committee next to COREPER. In contrast to the PSC, which is reviewed in the next section, the EFC has received very little attention in the academic literature so far (cf. Grosche and Puetter 2008). The EFC is a committee of capital-based top-level officials. The Commission and the ECB are represented too. The EFC is supported by a Brussels-based secretariat, and the committee delegates a part of its work to sub-committees and specialized ad-hoc working groups. It also relies on support from the EPC (see section 4.5.4). EFC meetings are prepared by the EFC alternates—the group of deputy EFC members. Many EFC members have the rank of deputy finance minister, and typically enjoy direct access to their relevant minister, and several of them also to their respective head of state or government. A prominent example is the former German state secretary Jörg Asmussen, who served on the EFC between 2008 and 2011 before becoming a member of the ECB's executive board and then again a government official. Asmussen was one of the masterminds behind the key crisis management decisions of the German government, and a close advisor to two finance ministers from different political parties and the chancellor. Many other EFC members have similar biographies and belong to the small group of European officials who rotate through the years between the top-level civil servant positions at member state and EU level. ECB president Mario Draghi even once acted as the EFC's president. His Italian colleague Lorenzo Bini Smaghi was a long-term member of the EFC, and its vice-president from 2003 until 2005. The senior finance ministry official worked under different finance ministers in Rome and then became a member of the ECB executive board in 2005. The above biographies reflect a key characteristic of the EFC as a committee, which combines epistemic community features with a focus on preparing broader political decision-making. EFC members have often known each other for a very long time, and share similar views on a range of economic issues. They have jointly participated in several episodes of difficult consensus seeking around highly controversial EU economic decisions ranging from the original creation of the SGP and its later modifications to complicated bailout decisions. Moreover, they are constantly involved in both policy development and implementation. The EFC functions as a sounding board for feedback from national-level administrations and as a venue for constant peer review. Quite importantly, the EFC is a crucial interface for Commission and member state interaction. The Commission is a key contributor to EFC debates. Its Directorate-General (DG) ECFIN prepares most of the substantial and analytical input to EFC discussions. EFC practice reflects the Commission's clipped policy initiation role in the field of economic governance. The Commission deliberately uses the EFC to test member state positions, and conversely the EFC is used by member state administrations to establish their own priorities in policy initiation *vis-à-vis* the Commission.

The EFC was set up by the Maastricht Treaty[122] and replaced the former Monetary Committee. The name change signalled the transition from an era of exchange rate policy coordination to one of coordinated economic policies. The Treaty endowed the EFC with far-reaching powers and linked it directly to the activities of the Council and the Commission. The EFC produces opinions upon the request of the two bodies and on its own initiative. The EFC is charged with the surveillance of national economic policies and is the key preparatory body on all matters related to SGP governance. The committee is a crucial interface between the Commission, the ECB, and national administrations, which are all represented around the table. The EFC president participates in ECOFIN Council and Eurogroup meetings. The committee deals with all crucial aspects of Eurogroup and ECOFIN Council discussion as far as they relate to intergovernmental policy coordination. It also oversees and is involved in the pre-negotiation of closely related legislative initiatives. The EFC thus effectively replaces COREPER's role as the final pre-negotiation body when it comes to the core economic policy coordination agenda. The Council's rules of procedure explicitly acknowledge the competing prerogatives of the EFC in comparison to COREPER.[123]

Despite the fact that the EFC is not a committee of Brussels-based officials, EFC meetings are frequent, and there is almost constant interaction between EFC members and their subordinated units in the national finance ministries, the Commission, and the ECB. The EFC has functioned as an important crisis manager since 2008. For example, as part of the first EU responses to the financial crisis, support for non-euro-area members needed to be organized. Latvia and Hungary received combined EU and International Monetary Fund support. An official involved in crisis management underlined that the EFC was crucial in this process:

> The EFC functioned very efficiently in this situation. We had weekly meetings and almost daily telephone conferences.[124]

---

[122] See Article 134, TFEU (Article 109c.2, TEC Maastricht).
[123] Article 19, Council Decision 2009/937/EU adopting the Council's Rules of Procedure, published in OJ L325/46.
[124] Interviewee PR-02/ECON, 3 November 2009.

The EFC also plays an increasingly important role in relation to the work of the European Council. A case in point is the Van Rompuy task force (see chapter 3.7). The new proximity of the EFC to the European Council also impacts on the committees meeting schedule. Extra meetings are scheduled or moved just to fit the preparatory process of European Council discussions.[125] In many ways the story of the EFC is increasingly the story of the Eurogroup Working Group—the euro-area arm of the EFC. Though EU crisis management revealed the existence of this group to a wider audience for the first time, its origins relate back to the early stages of euro-area governance when the Eurogroup was formed. The group comprises the EFC representatives from the euro-area countries, the Commission, and the ECB. Initially the Eurogroup Working Group focused on specific aspects of Eurogroup preparations such as briefing notes and agenda preparation, while substantial policy discussions related to Eurogroup deliberations took place in the full EFC (Puetter 2006: 74–5). Gradually the Eurogroup Working Group became a key venue for policy debates, reflecting the rise of the Eurogroup as the leading coordination forum of the euro area. Formally, the Eurogroup Working Group acted as a formation or sub-group of the EFC. It normally met after the full EFC meeting. The crisis as well as the acknowledgement of the Eurogroup in the Lisbon Treaty however accelerated the consolidation of the Eurogroup Working Group as a de facto euro-area EFC, effectively taking over core aspects of the EFC's role as the most senior technical and political committee in the field of economic governance. Most importantly the surge in Eurogroup Working Group's activity follows the expansion of the euro-area coordination agenda. The institutional construct of the Eurogroup Working Group implies that euro-area officials devote considerably more time to policy discussions than members of the full EFC. The Euro Summit of 26 October 2011 created the office of a full-time Eurogroup Working Group president, and called for the establishment of a 'more permanent sub-group of alternates/officials representative of the Finance Ministers, meeting more frequently under the authority of the President of the EWG.'[126] The new arrangements effectively converted the original EFC format of a committee of capital-based officials into a hybrid structure, combining elements of the old EFC working method with the PSC-model (see section 4.5.2) of a standing committee of Brussels-based member state officials who meet several times a week. The staff of the EFC secretariat now includes

---

[125] The *Financial Times* reported that a meeting of the 'euro working group', including EFC members and senior representatives of the heads, was convened to take place directly before the euro-area European Council meeting on 21 July 2011. The meeting was reportedly postponed from Wednesday evening to Thursday morning—just before the gathering of the heads—in order to reflect the outcome of the pre-negotiations between the French president Sarkozy and the German Chancellor Merkel in Berlin. See *Financial Times*, 'Barroso warns of Greece shockwaves', 20 July 2011.

[126] Statement, Euro Summit, 26 October 2011, Annex I, paras 7 and 8.

an additional sub-unit in charge of Eurogroup and Eurogroup Working Group preparation.

The change in the presidency regime constitutes a major institutional adjustment. Even prior to the October 2011 Euro Summit decision, the EFC and the Eurogroup Working Group had elected presidents. Indeed the EFC was the first senior coordination body to be based on a two-and-a-half-year presidency model from the beginning. EFC presidents were national finance ministry officials and served as chairs in a part-time capacity while receiving administrative support from the EFC secretariat and their own national administration. The October 2011 Euro Summit decision resulted in Thomas Wieser becoming the first full-time president of the Eurogroup Working Group, which he had previously chaired. Wieser's appointment, however, exacerbated the cleavage between the full EFC and the Eurogroup Working Group, with the latter becoming significantly upgraded and effectively more senior in status than the old core committee. This rift was partially healed in January 2012 when Wieser was elected as EFC president too.[127] The arrangement followed Van Rompuy's dual role as president of both the European Council and the Euro Summit. Again, the role of the president is interpreted mainly as internal. As Wieser put it:

> I am something like a marriage counsellor who tries—between two or several partners, if one accepts polygamy—to achieve a common understanding of things and seeks to make sure that operational implementation gets underway.[128]

How closely intertwined the work of the Eurogroup Working Group president with the work of the European Council president became is also evident from the geographical location of Wieser's office. It is to be found next to the offices of the cabinet members of the European Council president in the Council's Justus Lipsius building.

### 4.5.2 The PSC

> The PSC really runs foreign policy.[129]

The PSC was assigned a central role in foreign, security and defence policy-making by virtue of its Treaty mandate and related Council decisions, which characterize it as the 'linchpin' of CFSP decision-making.[130] The PSC is the

---

[127] Cf. Council Decision 2012/245/EU adopting the Council's Rules of Procedure, published in OJ L121/22, Annex, Articles 6–8.

[128] Interview with Deutschlandfunk radio, Hintergrund, 17 October 2012, own translation, <http://www.dradio.de/dlf/sendungen/hintergrundpolitik/1896250/> [accessed 17 October 2012].

[129] Interviewee PR-05/EXT, 24 November 2009.

[130] See Council Decision 2001/78/CFSP on setting up the PSC, 22 January 2001.

best researched senior-level committee among the new types of policy coordination committees introduced in the post-Maastricht era (Duke 2005; Juncos and Reynolds 2007; Wessel 2003). Many of the findings of existing research literature speak directly to the key proposition advanced by the analytical framework of deliberative intergovernmentalism. Christoph O. Meyer asks whether and how the PSC contributes to the emergence of a 'European strategic culture' (Meyer 2006: 112–37). Covering the period 2000–2005, Meyer provides a systematic review of the PSC environment and discusses key institutional features such as membership and the increased frequency of meetings.[131]

The PSC is identified as triggering profound changes in the way top foreign and security policy officials approach policy issues. It is found to be 'a multiplier of social influence, both through informal influence as well as peer pressure' (Meyer 2006: 136). Similarly, Jolyon Howorth (2011) identifies several key features of the PSC environment as conducive to consensus-oriented decision-making. Mai'a K. Davis Cross (2011) conceptualizes the PSC as an epistemic community. Chris Bickerton notices the political dimension of the PSC as an intergovernmental committee charged with reaching consensus on devising and implementing common policies, 'as it sits uncomfortably in a no-man's-land between intergovernmental and supranational policy-making' (Bickerton 2011: 178).

It is the informal institutionalization of the commitment to collective intergovernmental decision-making that characterizes the PSC as part of a wider process of institutional change in the post-Maastricht era as identified by deliberative intergovernmentalism. As Bickerton (2011: 180) writes: 'The function of these committees is not simply to maintain national vetoes over CFSP and CSDP. They are above all *consensus-generating machines*'.[132] Moreover, and this echoes the analysis of other key contexts for intergovernmental decision-making reviewed in this book, the PSC is considered to play a constitutive role for CFSP and CSDP decision-making, i.e. not only common European but also member state positions in foreign, security, and defence policy are formed increasingly through the committee process. Ana Juncos and Christopher Reynolds (2007: 147) conclude from their research on the PSC that 'PSC representatives are expressly not sent to Brussels simply to bargain over fixed, exogenously formed national preferences'. For the two authors 'the journey', i.e. the policy dialogue within the PSC, 'is as important as the destination' (Juncos and Reynolds 2007: 147).

---

[131] The findings show important parallels with the study of the informal Eurogroup as a forum that shaped an underlying working consensus on economic governance among finance ministers and senior officials during the first years of the euro area (see section 4.2 on the Eurogroup and Puetter 2006).

[132] Emphasis as in original text.

The PSC was first created as an interim committee by the Council in early 2000.[133] The decision was part of the implementation of a wider request from the European Council in December 1999 to establish a complex intergovernmental institutional infrastructure for governing the EU's foreign, security, and defence policy, which also includes the EU Military Committee and the EU Military Staff.[134] The PSC was then incorporated in the Treaty of Nice a year later and again formally mandated by the Council.[135] The PSC's mandate is broad. The committee is in charge of dealing with 'all aspects' of CFSP and CSDP decision-making.[136] Its activities are closely linked to those of the HR. The PSC has a general monitoring function as regards the international political situation and it coordinates reactions to crisis situations. The committee is assigned a central role in the preparation of policy debates within the FAC. It prepares opinions for the Council either upon request or on its own initiative—a prerogative also enjoyed by the EFC. The European Council also relies on direct PSC support. Even for the period covering the first half of the 2000s Hayes-Renshaw and Wallace (2006: 179) considered the input of the PSC into the process of European Council preparation to be 'significant' and highlighted the PSC's close involvement in the process of drafting European Council conclusions on foreign and security policy matters. Like the EFC, the PSC combines technocratic expertise with proximity to political decision-making at the level of ministers and the heads. The concentration on the latter dimension is confirmed by the PSC's oversight powers in relation to other specialized committees and Council working groups, which are in charge of CFSP and CSDP affairs.[137] As one participant in PSC meetings put it:

> The issues [the PSC is dealing with] are very strategic. The technical stuff is done by CIVCOM[[138]] and the [EU] Military Committee.[139]

Another official emphasized the PSC's political role by stating that 'the PSC is very useful as a clearing house',[140] particularly in crisis situations when conflicting positions between member states need to be reconciled or accommodated. Another interviewee commented on the political role of the PSC in day-to-day policy coordination by stating:

---

[133] See Council Decision 2000/143/CFSP.

[134] See European Council (1999a), para. 28 and Annex IV. Cross (2011) provides a detailed analysis of the EU Military Committee as an epistemic community. Compared to the political role of the PSC, which aims at support consensus formation at the highest political level, the EU Military Committee is much characterized by the technocratic expertise it assembles.

[135] See Article 25, TEU Nice (now Article 38, TEU) and Council Decision 2001/78/CFSP on setting up the PSC, 22 January 2001.

[136] Council Decision 2001/78/CFSP on setting up the PSC, 22 January 2001, Annex.

[137] On CSDP committees cf. Cross 2013.

[138] Committee for Civilian Aspects of Crisis Management.

[139] Interviewee PR-07/EXT, 12 November 2009.

[140] Interviewee PR-05/EXT, 24 November 2009.

I would say that PSC can solve around 90% of the issues which are controversial—the rest goes to GAERC [the General Affairs and External Relations Council].[141]

It is estimated that 70–80 per cent of the PSC agenda is prepared by working groups and other committees. CIVCOM and the Military Committee alone are considered to be responsible for 30–40 per cent of this preparatory work.[142] Moreover, a difference is detectable between the discussion of broader foreign policy issues and CSDP matters. The latter involve the entire range of organizational and operational aspects of EU missions and other practical activity, whereas broader foreign policy issues require a more strategic and political focus.[143] This implies that PSC ambassadors frequently need to go beyond pre-established positions when considering policy options within the committee. As one diplomat put it:

You need to have the guts to stand up and take a position in the committee and clarify things with your capital afterwards.[144]

Another diplomat explained:

This is one of the beautiful things about the PSC—that we often have proper discussions during the meetings. If you are not flexible this kills discussion.[145]

Yet it is understood that moving the discussion forward within the PSC very much depends on how ambassadors are linked with the top-level decision-makers in the capitals as otherwise a PSC decision 'falls apart in the Council—as it happens sometimes'.[146] As in the case of the EFC the selection of PSC ambassadors is therefore considered to be crucial:

PSC ambassadors are high in rank and able to talk to ministers and heads of government.[147]

It is considered to be counterproductive for PSC discussions if this is not the case, and if ambassadors 'are under extremely precise instructions by their capitals'.[148] Howorth (2011) shows that PSC members tend to have a very similar background in terms of education. His research reveals strong support among PSC members for the view that national and European interests are compatible in principle. PSC members are found to stay on the committee for

---

[141] Interviewee EU-05/EXT, 10 March 2009.
[142] Interviewee PR-12/EXT, 12 March 2009.
[143] The PSC's role in overseeing organizational and operational aspects of EU missions has been studied in detail by Cross (2011).
[144] Interviewee PR-09/EXT, 22 June 2009.
[145] Interviewee PR-18/EXT, 23 November 2009.
[146] Interviewee EU-24/EXT, 17 November 2011.
[147] Interviewee PR-13/EXT, 11 March 2009.
[148] Interviewee PR-18/EXT, 23 November 2009.

three years on average. During this time on the committee PSC members see each other on an almost daily basis.

The high frequency of meetings is a key characteristic of the PSC. It reflects the scope and intensity of intergovernmental policy dialogue within this policy area. Meyer's data on the first five years of the PSC show a rapid increase in the average number of meetings per month. Currently, the PSC schedules two or three formal meetings a week. These meetings are complemented by informal gatherings and lunches of PSC ambassadors. Ambassadors are said to spend only one day a week within their respective Permanent Representations without attending PSC-related meetings.[149] One diplomat described PSC routine as follows:

> We [the diplomats in the permanent representations] are always on call for the PSC. It works 24 hours. In 'normal diplomacy' [such as in the UN system] you have a different schedule. It is more administrative. The PSC cooperation is very close and complex on all foreign policy issues. It is a challenge to digest it.[150]

The ever-growing workload and the intensity of the PSC's meeting schedule may, however, also have adverse effects on the PSC's ability to generate consensus between national executives, as Cross (2011: 130) fears. One instrument for addressing the high workload and allowing more room for policy debates is the delegation of agenda coordination and procedural tasks to a special preparatory committee—the Nicolaidis Group. Each member state and the EEAS send a representative to the meetings. The preparatory body can also deselect purely procedural issues from the discussion agenda of the PSC and adopt them immediately.[151] The set-up of the Nicolaidis Group shares some institutional features with the EFC alternates and the new Brussels-based sub-group of the Eurogroup Working Group.

Unlike EFC meetings, PSC meetings bring together a relatively large group of participants. Member states are represented by their ambassador, the deputy PSC representative, and a competent counsellor from the Permanent Representation. PSC meetings might be attended by various officials from the EEAS, the Commission, and the Council Secretariat in addition to the senior representatives of these institutions. Participants are aware that the regular meeting format is not the most confidential, as one diplomat explained:

> What I say in the PSC is almost a public statement. I can be sure that the Russians will immediately know it.[152]

---

[149] Interviewee PR-18/EXT, 23 November 2009.
[150] Interviewee PR-08/EXT, 24 November 2009.
[151] Interviewees PR-03/EXT, PR-04/EXT, PR-12/EXT.
[152] Interviewee EU-01/EXT, 9 March 2009.

Again, institutional engineering has sought to address this issue. There are several restricted PSC formats—for example, the 'ambassador plus one' or 'ambassador plus two' configuration. These formats are used specifically to discuss secret and confidential aspects.[153] There are also so-called 'ambassador only' meetings as well as half-yearly retreats. Lunch meetings are a common informal format for discussion among the ambassadors.

Another adjustment of working methods that tries to address the growing workload and size of the committee is modification of the presidency regime. Initially the PSC presidency rotated with the Council presidency. The limits of this arrangement were noticed early on. It is reported that the Eurogroup—the first high-level intergovernmental forum to introduce a permanent president— was conceived as a template for the PSC.[154] As one official explained:

> Individual presidencies can create leadership but [with a permanent chair] we will gain in consistency and professionalism.[155]

It is also believed that a strong chair improves the performance of the PSC and better organizes parallel work on multiple tasks. The PSC chair is appointed by the HR. In November 2010 the Swedish diplomat Olof Skoog became the first permanent PSC chair. A participant in PSC meetings considered that this had impacted positively on the way the committee operated:

> The permanent chair has led to increased efficiency.[156]

At the time of his appointment Skoog had already gathered experience as Sweden's PSC ambassador for over three years, and had experience in chairing the PSC during the Swedish 2009 EU presidency.[157] The permanent PSC chair also acts a spokesperson in relation to the media and makes regular statements on the EU's policy stance in relation to positions adopted by the PSC and the Council. This gives the previously highly secretive committee a stronger public profile.

The complex administrative coordination infrastructure within the CFSP sector is mirrored by the organization of decision-making processes in national line ministries, though arrangements may vary between different member states. This also means that in many cases internal procedures and hierarchies have been adjusted and restructured. In several cases, responsibilities within the foreign ministry for EU affairs have been reorganized. Most importantly, so-called first- and third-pillar issues are dealt with by a separate

---

[153] Interviewee EU-11/EXT, 9 March 2009.
[154] Interviewee EU-11/EXT, 9 March 2009.
[155] Interviewee PR-05/EXT, 24 November 2009.
[156] Interviewee EU-24/EXT, 17 November 2011.
[157] See press release by the Swedish government, 18 November 2010, <http://www.sweden.gov. se/sb/d/13762/a/156013> [accessed 7 September 2012].

EU department or unit, whereas CFSP coordination is centralized in a dedicated unit. These units channel input from different country desks and directorates within the ministry into the EU coordination process. A high-ranking civil servant—the Political Director—is charged with overseeing the process and briefing the minister. The Political Director accompanies the ministers to FAC meetings. Ahead of FAC meetings the Political Director, together with the PSC ambassador, the head of cabinet, or a deputy minister, coordinates political decisions with the ministers.[158] Historically the group of political directors made up the PSC before it was transformed into a Brussels-based committee. The role of political directors thus resembles somewhat the role of deputy finance ministers in charge of Eurogroup and ECOFIN preparation who are members of the EFC. Political directors meet as an informal group to discuss broader and strategic issues. Typically, this happens in the context of informal lunches at the occasion of FAC meetings.

In many member states the Political Director instructs the PSC ambassador, and is the main contact point for the foreign minister. In addition, both the Commission and all member state foreign ministries have a so-called European correspondent, who oversees and coordinates day-to-day communication between the different branches of the ministry on the one hand, and the PSC ambassador and the staff in charge of PSC preparation at the Permanent Representation in Brussels on the other hand. In addition, these senior civil servants maintain close bilateral contacts with their counterparts in the other EU member states, the Commission, and the EEAS. European correspondents and their relevant units are seen to play a crucial role in mobilizing attention towards the EU agenda within national foreign ministries.[159] Most ministries have introduced 'centralized routines'[160] for all aspects of CFSP decision-making and their coordination. The experiences within the domestic setting in many ways mirror those within the PSC context. One member state official explained how the view on instructing PSC representatives had changed in the relevant capital:

> We also learned that our people in the PSC need to be informed about our red lines and do not require micromanagement.[161]

Another official from a different member state was even more assertive in rejecting the traditional diplomatic practice of written instructions:

> We don't do written instructions for detailed questions. The Political Director and the PSC ambassador work it out by phone and e-mail.[162]

---

[158] Interviewee, PR-05/EXT, 24 November 2009.  [159] Interviewee MS-11/EXT, April 2009.
[160] Interviewee MS-11/EXT, April 2009.  [161] Interviewee MS-14/EXT, 30 June 2009.
[162] Interviewee, PR-05/EXT, 24 November 2009.

The same official thought that the PSC ambassador had become 'a key actor on foreign policy' in the respective capital. The centrality of PSC decision-making also implied that domestic processes needed to follow the schedule of the committee and not the other way around. According to the official 'this increases the pressure to have very quick decision-making' in the capital. Finally, national line ministries increasingly need to adjust to the fact that they play a less important role with regard to CFSP agenda setting than previously; indeed they are rather at the receiving end. The office of the HR, the EEAS and, previously, the Council Secretariat are considered now to be more important than the national foreign ministries when it comes to setting objectives for discussions among ministers.[163] Pol Morillas (2011)—a Spanish diplomat familiar with PSC coordination—identified the dualism of stricter and more centralized agenda management by the HR on the one hand, and parallel insistence on a strictly intergovernmental process that gives member state administrations a central role on the other hand, as a defining element of EU foreign policy-making, following the Lisbon Treaty.

### 4.5.3 *The Policy Unit and the EEAS*

The above section showed the important role of dedicated expert committees in linking the top-level civil servant representatives of member state bureaucracies. The establishment of new areas of EU activity in the post-Maastricht period has led to the emergence of a new type of policy coordination comitology that is focused on facilitating consensus seeking while being located at the top of a complex intergovernmental bureaucratic infrastructure. Top-level committees play the lead role in coordinating the preparation and implementation of policy decisions in a decentralized policy-setting with the help of national line ministries and EU-level administrative resources such as the Commission's DG ECFIN. Yet with the expansion of the scope of the EU's new policy activities in the post-Maastricht era it has been impossible to avoid entirely the creation of additional and more integrated bureaucratic resources located at the EU level rather than within the member state capitals. Given the member states' reluctance to expand the administrative powers of the Commission the examples of two *de novo* types of bureaucratic set-up[164] deserve brief attention here: the Policy Unit and the EEAS. Both set-ups are not infrastructures for collective EU decision-making in the sense of European Council, Council, and senior expert committee contexts studied in this book.

---

[163] Interviewee MS-14/EXT, 30 June 2009.

[164] The role of *de novo* institutions within the context of the EU's post-Maastricht new intergovernmentalism is addressed in greater detail in Bickerton et al. (2015).

However, the Policy Unit and the EEAS are charged with providing administrative support to CFSP and CSDP policy coordination. The creation of the Policy Unit in 2000 represented a first small step in building an enhanced bureaucratic resource for CFSP and CSDP policy-making at the EU level. The creation of the EEAS by the Lisbon Treaty as an EU diplomatic service goes even further. In both cases the HR has been assigned direct oversight over the relevant bureaucratic structures, thus providing for some degree of bureaucratic autonomy. The prime functions of these administrative entities has never been to represent member state and Commission positions, but to carry out tasks delegated to them by the Council and the European Council, and to work in support of the HR.

The Policy Unit—called in full the Policy Planning and Early Warning Unit—was created on the basis of a declaration annexed to the Amsterdam Treaty,[165] located within the General Secretariat of the Council, and staffed with Brussels-based civil servants. It was charged with the monitoring and analysis of CFSP-related developments, forward planning, and early warning. The unit contributed to policy formulation in the Council through so-called policy option papers. The mandate of the Policy Unit clearly distinguished it from a classic supranational bureaucratic resource understood in terms of the Commission model. It was stipulated that '[t]he unit shall consist of personnel drawn from the General Secretariat, the Member States, the Commission and the WEU [Western European Union, the former West European security organization].'[166] Member states and the Commission were allowed to 'make suggestions to the unit for work to be undertaken',[167] but equally, were required to supply the Policy Unit with information required for policy planning. The Policy Unit was deliberately developed as an infrastructure that was as open as possible to member state influence in terms of personnel, politics, and agenda setting. As one official involved in the early phase of Policy Unit operation recalled, policy-makers at the time rejected an alternative institutional design as they feared a 'black box Brussels'[168]—a new administrative structure without access to member state resources such as intelligence and policy analysis capacities on which its own work would ultimately depend. The approach therefore needed to reflect the decentralized character of available foreign policy resources. As the same official explained:

> The capitals needed to be embedded [in the coordination process]. This is the key to successful coordination.[169]

---

[165] Declaration No. 6, Treaty of Amsterdam.
[166] Declaration No. 6, Treaty of Amsterdam, para. 3.
[167] Declaration No. 6, Treaty of Amsterdam, para. 4.
[168] Interviewee EU-13/EXT, 7 April 2009.
[169] Interviewee EU-13/EXT, 7 April 2009.

After creating the PSC the Policy Unit took on more analytical work and background briefing tasks. Crucially, Policy Unit personnel were now recruited on the principle of one unit member from each member state so as to further strengthen member state involvement in the process of policy formulation and design. EU enlargement thus led to significant increases in the number of unit personnel. Finally, the development of the Policy Unit revealed the demand for a different type of administrative support structure in the field of foreign policy coordination within the Council and the European Council context as opposed to classic domains of community method decision-making. In this new context of EU activity integrating analytical and strategic preparation, on the one hand, and procedural and logistical preparation as the traditional domain of the Council Secretariat, on the other, had become a central issue. The eventual merger of the Policy Unit with the old DG E for external affairs of the Council Secretariat spoke to this point and abolished the problem of partially overlapping administrative resources.

The establishment of the EEAS constitutes another major step in expanding the EU's coordination support infrastructure. The EEAS is an EU-level diplomatic service. Internally, it provides administrative support to policy planning, decision-making and implementation processes. Externally, the service supplies the diplomatic personnel for the global network of EU delegations. The EEAS essentially is a hybrid institution that combines supranational and intergovernmental elements. It integrates former branches and personnel from the Commission, the Policy Unit, and the Council Secretariat, as well as officials and diplomats from member states into one institution, which has the status of 'a functionally autonomous body of the European Union, separate from the General Secretariat of the Council and from the Commission',[170] and which is headed by the HR. The EEAS does not replace member state diplomatic resources but rather 'shall work in cooperation with the diplomatic services of the Member States' (Article 27, TEU). The EEAS expands the previously existing practice of coordinating the diplomatic activities of EU members within and towards third countries and international organizations. The EEAS is charged with supporting the HR 'in his/her capacity as President of the Foreign Affairs Council',[171] as well as in her role as vice-president of the Commission. The EEAS is thus a powerful bureaucratic resource for the EU's internal coordination process, and facilitates the HR's role as a proactive chair of the FAC and EU foreign policy agenda setter (see section 4.3 and Vanhoonacker and Pomorska (2013)). The EEAS equally supports the presidents

---

[170] Article 1.2, Council Decision 2010/427/EU establishing the organization and functioning of the EEAS, published in OJ L201/32.

[171] Article 2.1, Council Decision 2010/427/EU establishing the organization and functioning of the EEAS, published in OJ L201/30.

of the European Council and the Commission in their external relations activities.

The EEAS' organizational structure and staff recruitment policy is peculiar. The service is a separate and independent administrative entity, yet the overwhelming majority of its personnel came from previously existing branches of the Commission and the Council Secretariat. To this end a staff transfer took place in January 2011. The EEAS has absorbed the staff of the former DG External and Politico-Military Affairs of the Council Secretariat, including the former Policy Unit. Altogether 411 Council Secretariat officials have been transferred to the EEAS.[172] Thus, the EEAS has continued the integrated approach towards supporting Council decision-making, pursued with the merger of the Policy Unit and the external affairs branch of the Council Secretariat. The EEAS has also absorbed most of the previously existing Commission resources for external action. Alone 585 staff members from DG RELEX, 93 from DG Development Cooperation and another 436 Commission delegation officials have been transferred to the EEAS.

The EEAS organizational rules place much emphasis on developing the service as a vehicle for coordinating member state and existing EU-level resources rather than working on the principle of delegating executive competences to a genuinely supranational administration. The EEAS recruitment policy stipulates that 'staff from Member States [ . . . ] should represent at least one third of all EEAS staff at AD [administrator rank] level'.[173] Member states have amended national regulations for diplomatic personnel and ministerial officials so to guarantee reinstatement of these officials once they rotate out of the EEAS. In this way a considerable share of EEAS staff is exchanged with the member state administrations over time. The EEAS also recruits member state officials into permanent positions and works with seconded national experts, as is common practice in the Commission and Council Secretariat. For example, at the time that the 2011 rotation in the positions of heads of delegations was announced, the HR Catherine Ashton reported that '45 of the 149 management positions in EU delegations will be held by diplomats on secondment from national Foreign Affairs Ministries of the countries of the EU'.[174] Out of a total of 25 new appointments 16 positions of head of delegation were filled with diplomats from the member states, seven posts were

---

[172] EU press release, IP/10/1769, 21 December 2010, <http://europa.eu/rapid/press-release_IP-10-1769_en.htm?locale=en> [accessed 24 July 2013].
[173] Article 9, Council Decision 2010/427/EU establishing the organization and functioning of the EEAS, published in OJ L201/35.
[174] European Commission, press release IP/11/944, 'EU High Representative/Vice President Catherine Ashton appoints 25 new Heads of EU Delegations', Brussels, 3 August 2011.

taken up by EEAS staff, and two posts were occupied by Commission offi-cials.[175] The recruitment of diplomats on secondment from the foreign min-istries of the member states was also visible in the allocation of senior positions within the service, of which many were filled in late 2010 and in 2011.[176] The EEAS architecture is thus focused on constant coordination with all involved actors—member states and the Commission alike. As one official put it:

> We [the EEAS] do not have the intention to bypass the member states anyway because everybody knows that whatever you try to do in foreign affairs without the member states will only last for five minutes.[177]

The official also believed that the new EEAS structure made it easier to inte-grate Commission and intergovernmental decision-making. How radical a change it was became apparent during the rather bumpy launch of the new service. The hybrid EEAS model implied conflict on virtually all fronts almost by default. Smith (2013) even argues, because of its institutional complexity and the delays in Treaty reform, that the immediate effect of the introduction of the EEAS structure represented a de facto weakening of the EU's operational capability to carry out civil and military missions as unresolved disputes over bureaucratic resources and competences between the Commission, the Coun-cil, and individual member states hampered the creation of more rational and effective organization of the EEAS. Though an analysis of the actual operation of the EEAS is much beyond the scope of this book it can said that the main rationale behind the EEAS' organizational structure is indeed a systemic one—not solely the consideration of achieving immediate efficiency gains. The EEAS is an attempt to institutionalize the EU's new emphasis on expanding its own coordination support structures in Brussels and in relation to its international presence, as well as to integrate these activities with the more supranational domains of external activity under one roof. It reflects perfectly the post-Maastricht integration paradox. EEAS practice reveals core patterns of interaction that are predicted by deliberative intergovernmentalism. In their study of the attitudes of EEAS officials towards their institution, Ana Juncos and Karolina Pomorska (2013) reveal that there is a generally strong commit-ment towards the objective of establishing the service. Officials are over-whelmingly committed to pragmatism when it comes to overcoming differences and difficulties. This is remarkable given the difficulties in estab-lishing the EEAS and the bureaucratic rivalries that are inevitably associated with its peculiar personnel politics. Juncos and Pomorska's findings echo elite

---

[175] European Commission, press release IP/11/944, 'EU High Representative/Vice President Catherine Ashton appoints 25 new Heads of EU Delegations', Brussels, 3 August 2011.
[176] See e.g. Agence Europe, 'Three new directors at EEAS', 4 August 2011.
[177] Interviewee, EU-24/EXT, 17 November 2011.

orientations that could be observed in other institutional contexts studied within this book; their findings correspond with the proposition of deliberative intergovernmentalism that commitment to the coordination process is very high despite continuous differences about policy options and—as in the case of the EEAS—institutional design and reorganization. It is thus likely that the EEAS will be subject to further institutional engineering, which will focus primarily on improving its internal operation and its coordination potential rather than on changing its overall hybrid structure as a mixed supranational and intergovernmental bureaucracy. This study therefore echoes Smith's (2013: 13) expectation that 'EU policy élites will have to resort to other consensus-building mechanisms, such as networking, socialization and learning, for the foreseeable future', as the EEAS' complex institutional architecture will not be significantly altered. Such a trajectory of potential further EEAS development can also be inferred from the speech to the EP on the 2013 EEAS review report by Catherine Ashton. The HR emphasized the EEAS' main orientation, and rejected calls to look for stronger supranationalization as a means of increasing effectiveness:

> These recommendations will be designed to improve further the effectiveness of our Service which is widely judged already to have delivered a step change in EU foreign policy. But we should not delude ourselves—Lisbon left CFSP as intergovernmental and subject to unanimity decision-making: in situations where there is an absence of political will or an agreement amongst the Member States there are limits to what the Service can deliver. In that respect, the service supports me in my role both as High Representative and as Vice President of the Commission. This enables it to play an important coordination role on EU external policies.[178]

### 4.5.4 *Other Socio-economic Governance Committees*

Another trigger for the proliferation of expert committees that focus on consensus formation in the context of the development of coordination guidelines and multilateral surveillance processes was expansion of the EU's wider socio-economic governance agenda in the late 1990s and the launch of OMC processes under the Lisbon agenda. Three of the most prominent so-called 'OMC committees' deserve brief attention here though they are less senior in status than the EFC, the Eurogroup Working Group, or the PSC. Yet their basic institutional set-up is based on a similar rationale. Judged by its name and its original legal basis the first of these committees, the EPC is an old community committee. It was founded in 1974. However, the EPC underwent

---

[178] EEAS press release A 314/13, 12 June 2013, 'Statement by EU High Representative Catherine Ashton on EEAS Review', <http://www.consilium.europa.eu/uedocs/cms_data/docs/pressdata/EN/foraff/137458.pdf> [accessed 25 July 2013].

significant transformation after the introduction of the single currency and the launch of the Lisbon agenda.[179] One aspect of the EPC's new role is that it serves the analytical arm of the EFC in the context of the surveillance of member states' macroeconomic policies under EMU. While the EFC and the Eurogroup Working Group are focused on preparing the ground for the actual political decision-making within the Eurogroup and the ECOFIN Council, the EPC is concerned with forging agreement among policy experts from the member state administrations, the Commission, and the ECB. Since the launch of the Lisbon agenda the EPC has done much to shape the EU-level bureaucratic opinion in areas such as structural reform, active labour market policies, and specific policy challenges such as pension reform and environmental issues. In these areas the EPC's work intersects with the work of the other two committees that are discussed here: EMCO and SPC. The EPC also played an important role in reviewing the so-called Lisbon agenda and preparing the launch of the European Semester and EU2020. In June 2005 the EPC also set up a euro-area working group: the EPC-Eurogroup. This group is in charge of preparing specific input to Eurogroup decision-making, and can be considered as an attempt to enhance the Eurogroup's focus on medium- and long-term policy challenges and issues that require horizontal coordination with other Council formations.

EMCO was set up by the Amsterdam Treaty to support policy coordination in the EPSCO Council under the European Employment Strategy (EES). The committee was specifically created to deal with policy coordination instead of legislative matters, which constitute the other core aspect of the EPSCO agenda (see section 4.4).[180] The chair of EMCO participates in EPSCO meetings and there are EPSCO sub-groups, of which one is focused on supporting coordination processes and the other supplies analytical work on indicators for monitoring the employment situation and employment policies in the member states. The existence of sub-groups suggests that EMCO has a similar status to the EFC or the PSC. Yet the actual work of EMCO differs from the two top-level committees. In contrast to the PSC and the EFC, which have responsibility for the preparation of the dominant agenda items for the Eurogroup and ECOFIN, EMCO's work relates only to a fraction of the EPSCO agenda. It is also observed that EMCO's relatively low profile in contemporary EU socioeconomic governance is reflected in its membership. Once the fundamentals of the coordination process were established in the late 1990s many of the more senior members were lost. The EMCO process now is also considered to be more bureaucratic than in the first phase of EU employment policy

---

[179] For a further discussion of the reform of the EPC after the launch of the Lisbon agenda cf. Grosche and Puetter (2008).
[180] Interviewee EU-17/ECON, 15 November 2009.

coordination.[181] The low frequency of EPSCO meetings implies that EMCO essentially prepares the process of drafting and reviewing the so-called employment guidelines. The current coordination process is considered to be overloaded, owing to the need to prepare a new set of employment policy guidelines every year. This way room for meaningful policy debate is limited.[182] An episode in EU crisis management illustrates the difficulties EMCO has in playing a more forthcoming role. In the early phase of crisis management the EPC, rather than EMCO, was charged with preparing the special meeting on employment under the Czech Council presidency in the first half of 2009 (see section 4.4).[183]

The SPC is the other expert committee charged with supporting policy coordination within the EPSCO Council context. It too operates on the basis of the Treaty mandate (Article 160, TFEU), and is charged with the coordination of social inclusion and social protection policies.[184] It was created by the Treaty of Nice. It produces policy reports and adopts opinions. This means that the SPC by default can play even less of a political leadership role than EMCO, which is charged with preparing the employment guidelines.[185] The fact that two different committees deal with the EPSCO social and employment policy coordination portfolio rather than one is a source of difficulty—in particular given the limited focus on coordination issues in EPSCO. One official familiar with EPSCO discussions pointed to the gap between the two committees:

You often wonder whether these are the same 27 countries in both committees.[186]

As with EMCO and the other committees discussed in this section, the SPC chair participates in EPSCO meetings. Yet there are doubts about the influence of EMCO and SPC chairs in the context of EPSCO discussion. In the words of the above cited official:

They [the EMCO and SPC chairs] can't say much. The chairs don't have the delegates behind them.[187]

This brief overview of the three most important OMC committees shows how complex the bureaucratic infrastructure for policy coordination has become. In the case of the EPC institutional engineering led to an enhancement of its role. There is evidence that the EPC also pulls some of the social policy

---

[181] Interviewee EU-17/ECON, 15 November 2009.
[182] Interviewee EU-19/ECON, 25 June 2009.
[183] Interviewee EU-17/ECON, 12 March 2009.
[184] For a more in-depth analysis of SPC internal dynamics cf. Horvath (2008).
[185] Interviewee EU-19/ECON, 25 June 2009.
[186] Interviewee EU-22/ECON, 24 November 2009.
[187] Interviewee, EU-22/ECON, 24 November 2009.

coordination issues into its own portfolio. This essentially reflects the fact that finance ministers in the Eurogroup and ECOFIN have become the most important group of ministers, who also assume responsibility for the preparation of European Council coordination within the EU socio-economic governance domain. These developments are also reflected at the domestic level. The organization of line ministries in the overlapping areas of economic, employment, and social policy is of growing concern because of the evolution of the comitology process and coordination within the Council. One official explained that the economic and financial crisis especially triggered desire for adjustments within the domestic bureaucratic structure:

> Within our own government there is now a much higher awareness of the need for using the administrative machinery in [capital name deleted] and Brussels for preparing [country name deleted] positions on EU topics and for pre-coordinating with the partners. This attitude was absent before.[188]

Still, in most countries the picture is quite diverse. Coalition governments also make the reorganization of national portfolios according to the increasingly apparent hierarchy in Council decision-making difficult. Yet there are examples of member states in which '80% of Lisbon [i.e. the OMC] topics are under one ministry'.[189] Such structure is considered to make coordination 'easier'.[190]

## 4.6 Running the Council

The analysis so far demonstrated how much post-Maastricht attempts at institutional engineering have focused on adapting the functioning of the European Council and the Council to a new coordination agenda, and to make the institutions respond to the quest for consensus, which is characteristic of the new areas of EU activity. As much as the EU's new intergovernmentalism had repercussions for the work of the European Council and those Council formations that have immediate responsibility for the concerned policy areas, the overall institutional infrastructure of the Council is affected by the changing institutional dynamics. This section briefly traces the main consequences of new intergovernmentalism for the GAC, the rotating presidency of the Council, COREPER, and the General Secretariat of the Council as branches of Council activity that are charged with horizontal coordination and overall political and organizational leadership roles.

---

[188] Interviewee PR-14, 22 June 2009.
[189] Interviewee PR-17/ECON, 5 November 2009.
[190] Interviewee PR-17/ECON, 5 November 2009.

## 4.6.1 *The General Affairs Council*

Perhaps somewhat ironically, the set-up of the GAC, which was only consti-tuted as a functionally independent Council formation by the Lisbon Treaty (Article 16.6, TEU), reveals most clearly how much internal dynamics in the Council were changed by the increased importance of policy coordination within the new areas of EU activity as opposed to the Council's traditional role as a legislator. In principle the GAC is supposed to address a major problem in EU policy-making: the horizontal coordination of policy issues, which are dealt with in functionally separated Council formations. The functional sep-aration of this activity from the foreign affairs portfolio was meant to facilitate this task (see section 4.3). Already the Helsinki European Council in December 1999 had warned with a view to enlargement that the 'General Affairs Coun-cil's central responsibility for general horizontal issues'[191] would imply an ever more complex task in the future. At the time the European Council also underlined the role of the GAC in preparing European Council meetings. The Belgian minister of foreign affairs Steven Vanackere declared at the begin-ning of the Belgian 2010 EU presidency, which oversaw the first semester of Council decision-making under the Lisbon Treaty, that the development of the GAC was one of the priorities of its presidency. In particular he empha-sized the coordination role of this Council formation, both ahead of and after European Council meetings.[192] The GAC is formally in charge of prepar-ing all European Council meetings. It also holds a public debate on the 18-month work programme of each trio presidency of the Council (see section 4.6.2).[193] However, two structural features of post-Maastricht European Coun-cil and Council decision-making were identified in the earlier parts of this book that make it difficult for the GAC to play a central coordinating role: the proximity of the Eurogroup and ECOFIN and FAC to European Council decision-making, and the heads' ambition to personally oversee Council activ-ity within the context of the core coordination portfolios. As one official made it clear:

> The idea that the General Affairs Council prepares the European Council does not really work in foreign affairs and it does not work in economic governance. Member states do not really understand what the General Affairs Council is for. And, look who attends it now. It is not clear procedurally or substantially.[194]

---

[191] European Council (1999a), Annex III.
[192] Agence Europe, *Bulletin Quotidien Europe* 10188, 27 June 2010.
[193] Article 8.3, Council Decision 2009/937/EU adopting the Council's Rules of Procedure, published in OJ L325/35.
[194] Interviewee, EU-24/EXT, 17 November 2011.

As demonstrated in the earlier sections of this chapter and in the analysis of European Council decision-making, a series of steps in institutional engineering have led to greater administrative integration in the preparation of substantial policy issues on the one hand, and organizational aspects of European Council decision-making on the other hand. The Eurogroup and ECOFIN in the field of economic governance and the FAC in the external relations portfolio directly prepare European Council decision-making. In both policy domains, dedicated senior expert committees underpin this process. The analysis of the European Council agenda has revealed the importance of these domains in explaining the overall role of the European Council in contemporary EU decision-making. All this drastically limits any political role for ministers in the GAC. In any case such a role would contradict the ambition on part of the heads to control the activities of their ministers in the Council. This problem could be addressed only by a different composition of the GAC or outside of this framework, as one interviewee explained:

> The General Affairs Council is competing with ECOFIN. The question is whether the General Affairs Council will evolve to become the main coordination forum for the preparation of European Council meetings. It will be up to the member states to decide whether they will send the foreign ministers or personal representatives of the heads. Coalition arrangements or constitutional obstacles might make this all difficult to decide.[195]

During the first years after the Lisbon Treaty entered into force, the practice of line ministers taking part in GAC meetings was mixed, with some member states sending their foreign ministers as before and some sending their EU affairs ministers. Post-Lisbon, European Council practice indeed confirms that next to the dominance of the Eurogroup and the ECOFIN and FAC formations in European Council preparation, personal representatives of the heads are the key figures within this process. The work of the Van Rompuy task force highlighted for the first time the central role of such personnel representatives—the so-called Sherpas (see section 3.7). This approach was broadened and the Sherpa meetings, with a specific focus on economic governance, were convened ahead of European Council meetings. For example, two Sherpa meetings were convened ahead of the Spring European Council meeting in March 2013 to prepare the discussion. Moreover, the president's head of cabinet entertains regular conversations within the Sherpa network throughout the year. The Sherpa network plays an important role ahead of European Council meetings, and is considered to be essential to preparing the substantial aspects of individual agenda items. Only at the last stages of the preparations do COREPER and the GAC review and pre-discuss the European Council agenda.[196] There is little to

---

[195] Interviewee EU-07/ECON, 30 March 2010.     [196] Interviewee EU-25/GEN.

suggest that COREPER or the GAC reopen policy issues in the core economic governance and foreign affairs domains. Rather, the practice of regularly convening Sherpa meetings has become a central feature of the European Council's preparation regime.[197]

### 4.6.2 The Rotating Presidency of the Council

The rotating presidency is another key feature of the original Council architecture. Like the GAC, it has not remained unaffected by the rise of new intergovernmentalism within the context of the new areas of EU activity. This section moves the analysis of the presidency beyond the focus of principal–agent approaches on the novel formal leadership powers that the Lisbon Treaty assigned to the European Council president at the expense of the previously existing system of outright rotation (cf. Blavoukos et al. 2007). The post of the European Council president evidently implies a transformation in the role of the prime minister or president of the country holding the rotating presidency of the Council. Formally, the two presidencies coexist and mutually support each other. This, for example, is acknowledged by the seating order within the European Council. The relevant prime minister or president is seated next to the European Council president. However, the Lisbon Treaty remained vague on precisely how the relationship between the two representatives should be defined. The relationship between the two top-level representatives was therefore considered as a potential source of friction—in particular, because the new arrangements banned the head of state or government of the country holding the rotating Council presidency from the publicly recognizable role of an EU leader. One diplomat therefore expressed concern that member states might backtrack altogether from throwing their political weight behind the rotating presidency:

> The reduced role of the Prime Minister might imply that the presidency [of the Council] is seen as less attractive by the member states.[198]

The two terms of Van Rompuy's presidency did not provide much evidence for this. Several interviewees observed that at the time of Van Rompuy's first appointment as president of the European Council many members of the forum had not realized the consequences of the regime change. The Spanish Council presidency in the first half of 2010 was the first exposed to the new arrangements. As one official explained:

---

[197] This point was highlighted by Katarina Areskoug Mascarenhas, Sherpa and State Secretary to the Swedish prime minister Fredrik Reinfeldt with responsibility for European Council coordination, at a discussion at the Swedish Institute for European Policy Studies (SIEPS) in Stockholm, 8 October 2013.

[198] Interviewee PR-22/GEN, 1 June 2010.

In the Spanish government many people were not aware of what the Lisbon Treaty would mean. Many other Prime Ministers and presidents were also not aware of this. Could you see a Blair or Sarkozy in this game? The fact that all summits went to Brussels was a disaster for Zapatero.[199]

However, the transition proceeded rather smoothly. Van Rompuy did not compromise on his new prerogatives, and at the same time sought to establish a close working relationship with the rotating presidency. The transition was also facilitated by the fact that Belgium—Van Rompuy's home country— succeeded Spain in the presidency seat. The practice of the first trio presidency under the Lisbon Treaty (cf. Batory and Puetter 2013) not to establish a visible role for the head of state or government holding the rotating Council presidency was probably crucial in determining the way the relationship with the European Council president evolved from then on. Instead of undermining the authority of the European Council president by portraying themselves to the outside world as alternative leaders, member state prime ministers and presidents who represented the rotating presidency have so far been careful to restrict their own role to one that is essentially defined behind the scenes.

What is crucial to consider is that the rotating presidency of the Council is still an important actor within the field of legislative decision-making. Neither the new formal prerogatives of the European Council president nor his de facto role as a lead facilitator of top-level policy coordination within the new areas of EU activity changes this role. Moreover, in those areas where the EU's legislative and policy coordination agendas are closely interlinked, as with EMU institutional reform and banking union, close coordination with the rotating presidency of the Council is crucial for the European Council president. One official emphasized that there is still a clear division of labour between the European Council president and the rotating Council presidency when it comes to legislative decision-making:

The rotating [Council] presidency takes care of the negotiations of legal texts.[200]

The head of state or government representing the rotating presidency of the Council plays a crucial role in overseeing the work of the chairs of the different Council formations, and therefore becomes the main contact point for Van Rompuy as far as the relation between the Council and the European Council is concerned. As one official explained with reference to the Hungarian 2011 Council presidency:

---

[199] Interviewee EU-06/GEN, 3 June 2010.    [200] Interviewee EU-09/ECON, 4 July 2011.

> Van Rompuy has no direct links with Council chairs but he meets the Prime Minister—that means Orbán—a lot. Every time Orbán was in Brussels and then also in Budapest [they met].[201]

And another official explained:

> The role of the Prime Minister is interesting [under the Lisbon Treaty]. All the initiative now comes from Van Rompuy. There is coordination between the Prime Minister's cabinet and Van Rompuy's cabinet. He is very assertive. However, this will cause frustration [inside the administration of the country holding the Council presidency].[202]

The quote illustrates how far-reaching the role of the European Council president has become, and that with the European Council playing an increasingly important part in EU policy-making, national administrations sometimes have to adjust to a new pattern of coordination and decision-making. Some officials have therefore expressed concern that without clear incentives for individual heads representing the rotating Council presidency, they may not engage in 'mobilising political support'.[203] Indeed the experience so far has supported the idea that the readiness of Prime Ministers or presidents representing the rotating Council presidency to work closely with Van Rompuy and to devote energy to organizing support (both within their own administration and also among the other member states) is crucial to the European Council's ability to control and lead Council decision-making, especially in those areas where the policy coordination intersects with the EU legislative agenda.

Van Rompuy was considered to have been very well aware of these interdependencies, and was eager not to discourage individual heads from playing such an active role at the time their country held the rotating presidency of the Council. Instead of being challenged in his new role, Van Rompuy rather faced the opposite problem. For example, the Hungarian prime minister Viktor Orbán, who followed as the third representative of the rotating Council presidency after the change in the presidency regime in January 2011, reportedly turned down an offer by Van Rompuy to agree to a particular role for him during the term of the Hungarian Council presidency.[204] Personal commitment, which is unlikely to be rewarded by immediate political gains, on the part of individual heads who held the rotating presidency has therefore become a crucial factor in determining the political role of the Council presidency in the post-Lisbon period. The Danish Council presidency in the first half of 2012 was particularly praised in this regard. The Danish prime minister

---

[201] Interviewee EU-09/ECON, 4 July 2011.
[203] Interviewee PR-16/GEN, 3 June 2010.
[202] Interviewee MS-07/ECON, 20 May 2010.
[204] Interviewee EU-06/GEN, 3 June 2010.

Helle Thorning-Schmidt was thought to have been engaged in very efficient behind-the-scenes coordination.

The other key aspect in assessing the role of the rotating Council presidency in the post-Lisbon period is its role in agenda setting. In fact, the new emphasis on non-legislative Council decision-making had repercussions for the agenda setting role of the rotating presidency long before the Lisbon Treaty came into force. Chapter 3 has already revealed that the timing of European Council sessions in the post-Maastricht era became progressively less determined by the long-term planning priorities of the incoming rotating presidency. Similar changes can be identified with regard to the timing of Council sessions. Originally, the calendar and agenda of Council meetings very much followed the calendar of legislative decision-making. Council meetings were scheduled and prepared well in advance in order to allow for the completion of legislative dossiers. The internal Council rules of procedure even require each incoming Council presidency to announce the schedule of the planned meetings more than half a year before the actual presidency period.[205] Such planning still takes place. Within the EU legislative process the actual Council meeting is only one of the various steps that need to be taken. The schedule of the Council needs to be in tune with the schedules of the Commission, the EP, and comitology activities, as well as with the particular efforts of the rotating presidency to close a dossier. However, a different pattern has emerged with regard to the new areas of EU activity. In particular the meeting schedules of the EU's most senior Council formations, the ECOFIN Council and the FAC as well as the Eurogroup, show similar patterns to those revealed by the analysis of the European Council agenda. During the course of the year, numerous extra meetings are taking place and there are changes to the agenda that cannot be anticipated. Most importantly, coordination activity follows a different logic than the EU's legislative agenda. There are elements that establish regularity other than the legislative calendar, such as the adoption of annual policy guidelines and related review processes. Ad-hoc demand for collective decision-making arises whenever an issue requires collective action, rather than in response to an ongoing legislative process. As soon as a country violates the SGP, a foreign policy crisis situation requires a response, or the Union is faced with exceptional challenges culminating in a series of events such as high unemployment rates and a political crisis, decisions need to be taken. The early transition to a permanent presidency of the Eurogroup illustrates very well the ramifications for the role of the rotating presidency with regard to one dominant policy portfolio. All this implies that individual Council presidencies find it extremely difficult to

---

[205] Article 1.2, Council Decision 2009/937/EU adopting the Council's Rules of Procedure, published in OJ L325/35.

assert themselves as agenda-setters. This is not only due to the formal powers of the European Council president, but also to the fact that the European Council, the Eurogroup, and the FAC lead on important policy dossiers that impact on how the EU is perceived more broadly—internally and externally. This further helps us to understand why the rotating presidency of the Council has lost much visibility in contemporary EU politics, even though it still formally possesses leadership prerogatives in the legislative arena.

### 4.6.3 COREPER

COREPER has a privileged position in EU decision-making. It is mandated by the Treaty to act as the key preparatory body of the Council (Article 16.7, TEU). Most importantly, COREPER conducts reviews of all Council agenda items with legislative implications prior to Council meetings. This role is formally acknowledged by the Council's rules of procedure, which require the Council presidency to remove agenda items if 'Coreper has not completed its examination of draft legislative acts' a week before the actual meeting of the Council. This clause also puts COREPER above all other EU committees whenever legislative issues are concerned. Only 'considerations of urgency' allow the Council presidency to circumvent COREPER.[206] In addition, the importance of COREPER is highlighted by its role in preparing the so-called 'A points' on the Council agenda, which are approved without further debate within the Council unless a delegation raises last-minute objections. The crucial role of COREPER within Council decision-making is also acknowledged widely in the literature (cf. e.g. Hayes-Renshaw and Wallace 2006; Lewis 1998). COREPER ambassadors were long seen as the only ones who understand EU decision-making. They form a close community and are the main interlocutors for ministers and heads of state and government. However, COREPER is also not exempted from processes of post-Maastricht institutional change within the European Council and Council context. Its role as the central preparatory body for political decision-making within the two bodies has been seriously modified following the establishment of the new areas of EU activity and the rise of new intergovernmentalism. Formally, COREPER's Treaty mandate does not discriminate between legislative and non-legislative decision-making within the Council and stipulates in general terms that COREPER is 'responsible for preparing the work of the Council' (Article 16.7, TEU). However, the concrete procedural prerogatives quoted above, which are defined by the Council's rules of procedure, assign COREPER the role as an ultimate gatekeeper only in relation to legislative decision-making. This does not imply

---

[206] Article 3.5, Council Decision 2009/937/EU adopting the Council's Rules of Procedure, published in OJ L325/35.

that COREPER ambassadors have not been eager in the past two decades to fulfil their role as lead coordinators of all European Council and Council activity. It is only that they find it increasingly difficult, if not impossible, to exercise this role.

There are three main reasons for this. Firstly, the relevance of specialized top-level expert committees for policy coordination within the new areas of EU activity—notably the EFC, the Eurogroup Working Group, and the PSC—make it difficult for COREPER to exercise control over policy dossiers even if it has a chance to review them. Secondly, the importance of informal meeting formats as a key feature of new intergovernmentalism implies that COREPER ambassadors can no longer always follow all political discussion—a prerogative they enjoyed under the traditional Council and European Council working methods. Instead heads and ministers discuss among themselves or are accompanied by the relevant member of the specialized senior expert committee, as in Eurogroup meetings and most ECOFIN discussions. Thirdly and more generally, the dominance of agenda items that do not or only in a limited way relate to legislative activity make it very difficult for COREPER to insist on its procedural prerogatives. Interviews with senior officials outside COREPER who assist European Council, Eurogroup, and Council decision-making within the new areas of EU activity leave little doubt about the fact that COREPER does not fully control agenda preparation. As one of them explained by making reference to the European Council context:

> Some European Council conclusions on EMU are dealt with outside COREPER in order to preserve confidentiality.[207]

This remark is noteworthy as it is a standard procedure for COREPER to discuss European Council draft conclusions twice before a meeting of the heads.[208]

The wording of the Euro Summit rules of procedure also reveals how the chain of information works. The Eurogroup is put in charge of informing COREPER 'before and after meetings',[209] thus tacitly assuming that COREPER does not formally intervene with these matters anyway. How far-reaching the changes are is also detectable in criticism from within the Permanent Representations. As one diplomat mourned, with a view to the practice of giving more room to informal ECOFIN breakfast discussions:

> We have now ended with the breakfast agenda being actually longer than the regular ECOFIN meeting. This obviously means that COREPER II ambassadors are excluded from large parts of the discussion. This is not acceptable.[210]

---

[207] Interviewee EU-09/ECON, 4 July 2011.
[208] Interviewee EU-07/ECON, 7 April 2009.
[209] See Council of the European Union (2013: 2).
[210] Interviewee PR-02/ECON, 3 November 2009.

Similarly, the creation of the PSC has impacted on the role of COREPER. COREPER sees all PSC input that is tabled for discussion at the FAC.[211] However, COREPER effectively refrains from reopening issues that have been decided by the PSC. European Council preparation is seen as being somewhat difficult in terms of PSC and COREPER cooperation.[212] The PSC is considered to decide 'all substantial issues'[213] that are related to European Council discussions of CFSP issues. COREPER is also considered to watch jealously the regular informal lunch meetings in the context of FAC meetings of the capital-based political directors who oversee CFSP coordination and can be crucial in preparing political discussions among the ministers.[214] Finally, the increasing importance of Sherpas as personal representatives of the heads in the context of European Council preparation further diminishes the role of COREPER within this domain. Most importantly, this implies that the role of individual COREPER ambassadors as personal contact points for their respective heads and ministers on highly important issues in EU decision-making is reduced.

## 4.7 Conclusions

This chapter has demonstrated how the rise of the EU's new intergovernment-alism in the post-Maastricht era has triggered a process of profound institutional adjustment in Council decision-making. Most importantly, decision-making in policy areas governed through policy coordination rather than the classic community method follows a different logic. The analytical framework of deliberative intergovernmentalism helps us to better understand the link between the roles that were assigned to the three Council formations and the Eurogroup as key political forums for policy coordination on the one hand, and the push to improve the consensus generation capacity of these forums through a series of attempts at institutional engineering that were primarily focused on working methods on the other. This is not to say that the features of Council decision-making presented in this chapter are entirely new to analysts of Council decision-making. Contrary to the emphasis of rational choice institutionalists and other rationalist approaches to the relevance of formal leadership roles, voting and coalition building processes in the context of Council decision-making, the argument presented in this chapter is in agreement with research on the Council that emphasizes

---

[211] Interviewee PR-07/EXT, 12 November 2009.
[212] Interviewee EU-24/EXT, 17 November 2011.
[213] Interviewee PR-09/EXT, 22 June 2009.
[214] Interviewee EU-11/EXT, 9 March 2009.

the relevance of consensus and informal agreement-seeking as key features of Council decision-making—also in areas of community method decision-making (cf. Heisenberg 2007). However, what this chapter reveals is that the push to increase the consensus-generating capacity of Council decision-making is amplified by the growing importance of the new areas of EU activity in post-Maastricht EU decision-making. As the classic community method is no longer used to provide the procedural skeleton for collective decision-making, and as legal acts are no longer (or only to a very limited extent) used to codify the results of lengthy negotiations, ongoing policy dialogue around all key policy initiatives in the new areas of EU activity has become a key characteristic of Council decision-making. The emphasis on using decentralized resources rather than supranational capacities for policy initiation, development, and implementation has triggered the creation of ever more complex coordination structures that can levy political and administrative support in the capitals and among involved EU institutions. This explains the concentration on achieving and constantly renewing direct personal agreement among ministers and top-level civil servants within the relevant Council formations, the Eurogroup, and senior expert committees. In short, the Council is the main infrastructure within and around which these processes are constructed. This institution, in which member states are represented through government ministers, is no longer defined predominantly through its role as the EU's prime legislator—a role the Council increasingly has to share on an equal basis with the EP—but also through its role as the operational centre of the EU's new intergovernmentalism.

Deliberative intergovernmentalism as an analytical framework is not blind to the fact that the Council has always exercised crucial policy coordination functions, yet it emphasizes the particular historical context of the post-Maastricht era during which policy coordination has expanded to unprecedented levels, both in terms of scope and intensity. This explains why processes of institutional adjustment have been numerous and profound. The widening of EU coordination activity ever since Maastricht is reflected in increased Council activity. The creation of the Eurogroup has effectively doubled the frequency of meetings of euro-area finance ministers, as it has complemented rather than replaced ECOFIN meetings. Meetings have become longer and there is an increase in ad-hoc meetings over time. The creation of the FAC has freed meetings of foreign ministers from general EU affairs issues.

Deliberative intergovernmentalism as an analytical framework also allows for better understanding of how differences in institutional design impact on the relative performance of individual groupings of ministers to lead specific coordination processes successfully. The creation of the Eurogroup as a dedicated forum for informal policy dialogue is the most radical expression of the functional differentiation that can be observed with regard to the evolution of working practices within the Council environment since the second half of the 1990s. The case of ECOFIN shows that institutional engineering has led to the further institutionalization of different debating formats within one institution, which has both legislative and coordination functions. The case of the informal ECOFIN breakfast format, which has gained new importance in the context of the economic and financial crisis, shows that the quest for informal policy dialogue is crucially driven by decision-making uncertainty. The Council is an important environment for processes of preference formation, not simply a context for trading predefined positions—though the point here is not to deny this equally important dimension of Council decision-making, which has received much attention so far.

The trajectory of the reorganization of the FAC has also followed the idea that emphasis on face-to-face policy debate is crucial for CFSP and CSDP coordination. The policy coordination role of foreign ministers has been separated from other responsibilities concerning general EU affairs. Foreign ministers also meet on a monthly basis, and they regularly convene for informal meetings under the Gymnich format. Yet the FAC differs somewhat from the Eurogroup and ECOFIN. It is still heavier in procedural terms, and more officials have access to a greater range of the issues under discussion during a given meeting.

EPSCO is the least developed setting, with regard to the institutionalization of working methods aimed at enabling regular informal policy dialogue on key coordination issues. Yet the EPSCO Council is also the least successful policy coordination forum. The EPSCO experience shows how the absence of more radical institutional engineering, which leads to the creation of a dedicated space for policy deliberation about key coordination topics, is detrimental to the overall coordination process. Of course this is also a key political question, but the proximity of legislative decision-making (which tends to be cumbersome in social policy anyway) and policy coordination, as well as the coexistence of different policy portfolios represented by different ministers, certainly hampers EPSCO from taking a greater role in social and employment policy coordination. This equally makes it difficult for EPSCO to position itself in relation to the Eurogroup and ECOFIN, which show strong institutionalization in the practice of constant policy dialogue. Attempts by European Council president Van Rompuy to encourage closer EPSCO involvement from the top speak to this dilemma. The episode provides an interesting contrast to French president Sarkozy's visit to the Eurogroup, which he considered to be too influential and independent-minded.

Analysing the Council infrastructure invariably leads to the question of horizontal coordination between different policy portfolios, and thus different line ministries. Here the Council reforms so far have generated mixed results. The case of EPSCO reveals that above all the mega format of this Council formation has obvious detrimental effects on social and employment policy coordination, rather than any positive impact on horizontal coordination between the various portfolios represented within the EPSCO Council. The FAC shows a somewhat better record of managing horizontal coordination between representatives of different line ministries. This seems to be facilitated by the fact that foreign ministers are clearly positioned as the senior members within this Council formation with responsibility for overall political guidance on most of the external affairs issues. The HR acts as a single chairperson for the separate meetings of foreign affairs, defence, and development ministers. The meetings of trade ministers de facto represent a distinct activity, as they are chaired by the rotating Council presidency and do not overlap logistically with the foreign affairs meetings. However, this arrangement comes with some costs attached. The HR as a chair of the FAC and its subgroupings has to deal with a much broader agenda than the permanent chair of the Eurogroup, for example.

The expansion of coordination-related Council and Eurogroup activity coincides with the expanding role of the European Council in policy coordination. This means that we see similar institutional changes occurring in parallel in different settings. The Eurogroup and the FAC converge with the European Council as regards their respective presidency regimes. All three bodies are chaired by elected presidents and have abolished the rotation rule that characterized the Council presidency for so long. In each case consensus generation among the members of the relevant grouping is a key feature of the president's role. All presidents have been engaged in institutional engineering with the aim of refocusing debates and creating room for open policy debate. Like the position of the European Council president, the position of the Eurogroup president is focused on the internal role as a consensus-broker rather than the external representation function. The case of Catherine Ashton, the first HR to chair the FAC, illustrates how demanding the combination of a proactive internal role and substantial external representation commitments actually was.

The case of Eurogroup president Jean-Claude Juncker shows that a president who is focused on organizing the internal functioning of the coordination process may be more inclined to remind forum members of the consensus that the group has reached at previous stages. This constitutes a parallel with the case of European Council president Van Rompuy. The role of the EU's first HR Javier Solana as an external spokesperson without the responsibility of the chair represents the opposite example. ECOFIN and EPSCO are still chaired by the rotating presidency. The absence of a more permanent presidency arrangement is visible in both cases.

Enlargement has certainly been an important factor in triggering reforms of Council working methods, yet again reference to enlargement does not suffice to explain the dynamism and the overall direction of Council reform. Enlargement has exacerbated problems in Council organization, which were already apparent by the end of the 1990s. However, enlargement did not cause these problems in the first place. Individual steps in the reform process clearly revealed the link between the shifting focus of Council activity and the quest for particular working methods. Functional differentiation between various aspects of Council decision-making has increased radically with the rise of new intergovernmentalism. Legislative decision-making and policy coordination have emerged increasingly as distinct spheres of Council activity that have followed different organizational rules and patterns of interaction.

This leads to the next main finding. A highly complex and specialized administrative infrastructure, focused predominantly on preparing all work related to policy coordination within the new areas of EU activity of the relevant Council formations and, increasingly, the European Council, has emerged since the late 1990s. The PSC and the EFC as well as the EFC's euro-area offspring, the Eurogroup Working Group, are highly effective settings for consensus generation, linking the most senior administrative decision-makers of the member states and EU institutions. The institutional trajectories of these committees reflect the dramatic increases in coordination activity. The more recent creation of a Brussels-based Eurogroup Working Group sub-group, which is composed of alternate members, signals important parallels with the process of transforming the PSC into a Brussels-based committee. In both cases the question of how much a particular institutional design is able to generate political support within the capitals, while at the same time having the sheer administrative capacity for dealing with numerous and rapidly arising coordination requests, is central. In the sphere of social and employment coordination EMCO and the SPC show similar features of institutional design. One factor in explaining why they do not assume a role as prominent as the PSC, the EFC, and the Eurogroup Working Group may be the complicated institutional structure of EPSCO. The EMCO and the SPC simply lack the political attention that is characteristic of the work of the other committees. The case of the EPC, whose president was invited at some point to attend regular Eurogroup meetings, also shows that committees that are focused on analytical work can get political attention if the institutional setting is conducive to this. What all the above committees have in common is that they do much more than just providing venues for discussion in Brussels; they effectively lead intergovernmental networks of top-level civil servants within the member state administrations as well as within the Commission. The institutional design of the EEAS, as the boldest attempt so far to expand bureaucratic resources in the foreign affairs domain, reveals how crucial the integration of national-level and EU-level capacities has become. Politically, the EEAS structure reveals the importance of the mobilization of member state support, as this remains a constant rather than a one-off challenge in a decentralized policy-making set-up.

The rise of new intergovernmentalism and the emergence and consolidation of the structures discussed above has important repercussions for the overall process of Council organization and the question of political leadership within the Council. The Lisbon Treaty formally charged the GAC with horizontal coordination as well as European Council meeting preparation. The findings in this chapter show that both roles are only partially fulfilled by the GAC, though there is little doubt that the GAC matters with regard to the preparation of broader institutional issues for European Council discussion and the horizontal coordination of legislative decision-making. Yet when it comes to the key policy coordination dossiers related to the new areas of EU activity the role of GAC is limited. The Eurogroup and the ECOFIN and FACs especially have developed their own complex apparatus for portfolio preparation, and these processes are closely intertwined with the process of European Council preparation. The position of a permanent European Council president has further amplified such integration. The growing institutionalization of Sherpa coordination has moved the process further away from the GAC. This once again confirms a central proposition advanced by deliberative intergovernmentalism—namely the focus on direct personal agreement among the most important decision-makers within a given institutional context.

The institution of the rotating presidency has experienced significant change and effectively become a presidency in charge of EU legislative action. This largely bans the rotating presidency from assuming a more important role within the context of the most prominent coordination dossiers and consequently from receiving greater attention within the European Council context. The findings in chapter 3 help to understand why there was much less conflict between the newly created position of the permanent European Council president and the rotating presidency than some might have expected following the assignation of formal leadership roles by the Lisbon Treaty. European Council activity is dominated by the key coordination dossiers, not by legislative decision-making. Especially with regard to areas in which the policy coordination agenda and legislative decision-making intersect, the European Council president depends on close cooperation with the rotating presidency, which assumes key responsibilities in chairing legislative decision-making processes. Though Van Rompuy is assertive with regard to his prerogatives as chair of the European Council, he has been eager to establish a good working relationship with the heads of state or government representing the rotating presidency.

Finally, the new intergovernmentalism and the growing functional differentiation in Council decision-making have clearly left traces on COREPER. As it is one of the traditional power centres of EU politics, the top-level ambassadors see themselves excluded from key preparatory activities. Pre-negotiation of the economic governance and foreign affairs dossiers is taken almost completely out of their hands with most of the substantial policy issues being resolved and prepared for final adoption at the level of the PSC, the EFC, and the Eurogroup Working Group.

# 5

# New Intergovernmentalism and the Future of European Integration

Throughout this book the focus has been on how the post-Maastricht integration paradox triggered a series of particular institutional choices. The European Council and the Council of the European Union ('the Council') are at the centre of an institutional dynamic that is referred to here as new intergovernmentalism. The decisions at Maastricht and beyond to develop important new areas of EU activity outside the context of the classic community method have had a major impact on how the EU's core forums for member state representation and collective decision-making function. Next to the rise of the European Parliament (EP) to the status of a powerful co-legislator, the changes in the roles of the European Council and the Council in European Union (EU) decision-making represent perhaps the most remarkable institutional developments in the post-Maastricht era, though they have received much less attention so far. This study has taken seriously the distinction between policy coordination and intergovernmental agreement on the one hand, and legislative decision-making under the classic community method on the other hand. For the first time it has provided a comprehensive account of the European Council and the Council that traces the practical implications of this distinction and shows how a series of attempts at institutional engineering was triggered by the reinforced quest for consensus generation among member state governments and key supranational actors—notably the Commission. This final chapter discusses three broader issues that are directly related to the study of the European Council and the Council: the role of supranational actors, the challenge of democratic control, and the repercussions for integration theory.

First, the rise of new intergovernmentalism implies that institutional change is not restricted to the sphere of European Council and Council decision-making. It almost goes without saying that the leadership roles of the European Council and the Council in economic governance, foreign affairs, and social and employment policy coordination have implications for the way the roles of supranational actors are understood in post-Maastricht EU decision-making. A more detailed analysis of this issue is beyond the scope of this book. Such an endeavour would also require important modifications to the analytical framework. However, a few reflections on the role of supranational actors in the light of the main findings of this study are provided below. These reflections are intended to encourage further research on this issue. A first step in this direction is taken elsewhere (Bickerton et al. (2015)).

The second major issue related to the changing roles of the European Council and the Council in EU decision-making, which is considered in this chapter, is that of democratic control and the legitimacy of EU decision-making. Again, the main aim of this study was to understand processes of institutional change occurring within the European Council and Council environment. Yet the findings are certainly relevant to a discussion about the democratic control of EU decision-making. Most importantly, the rise of new intergovernmentalism raises the question whether it is still appropriate to understand the question of how to enhance democratic control of EU decision-making mainly in terms of classic community method decision-making. This is discussed in the second section of this chapter.

Finally, the account of the changing roles of the European Council and the Council in EU decision-making, presented here, takes issue with other interpretations of recent trends in the institutional development of the European Council and the Council. Most importantly, deliberative intergovernmentalism as an analytical framework has challenged especially rationalist interpretations, which refer either to enlargement or to the Lisbon Treaty or both, when explaining modifications to the ways in which the European Council and the Council operate in contemporary EU decision-making. In contrast, deliberative intergovernmentalism has validated insights into micro-institutionalist settings in EU governance that have been advanced by the literature on new modes of governance and foreign affairs policy coordination, while emphasizing the systemic dimension of these insights. Notably, deliberative intergovernmentalism challenges accounts that equate integration with community method decision-making.

## 5.1 The Role of Supranational Actors

It is already the case that in some areas, such as agricultural policy, national governments can decide hardly anything by themselves. I see no need in the coming years to transfer even more [decision-making] rights to the Commission in Brussels. Instead, like France's president François Hollande, I want better coordination in those policy fields that are crucial for

> strengthening our competitiveness: for example, policies on the labour market and pensions. Economic policy coordination in Europe is said to be far too weak; it needs to be strengthened, which is not the same as transferring more competences to Brussels. (German chancellor Angela Merkel)[1]

The decision against pursuing the development of the new areas of EU activity within the context of the classic community method inevitably implies that the previously established roles of supranational actors in EU integration are being reconsidered. The definition of the community method provided in chapter 2 emphasized the aim of establishing some form of autonomous supranational authority. The Commission embodies this principle as no other EU institution as it was assigned considerable powers in initiating, developing, and implementing EU policies. It acts as an agenda-setter in EU legislative decision-making. The Commission commands substantial administrative resources, which underpin its procedural prerogatives. The role of the Commission in post-Maastricht EU governance is not easy to understand. The review of the main Treaty provisions relating to the new areas of EU activity in chapter 1 certainly shows that many of the Commission's traditional procedural prerogatives are certainly lacking. Most importantly, the Commission's right of initiative is either non-existent or irrelevant because its legislative decision-making role is negligible. Or, where it occurs, the right of initiative is substantially modified, such as in the context of the excessive deficit procedure. The interview with German chancellor Angela Merkel referred to above shows that the reduced procedural prerogatives of the Commission correspond to contemporary political rhetoric by member state governments. There is certainly no appetite to change this situation in the foreseeable future. For example, a senior diplomat with long-term experience in the COREPER II portfolio explained with regard to the trajectory of post-Maastricht institutional changes:

> The Commission clearly lost out in economic policy and foreign affairs as it is no longer the main initiator.[2]

Moreover, the clipping or modification of traditional Commission prerogatives was accompanied by further modifications to internal Commission governance. The Lisbon Treaty's enthroning of the High Representative (HR) as a Commission vice-president and chair of the Foreign Affairs Council (FAC) documented this quite clearly. One interviewee who witnessed these changes in his/her day-to-day work explained that the Commission had been very well aware of the consequences of the Lisbon Treaty all along but had not

---

[1] Interview with *Der Spiegel*, 3 June 2013, print edition. Translation by the author.
[2] Interviewee PR-16/GEN, 3 June 2010.

comprehended the almost complete loss of its influence on agenda setting in the external affairs portfolio until it became a reality:

It was an institutional shock. It was bigger than anticipated.[3]

With the creation of the European External Action Service (EEAS) the Lisbon Treaty also stripped the Commission of many of its bureaucratic resources in the field of external relations (see chapter 4.5). The example of external relations however also shows that the Commission's role in the context of new intergovernmentalism is indeed ambivalent. To portray Commission influence within the new areas of EU activity as irrelevant would totally miss the point. The role of the Commission is illustrated by the fact that it did not entirely oppose the creation of the EEAS, which involved a considerable loss of Commission staff resources. Instead the Commission sought to influence the structure of the EEAS. By integrating parts of the Commission hierarchy into the EEAS the new service obtained a markedly supranational dimension. Caterina Carta (2012: 32–51) emphasizes the centrality of the Commission in EU external diplomatic representation in this regard. From the start the Commission has brought crucial knowledge to the service and process surrounding its development. This includes the Commission's existing experiences as a facilitator of consensus seeking among the member states and other EU-level actors. Even Commission president Barroso defended the new infrastructure, and insisted that 'the combination of Commission instruments, EEAS action and member states' cooperation can make a real difference[.]'[4] Also, since the creation of the EEAS the Commission has continued to control important community method tools in external affairs such as in the fields of development, trade, and emergency assistance (cf. Smith 2013).

The changing role of the Commission in EU external relations could perhaps best be described as one among many important actors. In political terms the Commission's role is perhaps comparable to the roles played by larger member states, which also commmand important resources. Thus, the Commission has itself become part of a larger policy coordination set-up. Its capacity to act autonomously has been further limited, but so has the capacity of others to act without the Commission. This role is reflected in the close integration of the Commission in the overall coordination process. The Commission neither chairs this process nor does it set the political agenda, but there are almost no aspects of external affairs in which the Commission is not involved. The hybrid structure of the EEAS that combines supranational and intergovernmental elements embodies this relationship. In many ways the EEAS institutionalizes the existing pragmatic approach to

---

[3] Interviewee EU-24/EXT, 17 November 2011.
[4] As quoted by Agence Europe, 5 September 2012.

policy coordination efforts between the European Council, the Council, and the Commission. As one official noted about the situation before the Lisbon Treaty came into force:

> The good thing about the Council–Commission relationship is that we always find a mostly good solution.[5]

And another colleague seconded:

> The EEAS will not be a dramatic change as we [the Commission and the Council] already cooperate very closely.[6]

Moreover, the case of external affairs shows how much the Commission has adjusted its own political approach to the new reality of post-Maastricht integration. For example, the Commission has so far avoided interfering with police and military matters. It has not pushed for an extension of its mandate into this domain, knowing that member states have strong reservations about it. As one EU official outlined:

> The Commission always kept away from engaging with the question of EU military missions.[7]

There are a number of parallels with the role of the Commission in economic governance. In the latter field too the Commission commands important policy-making resources, though it finds it difficult to act as an agenda-setter in a more pronounced way. The Commission does act as a watchdog in the context of the multilateral surveillance process and the excessive deficit procedure. It thus plays an important political role. At a bureaucratic level the Commission's Directorate-General for Economic and Financial Affairs (DG ECFIN) commands important analytical resources in relation to monitoring the economic situation and in the field of economic forecasting. DG ECFIN also hosts the Secretariat of the Economic and Financial Committee (EFC), the Economic Policy Committee (EPC), and the Eurogroup Working Group. The Commission supports the work of all three committees with policy background papers and analysis of all major coordination topics.

These administrative resources however do not imply that the Commission can act as a real agenda-setter during different stages of the policy process. Rather the political line is defined by the EFC as the main preparatory forum and then decided by the Eurogroup, the Economic and Financial Affairs Council (ECOFIN), and the European Council. The experience of crisis management reveals this very clearly. Though the Commission could claim some credit for having been among the first to give warnings on the lack of

---

[5] Interviewee EU-08/EXT, 23 June 2009.    [6] Interviewee EU-14/EXT, 25 June 2009.
[7] Interviewee EU-03/GEN, 23 November 2009.

awareness or preparedness of euro-area governments in relation to the threat of a severe economic and financial crisis, immediate crisis management efforts were launched elsewhere in 2008 and 2009. One official considered the EFC to have done most of the groundwork, though the same official also accepted that decision-making was done on the basis of crucial input provided by DG ECFIN.[8] A participant of ECOFIN meetings at the time underlined that the responsible commissioner for economic and financial affairs, Joaquín Almunia, kept silent during the early phase of crisis management:

> Almunia was very strong behind the scenes during the crisis but was not allowed by the Commission to be the public leader.[9]

Another official emphasized that the Commission needed to adapt to the decentralized governance setting. As it relied on rallying support among the member states, it was forced to present many of its ideas in behind-the-scenes contexts so as to avoid the impression that the EU is divided on particular issues. The official highlighted the example of rescue programmes for banks, in the context of which publicity needed to be avoided by all means.[10] The political salience of the economic governance portfolio for the Commission was finally highlighted in October 2011 with the appointment of Alumnia's successor Olli Rehn as vice-president of the Commission. Thus the new areas of EU activity came to be represented by two of the Commission's eight vice-presidents.

The crucial role of the Commission in connection with the various open method of coordination (OMC) procedures found attention in the literature early on (Borrás and Jacobsson 2004: 198). This role, however, varies between different policy areas, as Susana Borrás (2009) demonstrates in her analysis of the Commission's role in implementing the Lisbon strategy. Borrás identifies the field of employment policy as being the most prominent example for active Commission engagement. As with economic governance, Commission input is considered to be crucial for OMC committees with the Social Protection Committee being a case in point (cf. Armstrong 2011a: 95).

The findings so far suggest that with the rise of new intergovernmentalism it is becoming increasingly important for analysis of Commission decision-making to be based on more theoretically informed knowledge about the specific role of the Commission in the new areas of EU activity. The findings in chapter 3 certainly suggest that inter-institutional relations, notably the personal coordination between the presidents of the European Council and the Commission, focus to a large extent on the new areas of EU activity.

---

[8] Interviewee MS-05/ECON, 9 December 2009.
[9] Interviewee EU-04/ECON, 12 November 2009.
[10] Interviewee EU-18/ECON, 7 April 2009.

Studying the role of the Commission solely with a view to its role as a policy initiator in the EU legislative process would be certainly misleading in the post-Maastricht context. The changes in the role of the Commission also seem to be reflected in new research on how the Commission's role in EU integration is perceived from within the institution. Hussein Kassim and colleagues, most of whom are longstanding experts in the study of the Commission, reveal a diverse picture of how the political and administrative role of the Commission in contemporary EU policy-making is seen (Kassim et al. 2013).[11] To think of the Commission as an institution that primarily defines its task as driving for increased supranational autonomy and is blind to the reality of intergovernmental policy coordination seems to be at least problematic. This leads back to the interview with the German chancellor Merkel that was referred to at the beginning of this section. In the same interview Merkel also rejects calls for a directly elected Commission president. Instead Merkel invokes the image of the Commission president as a facilitator of policy coordination:

> I am of the view that it is good for keeping the institutional balance if the heads of state and government are also involved in this decision [of appointing the Commission president]. [...] Because I want the Commission president to be assigned a coordinating role as regards the policy decisions of national governments, I consider it inevitable that national heads of state and government are involved in his appointment.[12]

The other major supranational body that deserves particular attention in relation to understanding the new roles of the European Council and the Council is the EP. The remarkable rise of the EP to the status of a powerful co-legislator during the post-Maastricht period may at first sight run counter to the idea that the European Council and the Council assume a more central role in EU governance. Yet the integration paradox helps to explain why both developments—the rise in importance of the EP and the two intergovernmental bodies—can run in parallel. The development of the new areas of EU activity did not diminish the importance of EU-level legislative decision-making under the classic community method in previously established policy-making domains. The empowerment of the European Council and the Council as forums for day-to-day decision-making beyond the legislative process has occurred mainly within the new areas of EU activity. Here, indeed, the powers of the EP are more limited (see chapter 1). The empowerment of the EP occurs first and foremost with regard to its role as a legislator. Calls to

---

[11] Cf. also John Peterson's contribution on the Commission in Bickerton et al. (2).

[12] Interview with *Der Spiegel*, 3 June 2013, print edition. Translation by the author. In a similar vein, European Council president Herman Van Rompuy argued against the direct election of EU leaders. See Agence Europe, 3 December 2012.

extend the application of the community method to the new areas of EU activity were an obvious reaction to the rise of new intergovernmentalism. This position was exemplified by the following quote from a statement of the British Liberal MEP Sharon Bowles during the intensive period of European Council and Council decision-making related to crisis management and the institutional reform of EU economic governance:

> I would like to make a public appeal for full involvement of the Commission and the Parliament in future work towards improved working methods and enhanced crisis management. While I do appreciate that, at times, an intergovernmental approach is the only tool in emergency situations, institutional schemes are built through the Community method and should be the first choice wherever possible[.][13]

Bowles' statement serves as a good example of many other critical interventions by MEPs over the last two decades. Reference to the community method may be seen in many ways to constitute the major line of the EP's defence against the new intergovernmentalism. In this sense the European Council is referred to as the main counterpart of the EP. As one interviewee explained:

> Some MEPs perceive the European Council as a champion of intergovernmentalism.[14]

However, such an image of the EP might be misleading.[15] While there is no doubt that a number of senior MEPs are among the most prominent critics of the leading role assumed by the European Council and the Council, the EP has failed so far to mobilize clear majorities against the mainly intergovernmental institutional design of the new areas of EU activity. For example, the European Convention revealed that there were influential MEPs who understood themselves as defenders of the decentralized governance approach that is taken in the new areas of EU activity. At the time the former EP president Klaus Hänsch played a leading role as chair of the Convention's working group on economic governance and as a member of the Convention's praesidium, in reaching agreement that the existing decentralized approach in the field of economic governance was the preferred one and should be reasserted (cf. Puetter 2007a). In November 2013 a broad coalition of conservative and liberal MEPs succeeded in inserting explicit reference into an EP declaration at a European Council discussion on the social dimension of Economic and Monetary Union (EMU). The approved text stated that 'implementation of the social dimension of the EMU is subject to the subsidiarity principle and can be best achieved through the best practice method and the peer review method at European level'.[16]

---

[13] The British Liberal MEP Sharon Bowles, as quoted by Agence Europe, 27 July 2011.
[14] Interviewee EU-02/GEN, 4 July 2011.
[15] See the contribution by Johannes Pollak and Peter Slominski in Bickerton et al. (2).
[16] As quoted in Agence Europe, 21 November 2013.

Yet the EP did not remain inactive in relation to the new areas of EU activity. There are two major strategies that can be identified so far, which allow the EP to position itself in relation to specific policy developments at the level of the European Council and the Council no matter whether the pendulum swings more towards those MEPs who tend to back the decentralized approach towards decision-making within the new areas of EU activity or towards those who advocate the expansion of the community method. The first strategy is to engage the European Council and the Council by using the EP's law-making competences to influence decisions that are located at the intersection of policy coordination and EU legislative activity. This strategy implies that the EP's decisions affect the coordination process either directly or indirectly. There is evidence of this strategy in relation to both the economic governance and foreign affairs portfolios. For example, the so-called six-pack and two-pack of legislative reform proposals, which were adopted in response to the economic and financial crisis, required EP approval. Some of these powers had only been granted to the EP by the Lisbon Treaty. As one interviewee pointed out:

> The EP can now [after Lisbon] co-negotiate the Euro Plus Pact. That gives them a lot of influence.[17]

EP approval is also required in relation to the budget of the EEAS. For example, in 2010 the EP demanded stricter transparency and financial accountability requirements for the EEAS as well as guarantees for limiting the overall share of member state diplomats in the new service (Carta 2012: 144). However, no matter how important the EP becomes in these situations the parliament is hardly in a position to shape major coordination decisions in this way. The institutional reform of the economic governance setting constitutes a particular event. EEAS budget decisions are one-off events in the annual decision-making cycle.

This leads to the second strategy pursued by the EP. This is to function as an arena in which European Council and Council decision-making in the new areas of EU activity is scrutinized and debated publicly. An important example is the EP's Economic and Monetary Affairs Committee, which regularly hears the presidents of the Eurogroup and the ECOFIN Council. Similarly the committee regularly hears the European Central Bank's (ECB) president. The committee does not have formal powers over ECB policy either but it has become an important venue for reviewing ECB policy. The committee's powers are not restricted to hearing the representatives of EU decision-making bodies, as one official emphasized:

---

[17] Interviewee EU-09/ECON, 4 July 2011.

It is possible for the EP to invite national ministers to explain policy.[18]

The example of the Eurogroup shows that creating the position of elected president facilitates the EP's role in scrutinizing the work of intergovernmental policy coordination forums, as the relevant committee or the plenary can then relate to one particular individual on a regular basis. The HR has assumed a similar role. This is all the more important as the EP has repeatedly managed to assert itself as an important actor and an independent voice in EU external affairs. The EP's repeated interventions in response to the political conflict in Ukraine may serve as a case in point. In relation to specific EU responses to a foreign policy crisis, appearances of the HR before the EP are an important focal point for debate. Similarly, the creation of the office of a full-time European Council president has affected relations between the EP and the European Council. Not only is the European Council president obliged to present a report to the EP after each meeting—as is the president of the Euro Summit[19]—Van Rompuy has also been seen to welcome engagement with the EP. As one official explained:

Van Rompuy clearly sees that you can't circumvent the EP. He is very sympathetic to the idea of close involvement [of the EP].[20]

The same official also believed that MEPs engaged with Van Rompuy beyond the context of formal hearings:

In between debates [of the EP] access to Van Rompuy is much easier than was the case with the rotating presidency.

The official also thought that Van Rompuy was very well aware that the importance of the EP required a proactive approach towards potential criticism and conflict. For example, during the negotiations on the so-called six-pack, the European Council president sought to lobby for the European Council's position within the EP with help from his cabinet.[21]

## 5.2 The Challenge of Democratic Control

Though deliberative intergovernmentalism as an analytical framework is not focused on reviewing the democratic quality of European Council and Council decision-making, three major findings of this study have particular relevance for the debate about democratic control in the post-Lisbon EU. Reviewed

---

[18] Interviewee EU-09/ECON, 4 July 2011.
[19] Article 15.5, TEU and Article 12.5, TSCG respectively.
[20] Interviewee EU-02/GEN, 4 July 2011.     [21] Interviewee EU-02/GEN, 4 July 2011.

together these findings reveal a fundamental dilemma in contemporary EU decision-making.

First, the integration paradox pointed to the reservations that member state governments have towards the further empowerment of supranational actors. Concerns that citizens would reject further formal transfers of power either in referenda or by punishing ruling government parties in the next round of elections are certainly among the key factors informing such reservations. Indeed, the quoted interview data and statements from prominent EU leaders in the earlier chapters of this book rather suggest that the vast majority of the EU heads of state and government and senior cabinet ministers want to pursue integration in a way that allows them to portray themselves as being in direct control of EU decision-making. The efforts of the personal offices and administrations of the heads to acquire control of crucial government dossiers involving EU-level coordination matters speak particularly to this point. Controlling integration from the top—understood in terms of the hierarchy of domestic politics—is seen to respond to the EU's perceived deficits in accountability and legitimacy. The point here is not to judge whether this analysis is appropriate or misleading, but to highlight that specific political rhetoric in this case has led to very practical consequences for EU decision-making.

Second, the review of the European Council and the Council as lead forums in intergovernmental policy coordination has revealed the constitutive element of collective decision-making and demonstrated efforts in institutional engineering aimed at enhancing this dimension of the decision-making process. Many of the working methods applied by the European Council and the Council run counter to the idea of a publicly accessible debate. Rather, the decentralized governance setting depends very much on informal exchanges and collective processes of opinion formation behind closed doors. Otherwise the European Council and the relevant Council formations would largely fail to generate a viable working consensus. Many participants in Council meetings, for example, believe that opening up Council debates leads only to a situation in which ministers no longer engage in real discussions and 'are less ready to make compromises'.[22] The consequences of informal working methods for democratic control are very well identified in Deirdre Curtin's (2014) comprehensive account of what she refers to as 'executive dominance in European democracy'.[23] Secrecy, and the difficulties for national parliaments in following the often very quick pace of European

---

[22] Interviewee EU-21/ECON, 11 November 2009.
[23] Cf. also the definition of executive decision-making as all non-legislative EU decision-making in Curtin 2009.

Council and Council decision-making, are the main obstacles to greater accountability and transparency.

Third, the European Council, the Eurogroup, the ECOFIN Council and the FAC in particular deal increasingly with issues that have major implications for domestic politics. Thus the findings in this book challenge Moravcsik's (2002) 'defence' of the EU democratic deficit, which assumes that the EU deals mainly with issues of low electoral salience. This is clearly not the case when it comes to decisions that have severe ramifications at times on budgetary policy. The economic and financial crisis was not short of examples of national governments being ousted from power. Moreover, the very existence of euro-area financial assistance mechanisms implies that the Council finds it very difficult to stay away from controversial decisions. As one senior official pointed out:

> Because of the EFSF [European Financial Stability Facility] and the ESM [European Stability Mechanism] the Council is under much more pressure to be tough on surveillance.[24]

Even beyond the question of crisis management, the continuing intensification of budgetary policy coordination implies that European Council and Council guidelines on budgetary policy matter increasingly in domestic politics and policy—even during economically less difficult times. Similarly, it is unlikely that a greater EU role in foreign policy, including decisions about military intervention and larger-scale financial assistance, will remain irrelevant to electoral politics in at least a number of EU member states. Here again, the eagerness of the heads of state and government to control such policy dossiers directly is proof of this salience.

The problems with the current set-up are difficult to ignore. Each scenario represents a dilemma in its own right. Viewed together the identification of alternative institutional arrangements becomes even more problematic. With regard to the first scenario, direct personal involvement of the heads in a full range of EU-level decisions is far from a guarantee that the EU will be considered more responsive politically, as Mark Dawson and Floris de Witte (2013) highlight with reference to the evolving institutional architecture of economic governance following the euro crisis. Quite to the contrary, the European Council setting may at times render political decision-making and the distribution of responsibility entirely opaque. The second scenario however shows that there is little alternative to emphasizing the use of informal working methods. The new areas of EU activity depend on consensual agreement among national executives. Finally, denial of the problem is no alternative either.

---

[24] Interviewee EU-09/ECON, 4 July 2011.

Seen from the standpoint of constitutional politics the Maastricht Treaty and, even more remarkably now, the Lisbon Treaty left the EU with a messy arrangement. For example, for Christian Joerges, the European Council is a 'constitutional bogeyman'.[25] Indeed, this has been the underlying argument throughout this book. Neither the Maastricht Treaty nor the Lisbon Treaty provided the EU with a unified institutional architecture. Rather, both Treaties revealed the integration paradox. Most instances of institutional engineering that have been discussed throughout this book were not drafted at the negotiation tables of Intergovernmental Conferences or the European Convention. The changes in the internal functioning of the European Council and the Council and their roles in the wider process of EU policy-making occurred because of a persistent institutional dilemma as implied by the integration paradox. Treaty reform in some cases codified these changes. Yet the integration paradox also implies that alternative institutional options have not found political approval so far. Certainly, the scenario of converting the new areas of EU activity into domains of classic community method decision-making seems to be most unlikely at this point in time. Whether it would solve any of the underlying problems remains a matter of debate. What is important to note here—and this refers to the critique of Christian Joerges and others—is that so far the community method has not only served as a mechanism for delegation, but has also provided procedural legitimacy to collective decision-making. Though the Council was also not really known as a transparent institution in its role as a legislative body in the past, at least its final decisions acquired legality in EU law. This element is largely absent from the EU's new intergovernmentalism, though the Treaty does provide an overall procedural framework for policy coordination.

A different way to approach the reality of new intergovernmentalism is to enhance procedures for political contestation of European Council and Council decision-making.[26] The review of individual working practices in this regard and the discussion of alternative institutional options for enhanced accountability and transparency on the basis of the core features of the current institutional set-up is one way to approach this issue. For example, Ben Crum (2009) discusses the impact on the accountability of the European Council of introducing a permanent presidency. He argues that the office of permanent president allows for a more visible form of 'personalisation' (Crum 2009: 689) of those political responsibilities that are assigned to the European Council presidency. This personalization of the presidency is in turn considered to be conducive to greater accountability. The case of control through the EP, discussed in section 5.1, particularly vindicates this argument. The European

---

[25] The author would like to thank Christian Joerges for this comment.
[26] On the notion of enhanced political contestation, cf. Wiener 2008.

Council president has certainly become an important interlocutor in relation to the EP. However, as Van Rompuy has not opted for a more visible role outside Brussels and especially not *vis-à-vis* EU citizens, the status of the European Council presidency has been less relevant to the question of broader access to European Council decision-making beyond the EP.

Deirdre Curtin's (2014) critical review, quoted above, of what she refers to as executive dominance considers a number of pragmatic attempts that focus on enhancing accountability. Her proposals require some degree of further formalization but may very well be compatible with some of the core institutional aspects of the new intergovernmentalism—namely with the existence of dedicated forums for informal policy dialogue among the representatives of member state governments. Curtin also identifies the role played by the EP, but argues for a coordinated approach by the EP and national parliaments that aims to enhance scrutiny procedures. Such 'networked parliaments' (Curtin 2014: 30) would be in a better position to reduce information asymmetry and to challenge the heads and the relevant cabinet ministers in relation to their roles in European Council and Council decision-making. An example of this is the scheduling of regular parliamentary debates ahead of European Council meetings in all national parliaments. This has been far from standard practice in many EU member states for most of the post-Maastricht period. A key argument invoked by Curtin is that at present the notion of necessary secrecy remains largely unspecified. To put it differently and express it in terms of the analysis presented throughout this book: there is little to suggest that the use of informal working methods, which is a precondition for consensus generation among government representatives, as such requires members of national executives to be issued with a blank cheque for blocking all disclosure of policy documents and agenda-related information. Indeed, neither the introduction of the Eurogroup protocol by the Lisbon Treaty, which regulates the format of the meetings of the Eurogroup, nor the fact that the Eurogroup president reports regularly to the EP and that the group publishes its draft agenda, compromises the Eurogroup's informal working method. Nonetheless, these changes to the institutional status of the Eurogroup would have found little to no support in the early years of Eurogroup operation. Similarly, the relevant committees of the EP and of the national parliaments may want to scrutinize more closely the work of the EU's most influential policy coordination committees such the EFC, the Political and Security Committee (PSC), and the Eurogroup Working Group.

Debate about the democratic control of European Council and Council decision-making needs to be continued further and requires further research in this area. Insights into European Council and Council decision-making practices, which were provided through the earlier chapters of this book, can help this debate even though the analytical focus has not been on the question of democratic control. Moreover, the debate about democratic control is not primarily an academic debate, but has a very practical political dimension. The rise in importance of the European Council, the Eurogroup, and major Council formations dealing with the new areas of EU activity has inevitably provoked political reaction. This includes calls for an expansion of the community method to the new areas of EU activity, as well as attempts to increase control of the activities of the heads of state and government by the national parliaments and the EP through other mechanisms.

## 5.3 Deliberative Intergovernmentalism and Integration Theory

Deliberative intergovernmentalism has served as the analytical framework of this study of the European Council and the Council. This framework emphasizes the crucial importance of the evolution of the new areas of EU activity for understanding processes of institutional change within the European Council and Council context. As the journey through two decades of post-Maastricht EU integration, including numerous encounters with instances of institutional engineering, comes to an end, a few reflections are in order as to how this study speaks to European integration theory and the question of the future of integration more broadly.

At first sight this study may be considered to be at odds with classic integration theory. This interpretation of the story has so far led back to the definition of supranationalism and supranational institutions that was provided in chapter 2. Traditionally the EU's supranational bodies—notably the Commission and the Court of Justice, and later also the EP—have been understood as manifestations of pronounced supranational authority. In this sense the rise of importance of the European Council and the Council as far as their role within the new areas of EU activity is concerned may suggest a retreat from integration. Yet this is not the case.

It was Ernst Haas who provided generations of students of European integration with an important analytical compass when he conceptualized the then evolving European Community as a 'new centre, whose institutions possess or demand jurisdiction over the pre-existing national states' (Haas 1968: 16). Subsequently, for most analysts the key measure of progress in European integration has become the degree of authority that the community's supranational bodies—above all the Commission and the Court of Justice—are able to exercise, independently of the member states. This interpretation has been applied not only by neo-functionalists, but also their opponents who doubt that supranational decision-making powers have evolved to a large degree independently of explicit member state authorization. For the pre-Maastricht period this interpretation seems indeed to match very well the reality of the integration process. The community method served as the main mechanism for developing the single market, and it empowered the Commission and the Court of Justice.

However, this study also claims to be in line with Haas' general definition of the 'new centre' quoted above but it offers an important modification of the way this definition has been applied in most of the European integration studies literature that followed Haas. The post-Maastricht integration paradox implies that the notion of acquiring 'jurisdiction' is interpreted in a particular way. Collective political authority is constituted through procedures outside the classic community method. Having jurisdiction over the member states is not understood as having legal authority in the sense of EU law. Yet the new intergovernmentalism, which has evolved throughout the two decades of post-Maastricht integration and has formed the reference time period for this study of the European Council and the Council, has expanded the EU's influence over 'pre-existing national states'.

Therefore, deliberative intergovernmentalism warns against equating integration too certainly with the community method. While Haas was not much concerned with the juxtaposition of alternative methods of integration, later generations of integration scholars have tended to understand EU authority as authority that is constituted through the community method. This may have prevented EU scholarship from developing a more profound understanding of Europe's new intergovernmentalism during the post-Maastricht era. Despite the impact the debate about new modes of governance has had on the EU studies literature in general, it has had surprisingly little effect on theorizing the broader roles of the European Council and Council in EU integration and the internal functioning of these bodies. This is not to say that the phenomenon of coexisting supranational and intergovernmental decision-making structures has remained unnoticed. Scholars had detected the increasing relevance of such institutional dualism already during the period immediately following the Single European Act (cf. Cameron 1992). Yet the issue has remained a stepchild of European studies literature. Also Helen Wallace's (2002) explicit proposal to study the repercussions of this institutional dualism in Council decision-making was not heard. Moreover, perhaps one of the most important perspectives within post-Maastricht EU studies—the literature on Europeanization (cf. among many others Cowles et al. 2001; Olsen 2002; Schimmelfennig and Sedelmeier 2005) seems to have abandoned altogether the question of what constitutes political integration, as well as the analysis of transformative processes inside the EU's core institutional architecture.

Related to this point, deliberative intergovernmentalism cautions against juxtapositions of the community method and new intergovernmentalism as the progressive versus the destructive mode of EU decision-making. Ponzano,

241

for example, laments that the absence of Commission initiative in the context of new intergovernmentalism implies that 'there is no research in advance into the general interest that may be different from the sum of the interests of states that are taking part in the negotiation' (Ponzano 2011: 2). This presumes that member state preferences are not under any circumstances constituted through interaction at the EU level. The review of European Council and Council working methods suggests that such a view certainly requires qualification with regard to post-Maastricht new intergovernmentalism. Giving the Commission autonomy in the form of policy-initiating powers is certainly an institutional mechanism for addressing collective action problems, but so are mechanisms to create venues for open and informal policy dialogue at all levels of decision-making. Which mechanism is more efficient is certainly a question of legitimate concern. Yet identifying Commission autonomy outright as the sole institutional scenario that might allow advancements beyond lowest-common-denominator decisions may simply prevent a deeper analysis of contemporary European Council and Council decision-making practices.

As far as it relates to major strands in European integration theory, which offer explicit conceptualizations of the respective roles of intergovernmental and supranational bodies in EU decision-making, deliberative intergovernmentalism invokes a counterintuitive argument. Conceptualizing the integration paradox owes much more to the neo-functionalist tradition than it does to its rival, liberal intergovernmentalism. The rejection by member states of further major transfers of ultimate decision-making authority at Maastricht and beyond occurred because of the previous empowerment of the Commission and the Court of Justice. Without spillover dynamics and the ability of supranational actors to shift political loyalties towards the new centre and to shape policy independently of member states' original conceptions, it is difficult to comprehend the Maastricht Treaty and the institutional dualism that it established. Without strong supranational actors, European integration would never have reached a level that would have forced member state governments to confront the question of the ultimate goal of the integration process. Moreover, deliberative intergovernmentalism is developing an understanding of the European Council and the Council as decision-making bodies that were originally set up under, and owe most of their prevailing institutional practices to, the community method. Similarly, deliberative intergovernmentalism does not expect the Commission and the Court of Justice to depart fundamentally from previously established trajectories as far as their role in community method decision-making is concerned—though this aspect does require further research, as stated in section 5.1.

The fact that EU enlargement is not acknowledged as a more powerful factor in shaping post-Maastricht institutional change within the European Council and the Council context may be considered as an omission of deliberative intergovernmentalism—but it is effectively not. The integration paradox identified in chapter 1 revealed that the post-Maastricht quest for a reinforced consensus generation capacity among the EU's main forums for intergovernmental decision-making emerged independent of enlargement. It can indeed be argued that the Maastricht Treaty practically ignored enlargement, despite the fact that the prospect of it was blatantly clear to policy-makers.[27] This is not to say that EU enlargement did not serve as a key reference point in discussions about European Council and Council reform in the late 1990s and early 2000s. The point is rather to understand enlargement as a factor exacerbating existing problems in European Council and Council decision-making, which had their root causes elsewhere. Especially, reference to enlargement has not been found to be particularly conducive to revealing the direction and intensity of institutional change within the European Council and Council environment. Many of the reforms that were linked explicitly to enlargement, such as the reform of the qualified majority voting rule, had surprisingly little impact on the day-to-day operations of the two forums after 2004. Here, deliberative intergovernmentalism is better suited than rational choice institutionalist explanations, which focus on formal decision-making rules, to explain important changes in Council decision-making in the 2000s. The creation of the Eurogroup as an informal body and early modifications of the European Council working method, which occurred long before the 2004 enlargement, support this point further.

Moreover, deliberative intergovernmentalism can reveal the consequences of enlargement for European Council and Council decision-making beyond the idea that this process has led to an overcrowding of the two institutions. Enlargement in many ways represents the heyday of community method decision-making—something that is reflected in the analytical orientation of the Europeanization literature on EU accession. The adoption and transposition of EU regulations into national legislation has been the key political issue. This has also implied that political elites in the then accession countries conceived of EU decision-making primarily as being focused on producing enforceable legislative decisions. This may explain the under-appreciation of important policy coordination dossiers on the part of some representatives from these member states in the EU's main forums for intergovernmental decision-making, especially in the second half of the 2000s. The following comment by one diplomat from a member state, which joined the EU in 2004, illustrates this point particularly well:

---

[27] The author owes this point to comments by John Peterson.

I have been trying to convince my prime minister and my finance minister for many years now that [country name deleted] needs to do more on fiscal discipline. We simply need to comply with the European rules otherwise we are in trouble as we have no support here [in ECOFIN] and no credibility. But politicians do not understand this.... [I]f you warn them on this they only ask, what are the consequences if we don't comply with the recommendations? If they learn that there are no hard legal consequences they say: 'ok, so what? This means we can do it.'[28]

As demonstrated in chapter 4 the economic crisis was probably instrumental in reversing this attitude to coordination. The example of strong Polish intervention in the discussions about access to Eurogroup decision-making and the push to reinforce EU-wide economic governance through the expansion of informal policy debates within ECOFIN speak to this point.

Deliberative intergovernmentalism also remains largely silent on the question of which member states benefit most from the rise of new intergovernmentalism in the post-Maastricht era. For example, Youri Devuyst and others interpreted the Lisbon Treaty's focus on reinforcing the intergovernmental turn in EU decision-making as an empowerment of the larger member states (Devuyst 2008: 317). Again, the decision not to give more room to this aspect of European Council and Council decision-making in the context of this study is not to imply that it is not a relevant issue. The reason attempts by larger member states to dominate European Council decision-making are not interpreted as the main factor behind the empowerment of the European Council, the Eurogroup, and leading Council formations is simply that there is no evidence that only larger member states preferred to abandon the community method within the new areas of EU activity. While it is true that some countries, such as Belgium, tended to favour greater transfers of competences to the Commission compared with others, there is little evidence to suggest that this is true for smaller member states in general.

There is no doubt that throughout the two decades that were reviewed in this book the Franco–German partnership has made its presence felt, especially in the European Council context. There are numerous examples of the Chirac–Schröder, Merkel–Sarkozy, and Merkel–Hollande tandems being decisive in resolving difficult European Council negotiations. Yet there is the risk of overstating the role of individual leaders in determining the entire role of a particular institution. With reference to the debate about the potential role of the Franco–German partnership as a source of leadership in EU affairs William Paterson (2008: 89–91) warns against overstating the ability of individual countries or pairs of countries to provide solutions to a complex set of leadership problems surrounding the process of European integration.

---

[28] Interviewee PR-02/ECON, 3 November 2009.

Deliberative intergovernmentalism emphasizes especially that European Council and Council decision-making cannot be reduced to crisis decision-making, nor can analysis ignore the fact that unanimity decisions require more than the consent of two undoubtedly powerful partners who tend to pre-coordinate their positions. Rather the conclusion here is that larger member states seek to exercise their influence in the changed environment of the European Council and the Council, as they did and do within the context of community decision-making.

# List of Interviewees

All interviews in this book were carried out by the author or his research assistants between April 2009 and March 2013. Altogether more than 60 individuals were interviewed, some of them more than once. The names of those interviewees who gave their consent to this are listed below. All interviews were carried out on the basis of anonymity. Interviewee groups were coded according to institutional affiliation and the main policy dossier with which they were concerned. Interview reference codes throughout this book indicate this information and state the date of the interview. There are three groups of interviewees: officials employed by one of the European Union institutions ('EU'), diplomats from the permanent representations of the member states in Brussels ('PR'), and government officials in the member state capitals ('MS'). The portfolios and policy dossiers of the individual interviewees are indicated as 'ECON', 'EXT', and 'GEN'. These acronyms stand for socio-economic governance issues including euro area affairs and employment policy, external affairs including foreign policy, security, and defence issues, and general affairs including inter-institutional coordination respectively. All interview documentation remains on file with the author.

Mark Bentinck, Zsuzanna Beszteri, Hardy Boeckle, Rainer Breul, Helen Campbell, Didier Canesse, Richard Corbett, Robertus Cornelissen, Nick Dean, Fabrizio di Michele, Jacek Dominik, Olof Ehrenkrona, Reinhard Felke, Andrew Georges, Etienne Grass, Carl Hallergard, Alenka Jerkic, Michael Karnitschnig, Antii Kaski, Anikó Kátai, Andreas Kindl, Andras Kos, Cyryl Kozaczewski, Zoltan Martinusz, Malgorzata Mika-Bryska, Kalman Miszei, Katalin Nagy, Alex Naqvi, Jürgen Neisse, Franz Neueder, Karolina Nowak, Urszula Pallasz, Niina Pautola-Mol, Jose Costa Pereira, Stefan Pflueger, Carsten Pillath, Ursula Polzer, Pauliina Porkka, Michele Pranchere-Tomassini, Xavier Prats, Odile Renaud-Basso, Stéphanie Riso, Thomas Schieb, Bruno Scholl, Kristin Schreiber, Tibor Stelbaczky, Loukas Stemtiotis, Pirkka Tapiola, György Tatar, Max Uebe, Peter Van Kemseke, Andreas von Beckerart, Ursula Vossenkuhl, Hans-Bernhardt Weisserth, Richard Wright, Csaba Zalai.

# References

Abbott, K.W. and Snidal, D. (2000), 'Hard and soft law in international governance', *International Organization*, 54 (3), 421–56.

Adler, E. and Haas, P.M. (1992), 'Conclusion: epistemic communities, world order, and the creation of a reflective research program', *International Organization*, 46 (1), 368–90.

Armstrong, K.A. (1998), 'Legal integration: theorizing the legal dimension of European integration', *Journal of Common Market Studies*, 36 (2), 155–74.

Armstrong, K.A. (2008), 'JCMS symposium: EU governance after Lisbon', *Journal of Common Market Studies*, 46 (2), 413–26.

Armstrong, K.A. (2010), *Governing social inclusion: Europeanization through policy coordination* (Oxford: Oxford University Press).

Armstrong, K.A. (2011a), 'Law after Lisbon: legalization and delegalization of European governance', *Biennial Conference of the European Union Studies Association, 3–5 March* (Boston).

Armstrong, K.A. (2011b), 'The character of EU law and governance: from "community method" to new modes of governance', *Current Legal Problems*, 64 (1), 179–214.

Armstrong, K.A. (2013), 'The new governance of EU fiscal discipline', *European Law Review*, 38 (5), 601–17.

Armstrong, K.A. and Bulmer, S. (1998), *The governance of the single European market* (Manchester: Manchester University Press).

Batory, A. and Puetter, U. (2013), 'Consistency and diversity? The EU's rotating trio Council presidency after the Lisbon Treaty', *Journal of European Public Policy*, 20 (1), 95–112.

Begg, I. (2008), 'Economic governance in an enlarged euro area', *European Economy—Economic Papers* (311).

Bergström, C.F. (2005), *Delegation of powers in the European Union and the committee system* (Oxford Studies in European Law; Oxford: Oxford University Press).

Beyers, J. (2005), 'Multiple embeddedness and socialization in Europe: the case of Council officials', *International Organization*, 59 (4), 899–936.

Beyers, J. and Dierickx, G. (1998), 'The working groups of the Council of the European Union: supranational or intergovernmental negotiations?', *Journal of Common Market Studies*, 36 (3), 289–317.

Bickerton, C.J. (2011), 'Towards a social theory of EU foreign and security policy', *Journal of Common Market Studies*, 49 (1), 171–90.

Bickerton, C.J. (2012), *European integration: from nation-states to member states* (Oxford: Oxford University Press).

# References

Bickerton, C.J., Hodson, D., and Puetter U. (eds) (2015), *The new intergovernmentalism: states, supranational actors, and European politics in the post-Maastricht era* (Oxford: Oxford University Press).

Blavoukos, S., Bourantonis, D., and Pagoulatos, G. (2007), 'A president for the European Union: a new actor in town', *Journal of Common Market Studies*, 45 (2), 231–52.

Blom-Hansen, J. and Brandsma, G.J. (2009), 'The EU comitology system: intergovernmental bargaining and deliberative supranationalism?', *Journal of Common Market Studies*, 47 (4), 719–40.

Borrás, S. (2009), 'The politics of the Lisbon strategy: the changing role of the Commission', *West European Politics*, 32 (1), 97–118.

Borrás, S. and Jacobsson, K. (2004), 'The open method of co-ordination and the new governance patterns in the EU', *Journal of European Public Policy*, 11 (2), 185–208.

Börzel, T. (2010), 'European governance: negotiation and competition in the shadow of hierachy', *Journal of Common Market Studies*, 48 (2), 191–219.

Bulmer, S. (1996), 'The European Council and the Council of the European Union: shapers of a European confederation', *Journal of Federalism*, 26 (4), 17–42.

Bulmer, S. and Wessels, W. (1987), *The European Council: decision-making in European politics* (Houndmills, Basingstoke: Macmillan).

Bundesregierung (2013), *France and Germany—together for a stronger Europe of stability and growth*, press statement 187/13, Berlin, 30 May.

Bunse, S., Magnette, P., and Nicolaïdis K. (2005), 'Shared leadership in the EU: theory and reality', in Deidre Curtin, Alfred E. Kellermann, and Steven Blockmans (eds), *The EU constitution: The best way forward* (The Hague: Asser Press), 275–96.

Cameron, D.R. (1992), 'The 1992 initiative: causes and consequences', in Alberta M. Sbragia (ed.), *Euro-Politics: institutions and policymaking in the 'new' European Community* (Washington D.C.), 23–74.

Cameron, D.R. (1998), 'Creating supranational authority in monetary and exchange-rate policy: the sources and effects of EMU', in Wayne Sandholtz and Alec Stone Sweet (eds), *European Integration and Supranational Governance* (Oxford: Oxford University Press), 188–216.

Cardwell, P.J. (2009), *EU external relations and systems of governance: the CFSP, Euro–Mediterranean partnership and migration* (London: Routledge).

Carrubba, C.J. and Volden, C. (2001), 'Explaining institutional change in the European Union: what determines the voting rule in the Council of Ministers', *European Union Politics*, 2 (1), 5–30.

Carta, C. (2012), *The European Union diplomatic service: ideas, preferences and identities* (Oxon: Routledge).

Christiansen, T., Jørgensen, K.E., and Wiener A. (2001), 'Introduction', in Thomas Christiansen, Knud Erik Jørgensen, and Antje Wiener (eds), *The social construction of Europe* (London: Sage), 1–19.

Commission of the European Communities (1990), 'One market, one money', *European Economy*, 44, 1–347.

Council of the European Union (1999), *Operation of the Council with an enlarged Union in prospect: report by the Working Party set up by the Secretary-General of the Council (as reproduced by CVCE)*, SN 2139/99, Brussels.

Council of the European Union (2001), *Interim report from the Secretary-General/High Representative: preparing the Council for enlargement*, 15100/01, POLGEN 38, Brussels, 7 December.

Council of the European Union (2002a), *Report by the Presidency: measures to prepare the Council for enlargement. Submitted to the European Council (Seville, 21–2 June 2002)*, 9939/02, POLGEN 25, Brussels, 13 June.

Council of the European Union (2002b), *Report from the presidency: reform of the Council presidency. Submitted to the European Council (Copenhagen, 12–13 December 2002)*, 15406/02, POLGEN 76, Brussels, 10 December.

Council of the European Union (2013), *Rules for the organisation of the proceedings of the Euro Summits*, Brussels, 14 March.

Cowles, M.G., Caporaso, J.A., and Risse, T. (eds) (2001), *Transforming Europe: Europeanisation and domestic change* (Ithaca, NY: Cornell University Press).

Cross, M.a.K.D. (2011), *Security integration in Europe: how knowledge-based networks are transforming the European Union* (Ann Arbor, MI: University of Michigan Press).

Cross, M.a.K.D. (2013), 'The military dimension of European security: an epistemic community approach', *Millennium*, 42 (1), 45–64.

Crum, B. (2009), 'Accountability and personalisation of the European Council presidency', *European Integration*, 31 (6), 685–701.

Curtin, D. (2009), *Executive power of the European Union: law, practices, and the living constitution* (Oxford: Oxford University Press).

Curtin, D. (2014), 'Challenging executive dominance in European democracy', *Modern Law Review*, 77 (1), 1–32.

Dann, P. (2010), 'The political institutions', in Armin von Bogdandy and Jürgen Bast (eds), *Principles of European constitutional law* (2nd edn; Oxford: Hart Publishing), 237–73.

Dawson, M. and de Witte, F. (2013), 'Constitutional balance in the EU after the euro-crisis', *Modern Law Review*, 76 (5), 817–44.

De la Porte, C. (2002), 'Is the open method of coordination appropriate for organising activities at European level in sensitive policy areas?', *European Law Journal*, 8 (1), 38–58.

De Schoutheete, P. (2011), 'Decision-making in the Union', *Notre Europe Policy Brief* (24). <http://www.notre-europe.eu/uploads/tx_publication/Bref24-DeSchoutheete-EN.pdf> [accessed 28 April 2014].

De Schoutheete, P. (2002), 'The European Council', in John Peterson and Michael Shackleton (eds), *The institutions of the European Union* (1st edn; Oxford: Oxford University Press), 21–46.

Dehousse, R. (2013), 'The community method, the EU's "default" operating system', *Notre Europe Synthesis*, 1–4. <http://www.notre-europe.eu/media/communitymethod-synthesis-ne-jdi-feb13.pdf?pdf=ok> [accessed 28 April 2014].

Dehousse, R., Boussaguet, L., and Jacquot, S. (2010), 'From integration through law to governance: has the course of European integration changed?', in Henning Koch et al. (eds), *Europe: the new legal realism* (Copenhagen: Djøf Publishing), 153–69.

Denza, E. (2002), *The intergovernmental pillars of the European Union* (Oxford: Oxford University Press).

# References

Devuyst, Y. (2008), 'The European Union's institutional balance after the Treaty of Lisbon: "community method" and "democratic deficit" reassessed', *Georgetown Journal of International Law*, 39 (2), 247–325.

Devuyst, Y. (2012), 'The European Council and the CFSP after the Lisbon Treaty', *European Foreign Affairs Review*, 17 (3), 327–50.

Dinan, D. (2012), 'The arc of institutional reform in post-Maastricht treaty change', *Journal of European Integration*, 34 (7), 843–58.

Duke, S. (2005), 'The Linchpin COPS: assessing the workings and institutional relations of the Political and Security Committee', *EIPA Working Paper*, No. 5/2005.

Dyson, K. and Featherstone, K. (1999), *The road to Maastricht: negotiating economic and monetary union* (Oxford: Oxford University Press).

Elgström, O. and Jönsson, C. (2000), 'Negotiation in the European Union: bargaining or problem-solving', *Journal of European Public Policy*, 7 (5), 684–704.

Elster, J. (ed.), (1998), *Deliberative democracy* (Cambridge: Cambridge University Press).

Eriksen, E.O. (2000), 'Deliberative supranationalism', in Erik Oddvar Eriksen and John Erik Fossum (eds), *Democracy in the European Union: integration through deliberation?* (London: Routledge), 42–64.

European Commission (2001), *European governance—a White Paper*, COM(2001) 0428 final, Brussels, 25 July.

European Commission (2012), *Communication: a blueprint for a deep and genuine economic and monetary union: Launching a European debate*, COM(2012) 777 final/2, Brussels, 30 November.

European Convention (2002), *Final Report of Working Group VI on Economic Governance*, CONV 357/02, Brussels, 21 October.

European Council (1994), *Presidency conclusions*, SN 00300/94EN, Essen, 9–10 December.

European Council (1996), *Presidency conclusions*, 00401-x/96, Dublin, 16 December.

European Council (1997a), *Presidency conclusions*, SN 300/1/97 REV 1, Luxembourg, 20–21 November.

European Council (1997b), *Presidency conclusions*, SN 400/97, Luxembourg, 12–13 December.

European Council (1998), *Presidency conclusions*, 00150/1/98 REV1, Cardiff, 15–16 June.

European Council (1999a), *Presidency conclusions*, SN 300/99, Helsinki, 10–11 December.

European Council (1999b), *Presidency conclusions*, 150/99, Cologne, 3–4 June.

European Council (2000), *Presidency conclusions*, 100/1/00, Lisbon, 23–24 March.

European Council (2002), *Presidency conclusions*, 13463/02, Seville, 21–22 June.

European Council (2009), *Presidency conclusions*, 7880/1/09 REV 1, Brussels, 19–20 March.

European Council (2010a), *Conclusions*, EUCO 7/10, Brussels, 25–26 March.

European Council (2010b), *Conclusions*, 25/1/10 REV 1, Brussels, 28–29 October.

European Council (2010c), *Conclusions*, EUCO/1/10, REV 1, CO EUR 21, CONCL 5, Brussels, 16–17 December.

European Council (2011), *Conclusions*, EUCO 52/1/11, REV 1, CO EUR 17, CONCL 5, Brussels, 23 October.

European Council (2012a), *Conclusions*, EUCO 205/12, Brussels, 14 December.

European Council (2012b), *Conclusions*, EUCO 156/12, CO EUR 15, CONCL 3, Brussels, 18–19 October.

European Council (2012c), *Conclusions*, EUCO 76/12, Brussels, 29 June.

European Council (2013), *The European Council in 2012*. Report by the President of the European Council, Herman Van Rompuy, Brussels, January 2013.

Farrell, H. and Héritier, A. (2003), 'Formal and informal institutions under codecision: continuous constitution-building in Europe', *Governance*, 16 (4), 577–600.

Farrell, H. and Héritier, A. (2007), 'Codecision and institutional change', *West European Politics*, 30 (2), 285–300.

Fernández, A.M. (2008), 'Change and stability of the EU institutional system: the communitarization of the Council presidency', *European Integration*, 30 (5), 617–34.

Galloway, D. and Westlake, M. (2004), *The Council of the European Union* (3rd edn; London: John Harper Press).

Gros, D. and Thygesen, N. (1998), *European monetary integration: from the European Monetary System to Economic and Monetary Union* (2nd edn; London: Longman) XIV, 574 S.

Grosche, G. and Puetter, U. (2008), 'Preparing the Economic and Financial Committee and the Economic Policy Committee for enlargement', *Journal of European Integration*, 30 (4), 529–45.

Haas, E.B. (1968), *The uniting of Europe: political, social, and economic forces 1950–1957* (2nd edn; Stanford, CA: Stanford University Press).

Habermas, J. (1995), *Theorie des kommunikative Handelns* (Frankfurt am Main: Suhrkamp).

Häge, F.M. (2008), 'Who decides in the Council of the European Union?', *Journal of Common Market Studies*, 46 (3), 533–58.

Hayes-Renshaw, F., Van Aken, W., and Wallace, H. (2006), 'When and why the EU Council of Ministers votes explicitly', *Journal of Common Market Studies*, 44 (1), 161–94.

Hayes-Renshaw, F. and Wallace, H. (2006), *The Council of Ministers* (Houndmills, Basingstoke: Palgrave).

Heisenberg, D. (2007), 'Informal decision-making in the Council: the secret of the EU's success?', in Sophie Meunier and Kathleen R. McNamara (eds), *Making history: European integration and institutional change at fifty* (Oxford: Oxford University Press).

Héritier, A. (2007), *Explaining institutional change in Europe* (Oxford: Oxford University Press).

Hervey, T.K. (1998), *European social law and policy* (European law series; London: Longman) 228.

Hinarejos, A. (2009), *Judicial control in the European Union. reforming jurisdiction in the intergovernmental pillars* (Oxford Studies in European Law; Oxford: Oxford University Press).

Hix, S. and Høyland, B. (2011), *The political system of the European Union* (3rd edn; Houndmills, Basingstoke: Palgrave Macmillan).

Hodson, D. (2011), *Governing the euro area in good times and bad* (Oxford: Oxford University Press).

Hodson, D. and Maher, I. (2001), 'The open method as a new mode of governance: the case of soft economic policy co-ordination', *Journal of Common Market Studies*, 39 (4), 719–46.

Hodson, D. and Puetter, U. (2013), 'The European Union and the economic crisis', in Michelle Cini and Nieves Pérez-Solórzano Borragán (eds), *European Union Politics* (4th edn; Oxford: Oxford University Press), 367–79.

Horvath, A. (2008), 'From policy to politics? Informal practices within the Social Protection Committee after the enlargement', *Journal of European Integration*, 30 (4), 545–61.

Hosli, M.O. (1996), 'Coalitions and power: effects of qualified majority voting in the Council of the European Union', *Journal of Common Market Studies*, 34 (2), 255–73.

Howorth, J. (2011), 'Decision-making in security and defence policy: towards supranational intergovernmentalism?', *KFG Working Paper Series* (no. 25).

Jacobsson, K. and Vilfell, Å. (2007), 'Deliberative transnationalism? Analysing the role of committee interaction in soft coordination', in Ingo Linsenmann, Christoph Meyer, and Wolfgang Wessels (eds), *Economic government of the EU: a balance sheet of new modes of policy co-ordination* (Houndmills, Basingstoke: Palgrave Macmillan), 163–86.

Jentleson, B.W. and Ratner, E. (2011), 'Bridging the beltway-ivory tower', *International Studies Review*, 13, 6–11.

Joerges, C. (2002), '"Deliberative supranationalism"—two defences', *European Law Journal*, 8 (1), 133–51.

Joerges, C. and Neyer, J. (1997), 'Transforming strategic interaction into deliberative problem-solving: European comitology in the foodstuffs sector', *Journal of European Public Policy*, 4 (4), 609–25.

Joerges, C. and Rödl, F. (2009), 'Informal politics, formalised law and the social deficit of European integration: reflections after the judgements of the ECJ in Viking and Laval', *European Law Journal*, 15 (1), 1–19.

Juncker, J.-C. (2010), *Letter from the President of the Eurogroup to Euro Area Finance Ministers, the European Commissioner for Economic and Financial Affairs and the President of the European Central Bank*, Luxembourg, 15 January.

Juncos, A. and Pomorska, K. (2006), 'Playing the Brussels game: strategic socialisation in CFSP Council Working Groups', *European Integration online Papers*, 10 (11).

Juncos, A.E. and Pomorska, K. (2013), '"In the face of adversity": explaining the attitudes of EEAS officials vis-à-vis the new service', *Journal of European Public Policy*, 20 (9), 1332–49.

Juncos, A. and Reynolds, C. (2007), 'The Political and Security Committee: governing in the shadow', *European Foreign Affairs Review*, 12 (2), 127–47.

Kassim, H., et al. (2013), *The European Commission of the twenty-first century* (Oxford: Oxford University Press).

Keohane, R.O. and Hoffmann, S. (1991), 'Institutional change in Europe in the 1980s', in Robert O. Keohane and Stanley Hoffmann (eds), *The new European community: decisionmaking and institutional change* (Boulder, CO: Westview Press), 1–39.

Kollman, K. (2003), 'The rotating presidency of the European Council as a search for good policies', *European Union Politics*, 4 (1), 51–74.

König, T. and Proksch, S.-O. (2006), 'Exchanging and voting in the Council: endogenizing the spatial model of legislative politics', *Journal of European Public Policy*, 13 (5), 647–69.

Kuhn, H. (1995), *Die soziale Dimension der Europäischen Gemeinschaft* (Berlin: Duncker und Humboldt).

Leibfried, S. and Pierson, P. (1992), 'Prospects for Social Europe', *Politics & Society*, 20 (3), 333–66.

Lempp, J. and Altenschmidt, J. (2008), 'The prevention of deadlock through informal processes of "supranationalization"', *Journal of European Integration*, 30 (4), 511–26.

Lenschow, A. (2002), 'New regulatory approaches in "greening" EU policies', *European Law Journal*, 8 (1), 19–37.

Lewis, J. (2013), 'The Council of the European Union and the European Council', in Michelle Cini and Nieves Pérez-Solórzano Borragán (eds), *European Union Politics* (Oxford: Oxford University Press), 142–58.

Lewis, J. (1998), 'Is the "hard bargaining" image of the Council misleading? The Committee of Permanent Representatives and the local elections directive', *Journal of Common Market Studies*, 36 (4), 479–504.

Lewis, J. (2010), 'How institutional environments facilitate cooperative negotiation styles in EU decision-making', *Journal of European Public Policy*, 17 (5), 648–64.

Majone, G. (1997), 'From the positive to the regulatory state', *Journal of Public Policy*, 17 (2), 139–67.

Majone, G. (2005), *Dilemmas of European integration: the ambiguities and pitfalls of integration by stealth* (Oxford: Oxford University Press).

Marcussen, M. (2000), *Ideas and elites: the social construction of Economic and Monetary Union* (Aalborg: Aalborg University Press).

Mattila, M. (2004), 'Contested decisions: empirical analysis of voting in the European Union Council of Ministers', *European Journal of Political Research*, 43 (1), 29–50.

Merkel, A. (2010), *Rede anlässlich der Eröffnung des 61. akademischen Jahres des Europakollegs Brügge*, Bruges, 2 November.

Meyer, C.O. (2006), *The quest for a European strategic culture: changing norms on security and defence in the European Union* (New York: Palgrave Macmillan).

Moravcsik, A. (1991), 'Negotiating the Single European Act: national interests and conventional statecraft in the European Community', *International Organization*, 45 (1), 19–56.

Moravcsik, A. (1993), 'Preferences and power in the European Community: a liberal intergovernmentalist approach', *Journal of Common Market Studies*, 31 (4), 473–524.

Moravcsik, A. (1998), *The choice for Europe: social purpose and state power from Messina to Maastricht* (Ithaca, NY: Cornell University Press).

Moravcsik, A. (2002), 'In defence of the "democratic deficit": reassessing legitimacy in the European Union', *Journal of Common Market Studies*, 40 (4), 603–24.

Morillas, P. (2011), 'Institutionalization or intergovernmental decision-taking in foreign policy: the implementation of the Lisbon Treaty', *European Foreign Affairs Review*, 16 (2), 243–57.

Müller-Brandeck-Bocquet, G. and Rüger, C. (eds) (2011), *The High Representative for the EU foreign and security policy: review and prospects* (Baden/Baden: Nomos).

Nederlof, D., Reestman, J.-H., and Vandamme, T. (2012), 'The European Council and national executives: segmentation, consolidation and legitimation', *European Constitutional Law Review*, 8 (2), 165–71.

Neyer, J. (2006), 'The deliberative turn in integration theory', *Journal of European Public Policy*, 13 (5), 779–91.

Nuttall, S.J. (1992), *European Political Co-operation* (Oxford: Clarendon Press).

Olsen, J.P. (2002), 'The many faces of Europeanization', *Journal of Common Market Studies*, 40 (5), 921–52.

Paterson, W.E. (2008), 'Did France and Germany lead Europe? A retrospect', in Jack Hayward (ed.), *Leaderless Europe* (Oxford: Oxford University), 89–110.

Pernice, I. (1999), 'Multilevel constitutionalism and the Treaty of Amsterdam: European constitution-making revisited?', *Common Market Law Review*, 36 (4), 703–50.

Peterson, J. (1995), 'Decision-making in the European Union: towards a framework for analysis', *Journal of European Public Policy*, 2 (1), 69–93.

Pochet, P. (2004), 'The nature of the open method of co-ordination', in Robert Salais and Robert Villeneuve (eds), *Europe and the politics of capabilities* (Cambridge: Cambridge University Press), 185–201.

Ponzano, P. (2011), 'Community and intergovernmental method: an irrelevant debate?', *Notre Europe Policy Brief*, No. 23. <http://www.notre-europe.eu/uploads/tx_publication/Bref23-Ponzano-EN.pdf> [accessed 28 April 2014].

Puetter, U. (2004), 'Governing informally: the role of the Eurogroup in EMU and the Stability and Growth Pact', *Journal of European Public Policy*, 11 (5), 854–70.

Puetter, U. (2006), *The Eurogroup: how a secretive circle of finance ministers shape European economic governance* (Manchester: Manchester University Press).

Puetter, U. (2007a), 'Intervening from outside: the role of EU finance ministers in the constitutional politics', *Journal of European Public Policy*, 14 (8), 1293–310.

Puetter, U. (2007b), 'Providing venues for contestation: the role of expert committees and informal dialogue among ministers in European economic policy coordination', *Comparative European Politics*, 5 (1), 18–35.

Puetter, U. (2009), *Die Wirtschafts- und Sozialpolitik der EU* (Vienna: Facultas WUV/UTB).

Puetter, U. (2012a), 'The latest attempt at institutional engineering: the Lisbon Treaty and deliberative intergovernmentalism in EU foreign and security policy coordination', in Paul James Cardwell (ed.), *EU external relations, law and policy in the post-Lisbon era* (The Hague: TMC Asser Press), 17–34.

Puetter, U. (2012b), 'Europe's deliberative intergovernmentalism: the role of the Council and European Council in EU economic governance', *Journal of European Public Policy*, 19 (2), 161–78.

Quaglia, L. and Moxon-Browne (2006), 'What makes a good EU presidency? Italy and Ireland compared', *Journal of Common Market Studies*, 44 (2), 349–68.

Risse, T. and Kleine, M. (2010), 'Deliberation in negotiations', *Journal of European Public Policy*, 17 (5), 708–26.

Ross, G. (1995), *Jaques Delors and European Integration* (Cambridge: Polity Press).

Sabel, C.F. and Zeitlin, J. (2008), 'Learning from difference: the new architecture of experimentalist governance in the EU', *European Law Journal*, 14 (3), 271–327.

Sandholtz, W. (1993), 'Choosing Union: monetary politics and Maastricht', *International Organization*, 47 (1).

Sandholtz, W. and Stone Sweet, A. (eds) (1998), *European integration and supranational governance* (Oxford: Oxford University Press).

Sartori, G. (1994), *Comparative constitutional engineering: an inquiry into structures, incentives, and outcomes* (New York: New York University Press).

Scharpf, F.W. (1988), 'The joint decision-trap: lessons from German federalism and European integration', *Public Administration*, 66 (3), 239–78.

Scharpf, F.W. (2001), 'European governance: common concerns vs. the challenge of diversity', *MPIfG Working Paper*, 01 (6).

Scharpf, F.W. (2003), 'Problem-solving effectiveness and democratic accountability in the EU', *MPIfG Working Paper*, 03 (1).

Scharpf, F.W. (2006), 'The joint-decision trap revisited', *Journal of Common Market Studies*, 44 (4), 845–64.

Schimmelfennig, F. and Sedelmeier, U. (eds) (2005), *The Europeanization of Central and Eastern Europe* (Ithaca, NY: Cornell University Press).

Schmidt, V.A. and Radaelli, C.M. (2004), 'Policy change and discourse in Europe: conceptual and methodological issues', *West European Politics*, 27 (2), 183–210.

Schneider, G. (2008), 'Neither Goethe nor Bismarck: on the link between theory and empirics in Council decision-making studies', in Daniel Naurin and Helen Wallace (eds), *Unveiling the Council of the European Union. Games governments play in Brussels* (Houndmills, Basingstoke: Palgrave Macmillan), 277–89.

Shaw, J., Hunt, J., and Wallace, C. (2007), *Economic and social law of the European Union* (Houndmills, Basingstoke: Palgrave Macmillan).

Sherrington, P. (2000), *The Council of Ministers: political authority in the European Union* (London: Pinter).

Smismans, S. (2004), *Law, legitimacy, and European governance: functional participation in social regulation* (Oxford: Oxford University Press).

Smismans, S. (2008), 'New modes of governance and the participatory myth', *West European Politics*, 31 (5), 874–95.

Smith, M.E. (2013), 'The European External Action Service and the security-development nexus: organizing for effectiveness or incoherence?', *Journal of European Public Policy*, 20 (9), 1299–315.

Snyder, F. (1994), 'Soft law and institutional practice in the European Community', in Stephen Martin (ed.), *The construction of Europe: essays in honour of Emile Noel* (Dordrecht: Kluwer Academic Publishers), 197–226.

Stacey, J. (2010), *Integrating Europe: informal politics and institutional change* (Oxford: Oxford University Press).

Stone Sweet, A., Sandholtz, W., and Fligstein, N. (eds) (2001), *The institutionalization of Europe* (Oxford: Oxford University Press).

Streeck, W. (1995), 'Neo-voluntarism: a new European social policy regime?', *European Law Journal*, 1 (1), 31–59.

Tallberg, J. (2006), *Leadership and negotiation in the European Union* (Cambridge: Cambridge University Press).

Tallberg, J. (2008), 'Bargaining power in the European Council', *Journal of Common Market Studies*, 46 (3), 685–708.

Tallberg, J. (2010), 'Explaining the institutional foundations of European Union negotiations', *Journal of European Public Policy*, 17 (5), 633–47.

Thomas, D.C. (2009), 'Explaining the negotiation of EU foreign policy: normative institutionalism and alternative approaches', *International Politics*, 46 (4), 339–57.

Thomas, D.C. (ed.), (2011), *Making EU foreign policy: national preferences, European norms and common policies* (Houndmills, Basingstoke: Palgrave Macmillan).

Thym, D. (2011), 'The intergovernmental constitution of the EU's foreign, security and defence executive', *European Constitutional Law Review*, 7 (3), 453–80.

Trubek, D.M. and Mosher, J.S. (2003), 'New governance, employment policy, and the European social model', in Jonathan Zeitlin and David M. Trubek (eds), *Governing work and welfare in a new economy: European and American experiments* (Oxford: Oxford University Press), 33–58.

Tsebelis, G. and Garrett, G. (2001), 'The institutional foundations of intergovernmentalism and supranationalism', *International Organization*, 55 (2), 357–90.

Uçarer, E.M. (2013), 'The area of freedom, security, and justice', in Michelle Cini and Nieves Pérez-Solórzano Borragán (eds), *European Union Politics* (4th edn; Oxford: Oxford University Press), 281–95.

Ungerer, H. (1997), *A concise history of European monetary integration: from EPU to EMU* (Westport, CT: Quorum Books) XII, 338 S.

Van Rompuy, H. (2010a), *Not renationalisation of European politics, but Europeanisation of national politics*, address given at the invitation of 'Notre Europe', Paris, Grand amphi de Sciences-Po, PCE 191/10, Paris, 20 September.

Van Rompuy, H. (2010b), *The challenges for Europe in a changing world*, speech delivered at the College of Europe, European Council press release PCE 34/10, Bruges, 25 February.

Van Rompuy, H. (2012a), *Towards a genuine Economic and Monetary Union*, report by President of the European Council Herman Van Rompuy, EUCO 120/12, PRESSE 296, PR PCE 102, Brussels, 26 June.

Van Rompuy, H. (2012b), *Towards a genuine Economic and Monetary Union*, Brussels, 5 December.

Van Rompuy, H. (2012c), *Towards a genuine Economic and Monetary Union: interim report*, Brussels, 12 October.

Van Rompuy, H. (2013), *Driving Europe's recovery—the way forward*, speech to the Irish Business and Employers Confederation, EUCO 7/13, PRESSE 4, PR PCE 4, Dublin, 9 January.

Vanhoonacker, S. and Pomorska, K. (2013), 'The European External Action Service and agenda-setting in European foreign policy', *Journal of European Public Policy*, 20 (9), 1316–31.

Verdun, A. (1999), 'The role of the Delors Committee in the creation of EMU: an epistemic community?', *Journal of European Public Policy*, 6 (2), 308–28.

Von Bogdandy, A. (2010), 'Founding principles', in Armin Von Bogdandy and Jürgen Bast (eds), *Principles of European constitutional law* (Oxford: Hart Publishing), 11–54.

Waldschmitt, E. (2001), *Die europäische Sozialunion: ordnungspolitischer Prüfstein des europäischen Integrationsprozesses* (Europäische Hochschulschriften Reihe 5, Volks- und Betriebswirtschaft; 2822; Frankfurt am Main: Lang) XIII, 189 S.

Wallace, H. (2000), 'The institutional setting: five variations on a theme', in Helen Wallace and William Wallace (eds), *Policy-making in the European Union* (4th edn; Oxford: Oxford University Press), 3–37.

Wallace, H. (2002), 'The Council: an institutional chameleon?', *Governance*, 15 (3), 325–44.

Werts, J. (1992), *The European Council* (Amsterdam: North Holland).

Werts, J. (2008), *The European Council* (London: John Harper Publishing).

Wessel, R.A. (2007), 'The multilevel constitution of European foreign relations', in Nikolaos Tsagourias (ed.), *Transnational constitutionalism: international and European models* (Cambridge: Cambridge University Press), 160–206.

Wessel, R.A. (2003), 'The state of affairs in EU security and defence policy: the breakthrough in the Treaty of Nice', *Journal of Conflict & Security Law*, 8 (2), 265–88.

Wessel, R.A. (2008), 'The European Council: a bigger club, a similar role?', in Edward Best, Thomas Christiansen, and Pierpaolo Settembri (eds), *The institutions of the enlarged European Union* (Cheltenham: Edward Elgar), 16–33.

Wessel, R.A. (2001), 'Nice results: the Millennium IGC in the EU's evolution', *Journal of Common Market Studies*, 39 (2), 197–219.

Wessels, W. (2014), *The European Council* (Houndmills, Basingstoke: Palgrave Macmillan).

Wessels, W. and Bopp, F. (2008), 'The institutional architecture of CFSP after the Lisbon Treaty—constitutional breakthrough or challenges ahead?', *Liberty and Security Research Paper* (10). <http://www.ceps.eu/files/book/1677.pdf> [accessed 28 April 2014].

Wessels, W. and Traguth, T. (2010), 'Der hauptamtliche Präsident des Europäischen Rates: "Herr" oder "Diener" im Haus Europa?', *Integration*, 33 (4), 297–311.

Wiener, A. (2007), 'The dual quality of norms and governance beyond the state: sociological and normative approaches to "interaction"', *Critical Review of International Social and Political Philosophy*, 10 (1), 47–69.

Wiener, A. (2008), *The invisible constitution of politics: contested norms and international encounters* (Cambridge: Cambridge University Press).

Wrantjen, A. (2010), 'Between bargaining and deliberation: decision-making in the Council of the European Union', *Journal of European Public Policy*, 17 (5), 665–79.

Zimmer, C., Schneider, G., and Dobbins, M. (2005), 'The contested Council: conflict dimensions of an intergovernmental EU institution', *Political Studies*, 53 (2), 403–22.

# Index